CONTENTS

INTRODUCTION

Co-sponsors of the 2002 Dwight D. Eisenhower National Security Conference were the Woodrow Wilson International Center for Scholars, the Peter F. Drucker Foundation for Nonprofit Management, the Conference Board, the Lexington Institute, the Office of the Secretary of Defense for Net Assessment, and the United States Army. This two-day event was held at the Ronald Reagan Building and International Trade Center in Washington, D.C., on September 26th and 27th. The conference, which culminated the 2002 Dwight D. Eisenhower National Security Series, focused on identifying the opportunities and challenges for national security in the twenty-first century and the capabilities needed to anticipate those challenges and to seize those opportunities for greater security and prosperity in the future.

The conference consisted of five addresses and four panel discussions. Mr. David Gergen, Editor-at-Large, *U.S. News & World Report*, and Professor, John F. Kennedy School of Government, Harvard University; Mr. Dick Grasso, Chairman, New York Stock Exchange; the Honorable Norman Y. Mineta, Secretary of Transportation; Mrs. Frances Hesselbein, Chairman of the Board of Governors, Peter F. Drucker Foundation for Nonprofit Management; and General Richard B. Myers, Chairman, Joint Chiefs of Staff, addressed the conference.

The first panel addressed today's security environment and the new context for global security. The Conference Board sponsored the panel and the Conference Board's Senior Vice President and Chief Economist, Ms. Gail D. Fosler, moderated. Panelists included the Honorable Jerry Lewis (R-Calif.), Chairman, Defense Appropriations Subcommittee; Professor Douglass C. North, Spencer T. Olin Professor of Arts and Sciences, Washington University, St. Louis; Ms. Anne O. Krueger, First Deputy Managing Director, International Monetary Fund; and Dr. Stephen J. Flanagan, Director, Institute for National Strategic Studies, National Defense University.

The second panel, sponsored by the Woodrow Wilson International Center for Scholars, focused on security cooperation. The debate centered on how much the United States should work with others in a globalized world; should United States foreign policy be unilateral or multilateral? Dr. Robert S. Litwak, Director, International Studies, Woodrow Wilson International Center for Scholars, chaired the panel. Panelists included Dr. G. John Ikenberry, Peter F. Krogh Professor of Geopolitics and Justice in World Affairs, School of Foreign Service, Georgetown University; Dr. Charles Krauthammer,

Syndicated Columnist, the *Washington Post*; Dr. Thérèse Delpech, Director of Stratégie Affairs, Commissariat de l'Energie Atomique, France; and Dr. Yoichi Funabashi, chief diplomatic correspondent and columnist, *Asahi Shimbun*, Japan.

The third panel focused on the military instrument of national power and the capabilities the military needs to develop to successfully operate in the current and future global security environment. The Lexington Institute sponsored this panel and its Chief Operations Officer, Dr. Loren B. Thompson, moderated the discussion. Panelists included Dr. Michael E. O'Hanlon, Senior Fellow, Brookings Institution; Dr. David Johnson, Senior Policy Analyst, RAND; Dr. Hans Binnendijk, National Defense University; and Major General James M. Dubik, Director for Joint Experimentation (J9), Joint Forces Command.

The Peter F. Drucker Foundation for Nonprofit Management sponsored the fourth and final panel, which focused on the other capabilities that must be developed for successful international efforts. Ambassador Peter W. Galbraith, National War College, chaired the panel whose panelists included General Montgomery C. Meigs, Commanding General, United States Army, Europe, and 7th Army; Mr. Howard Roy Williams, President and Chief Executive Officer, Center for Humanitarian Cooperation; and Ambassador Robert B. Oakley, Distinguished Fellow, Institute for International and Strategic Studies, National Defense University.

SUMMARY

Key Outcomes

Throughout the 2002 Dwight D. Eisenhower National Conference, discussions among the participants and the attendees centered on the 2002 Series theme: *Anticipating Challenges, Seizing Opportunities, Building Capabilities.* By beginning the conference with a discussion of today's security environment and comparing it to the post–World War II period, the participants set the stage for a broader discussion of security policy and required capabilities in the current and future security context. Distilled from this discussion was the essential need for principled, effective, and collaborative leadership in all types of organizations.

Anticipating Challenges, Seizing Opportunities

Today's Global Security Environment

Dr. Loren B. Thompson, the Lexington Institute, opened the conference by expressing the sentiment shared by many of the ensuing speakers that the global landscape has changed tremendously during the last two decades. The Cold War ended. The information revolution arrived. The delicate balance of terror gave way to a world of unpredictable and diverse dangers. Open markets and democratic processes gradually became globalized. But, by most measures, today is the best moment in human history. It is a time of unparalleled freedom, economic expansion, longevity, and opportunity.

Nevertheless, attendees were frequently reminded that the world remains a dangerous place with authoritarian regimes and criminal interests whose combined influence extends the envelope of human suffering. This influence fosters an environment for extremism and the drive to acquire asymmetric capabilities and weapons of mass destruction. As Ms. Gail D. Fosler, the Conference Board, stated, we face an environment that has become enormously more complex. We face a series of weapons of various types of destruction that provide huge diversity in the possible combinations of threats and the possible responses.

The Honorable Jerry Lewis, Defense Appropriations Subcommittee, and the Honorable Norman Y. Mineta, Secretary of Transportation, addressed the balances that must be maintained between national security and finite fiscal resources and between security and individual liberties. As Congressman

Lewis stated, at this moment the challenges could not be more serious, and there is significant pressure to prioritize national defense spending as Congress appropriates federal resources across a variety of competing needs. Secretary Mineta highlighted the other balance when he said that our ability to respond to the dynamic challenges of this war on terrorism rests upon the very virtues that we seek to defend: liberty, democracy, and free and open markets.

Post–World War II Security Environment

Many speakers found it useful to look to the post–World War II era for examples and lessons that apply in today's environment. While many similarities were evident between the two eras, the consensus was that today's environment is more dissimilar to that of President Eisenhower than not. But the way in which President Eisenhower and other leaders responded and behaved provided enlightening insights that are relevant today.

Mr. David Gergen, *U.S. News & World Report*, believes there are certainly clear parallels between Eisenhower's time after World War II and our own time. Then, as now, an era of fateful conflict was concluded and the United States emerged not only triumphant but also ascendant. In both eras, new threats appeared and endangered our hopes for peace. In Eisenhower's time, it was the Iron Curtain and Soviet expansion. Today, it is terrorism, the threat of weapons of mass destruction, and super-empowered nonstate actors. Then, as now, we needed a new strategy to address new threats, and we needed to reorganize major elements of our military establishment. Both times called for leadership that was strong, wise, moral, and uniting.

Chairman of the Joint Chiefs of Staff General Richard B. Myers echoed this comparison and stated that the security environment that President Eisenhower faced was unprecedented when he took office. He had a conventional conflict under way while having to simultaneously prepare for a potential global nuclear conflict. However, General Myers said today we have the opposite situation: we are involved in a global nonconventional war, fighting against terrorists, while having to prepare for a potential regional war.

Globalization

Globalization fueled by the information revolution remains a defining force in today's security environment. While participants debated the impact and ramifications of globalization, most agreed to the definition provided by Ms. Anne O. Krueger of the International Monetary Fund. She defined globalization as the process of integration across nations through the spread of ideas; the sharing of technological advances; trade in goods and services; and the movement of labor and capital across national boundaries.

Ms. Krueger also highlighted many of the benefits that have accrued as a result of globalization. She stated that the international community can do more today about poverty and act more quickly than ever before. Access to the buoyant international market has greatly facilitated faster growth for poor people in poor countries. It has permitted the degree of reliance on comparative advantage and a division of labor when things are going well that was not possible in the nineteenth century. The rapid growth in international trade and in the supportive services has resulted in a significant increase in what developed countries can provide to developing countries to do things right and do them quickly, without incurring the huge costs.

Professor Douglass C. North, Washington University, discussed globalization in broader, historic terms. He sees globalization not as an unstoppable worldwide trend but as a product of a belief system in the Western world. This system encouraged the development of impersonal exchange, large markets, productivity growth, and the technological miracles that are becoming a significant part of the world today. However, as demonstrated in the Moslem world since the thirteenth century, a belief system that evolves underlies not only choices that make us productive but also choices that lead equally to violence, to fanaticism, and to religious extremism.

Dr. Stephen J. Flanagan, National Defense University, discussed what he considers the dark side of globalization. As information and economic capabilities continue to expand, they are placing more demands on our security abilities. For example, an interlocking link exists between the activities of organized crime in trafficking of drugs, people, and weapons, which is overlapping and sometimes creating alliances of convenience with terrorist groups. He believes we have an obligation to get at the sources of this rage and despair and to narrow the prosperity gap. He stated that we should work at ways to restore the sense of hope among many countries in the world. Dr. Flanagan stated that the United States has to enhance public diplomacy to better explain America's purpose in the world and to counter misinformation about the nature of its power. He stated that all of these strategic elements need to be much better integrated if we are to succeed in our efforts to promote global peace and security.

Security Strategies

Each panel discussion and discussions following each address eventually turned to the need to best meet the challenges and exploit the opportunities of this environment. Recently published Bush administration documents, including *The National Security Strategy* and *The National Strategy for Homeland Security*, gave this discussion both context and reference.

As the senior administration official present, Secretary Mineta highlighted the key points of the just-published *National Security Strategy*. To emphasize the departure from President Eisenhower's era, he emphasized that this security strategy is based upon a doctrine of preempting the new threats to our national security rather than relying exclusively on the Cold War era doctrines of containment and deterrence.

Mr. Gergen opened the debate regarding this doctrine of preemption and capability for unilateral action with historical references to President Eisenhower. Mr. Gergen underscored Eisenhower's commitment to internationalism, to collective security, and to solving problems through the United Nations. He noted Eisenhower's commitment to solving international problems and that he believed the way to do this was through international agencies. President Eisenhower concluded that the United States should extend its view of the rule of law across the world. Our best protection, he said, lies in a set of rules, norms, and agencies in which all nations join, and in which the United States provides the leadership and the moral vision.

The Woodrow Wilson International Center for Scholars expanded this discussion and made it the focal point of its panel. Dr. G. John Ikenberry, Georgetown University, stressed that this strategy could be a fundamental challenge to U.S. relations with its major European and Japanese allies. Assertive American unilateral policies related to the war on global terrorism could undermine the grand strategic bargain between the United States and its Western partners, which created the most stable and prosperous international order in history. A key element of that post–World War II strategy was American strategic restraint—embedding U.S. power in multilateral security and economic institutions. That characteristic made the exercise of American power less threatening and more legitimate to other states. Dr. Thérèse Delpech, Commissariat de l'Energie Atomique, and Dr. Yoichi Funabashi, *Asahi Shimbun*, agreed that it was essential to develop new rules governing the use of force that take into account the increased proliferation of weapons of mass destruction by hostile states and nonstate actors.

However, Dr. Charles Krauthammer, the *Washington Post*, argued that collapse of the Cold War bipolar system had created an unprecedented "unipolar moment" that American policymakers should unabashedly seize to reshape international affairs and safeguard U.S. supreme national interests. The new American unilateralism, in fact, predates the September 11th attacks and is evidenced in the Bush administration's policies toward the Kyoto Protocol on Climate Change and multilateral arms control agreements. The September 11th attacks underscored the horrific and unacceptable consequences of a mass casualty attack perpetrated by an undeterrable terrorist group. Meeting the diverse threats posed by rogue states and global terrorism may require the United States to undertake preemptive military action unfettered by the constraints of multilateral institutions.

Building Capabilities

National Power

As the discussion shifted from describing today's environment and appropriate strategies to focusing on the capabilities needed for effective action, it became clear that the definition of national power has changed along with the broader security context. The elements of national power—diplomatic, informative, military, and economic—are no longer discrete but are interrelated, interdependent, and inseparable.

Mr. Dick Grasso, Chairman of the New York Stock Exchange, highlighted this change with his discussion about the mutual dependence of economic growth and development and strong national security. He stated that there is no private economy without a great military, and there is no national defense without great private economy.

Secretary Mineta's description of the Department of Homeland Security reinforced this theme by stating that the President's plan recognizes that we are fighting a new kind of enemy—one that plots to turn our twenty-first century technology, transportation, and economy against us. This new enemy and this new environment justify the largest reorganization of the federal government in more than 50 years.

Military Transformation

Most participants agreed that the spectrum of likely military operations describes a need for joint, combined, and multinational formations for a variety of missions extending from humanitarian assistance and disaster relief to peacekeeping and peacemaking to major theater wars, including conflicts involving the potential use of weapons of mass destruction. As General Myers stated, the military must be able to respond to the President when he asks the joint force to do something. The military must be able to rapidly and decisively enter any situation, analyze it, and achieve its objectives.

General Myers highlighted three essential elements of transformation: intellectual, cultural, and technological. He stated that, in the past, we participated in segregated warfare. In the future, we have to consider how to integrate all of the elements the services bring to the fight into a joint operating architecture. The Department of Defense is working on a joint concept of operations to explain how the military will fight. This concept will be used to test potential systems against an operational architecture.

Dr. Hans Binnendijk, National Defense University, looked at military transformation from a historical perspective and said that over the last 700 years there have been at least a dozen "revolutions in military affairs," which he defined as moments of rapid technological progress leading to new operational concepts and organizational structures. However, Dr. Michael E. O'Hanlon, Brookings Institution, challenged the central premise of the transformation movement—the notion that rapid technological advances will facilitate new concepts of operation and organizational constructs. Patterns of military change in the present era are uneven, he suggested, reflecting both continuity and discontinuity with the past.

Major General James M. Dubik, Joint Forces Command, argued that while "materiel solutions"—new technology and systems—are critical to transformation, they may not be as important as effective training, organization, doctrine, and leadership development. He called for greater "inclusiveness" in the transformation process to involve the service bureaucracies, combatant commanders, other federal agencies, and foreign allies—all of whom might have roles to play in future military operations.

From an economic perspective, Mr. Grasso of the New York Stock Exchange maintains that the United States must invest more in defense to meet potential threats today and tomorrow. He stated that the current 3.8 percent of gross domestic product (GDP) invested in defense must be increased dramatically to sustain the inextricable link between economic performance and national defense. Mr. Grasso also believes that the military retirement system must be transformed so that the nation supports, for the rest of their lives, citizens who provide a career of service to their country.

International Efforts

As the military transforms to meet the challenges of tomorrow's security environment, other public, private, and international organizations are also changing how they operate and how they interact within the international community. The final panel, co-sponsored by the Peter F. Drucker Foundation for Nonprofit Management, focused on the capabilities needed for successful international efforts.

General Montgomery C. Meigs, Commanding General, United States Army, Europe, and 7th Army, stated that to create a common effort in civil-military peacekeeping or peace-enforcement situations, three basic elements were essential: common goals and coordinated ends reached through consensus, the building of trust between the key players, and a willingness on the part of the military to lead from behind.

Mr. Howard Roy Williams, President and Chief Executive Officer, Center for Humanitarian Cooperation, asked how you get communities with different cultures, histories, and languages to come together for the common good. He suggested setting up channels of communication between the communities. The military must learn that the causes nongovernmental organizations (NGO) are engaged in are very precious to them, they are willing to risk their lives in order to maintain them, and conflict prevention must be a function of a lot of micro-efforts pulling together to accomplish a much larger goal. Awareness of these micro-efforts and seeing them as part of the larger picture would go far in improving coordination efforts.

While supportive of the need to work together and communicate consistently and clearly, Ambassador Robert B. Oakley, National Defense University, stated that the need for public security will constantly be challenged by the two different approaches to increasing public security internationally: the soft approach, through humanitarian efforts, and the hard approach, through military, intelligence, and policing efforts. The military must take a hard-line approach to these public security threats, which sets them apart from the NGO community.

Essential Nature of Effective Leadership

Throughout the discussions of security environments, economic expansion, security cooperation, and transformation, the one theme that was consistent among all of the participants was the need for effective, values-based leadership. Just as the leaders in Eisenhower's era developed the appropriate strategies, exercised the needed wisdom, and lived the right example, today's organizations—public and private—need leaders who have a strong sense of values, who treat others with dignity and respect, who are accustomed to hard work, who are courageous, who thrive on responsibility, who know how to build and motivate teams, and who are positive role models for all around them.

The example of President Eisenhower is especially relevant as we look at the type of leaders we need today. As Mr. Gergen explained, President Eisenhower learned a collaborative style of leadership while playing and coaching football in his early days at West Point and while in the Army. It was this approach that he brought to military and political leadership—to insist upon close teamwork and to serve as coach to everyone in the organization. Mr. Gergen quoted Stephen Ambrose, renowned historian and Eisenhower biographer, who said that another element of the leadership quality that he respected so much beyond the teamwork was that Eisenhower always made sure that others shared the credit.

Mrs. Frances Hesselbein, Chairman of the Board of Governors, Peter F. Drucker Foundation for Nonprofit Management, provided an apt definition of leadership today when she said we define leadership in our own terms and that leadership is a matter of how to be, not how to do. She continued to say that leaders in all sectors are finding old answers do not fit the new questions. Across all sectors, there are common questions, common challenges, and a call for principled leadership. Mr. Dick Grasso reiterated this call when he discussed the challenge of reestablishing trust and confidence in the markets and in corporate leaders after recent corporate scandals.

The specific challenge of leading in a time of change was mentioned throughout the conference. General Eric K. Shinseki, Chief of Staff, United

States Army, said that change confronts our biases, it undercuts our most closely held beliefs; it challenges our willingness to take risks. Yet it is essential if we are to grow and remain relevant. Change is the most difficult thing that any institution can undertake and it demands strong, visionary leadership. Mrs. Hesselbein echoed this sentiment, saying that the challenge for leaders today in any type of organization is to successfully manage change, lead change, create change.

Closing

In President Eisenhower's words, an objective of the Dwight D. Eisenhower National Security Series is to "help promote . . . a common knowledge and understanding of the critical issues of our time." While discussing and debating contemporary and future national security issues of our times, this distinguished group of speakers fulfilled this objective and substantively contributed to a critical examination of more effective means to focus the instruments of national power.

Full transcripts, video, and audio presentations from the conference can be found at *www.eisenhowerseries.com*. Themes and schedules for future events are also located at this website.

CONFERENCE CHARTER

National Security for the Twenty-First Century— Anticipating Challenges, Seizing Opportunities, Building Capabilities

The end of the Cold War, the prevalence of information technology, and the expansion of the global economy provide unprecedented challenges and opportunities for national security. National security organizations, policies, and relationships must transform to meet these challenges and exploit these opportunities. A continuing, open dialogue among these organizations is essential. The Dwight D. Eisenhower National Security Conference strives to contribute substantially to this dialogue.

This year's conference is the culmination of our first Dwight D. Eisenhower National Security Series. This annual series is a broad fora of events and papers designed to engage the national security community in a broad and unique dialogue that identifies and promotes new ways to focus national power to meet the full range of twenty-first century security challenges. Participants and audiences will continue to include a wide range of current and former national security policymakers, senior military officials, congressional leaders, internationally recognized security specialists, corporate and industry leaders, and the national media.

The theme for this year's conference and series is National Security for the Twenty-First Century—Anticipating Challenges, Seizing Opportunities, Building Capabilities. This broad construct allowed our co-sponsors to pursue a variety of related issues that are critical to national security. This year's conference will culminate and expand upon these ongoing efforts.

The events of 2001 made clear the dramatic evolution in threats to national security, as well as the urgent necessity to rapidly organize to eliminate them. Fully anticipating future challenges and seizing opportunities in this new environment require new approaches to achieving strategic objectives and fulfilling global responsibilities and commitments.

The conference's opening address draws lessons from President Eisenhower's legacy that remain relevant in today's security environment. Like today, leaders in the post–World War II era faced a vastly changed national security environment and endeavored to develop appropriate responses that met those challenges and exploited technological and geopolitical opportunities.

Panel I builds on this address with a discussion of today's security environment. It not only explores the new global security environment, it also provides the context for the remainder of the conference.

The luncheon address focuses on the interdependence between a nation's economic vitality and its national security; each propels the other. Strong economies produce the infrastructure and wherewithal that grant strong militaries a competitive advantage. Likewise, strong militaries produce the tranquility and predictability that grant strong economies a competitive advantage. National leaders must continue to balance these mutually interdependent requirements.

Panel II focuses on security cooperation and on the appropriate balance of multilateralism and unilateralism in United States foreign policy from both an American and an international perspective.

The keynote address highlights both the challenges and opportunities of the current security environment while including a discussion of the capabilities needed for national security in the twenty-first century. This address focuses specifically on homeland security and how we, as a nation, are adapting our existing and new institutions, policies, and organizations to meet the challenges of our day.

The morning address offers a corporate perspective on the challenge of managing change in large, complex organizations. Rarely is transformation an internal event. Rather, it usually occurs as part of a larger, externally driven force. As a result, a particular organization's transformation is usually tied to a market or interagency transformation. Taken in today's context, transformation must be an imperative not only to the military but also to other public and private agencies as we attempt to achieve a new security vision.

This discussion set the context for Panel III's discussion on the transformation of the military instrument of national power, as well as Panel IV's discussion on building other capabilities for international efforts.

Finally, the closing address revisits the issue of transformation by placing military transformation into a broader context of transforming international organizations and the efforts those organizations initiate.

OPENING ADDRESS

WHY EISENHOWER? IKE AND TODAY'S NATIONAL SECURITY ENVIRONMENT

Mr. David Gergen, Editor-at-Large, *U.S. News & World Report*, and Professor, John F. Kennedy School of Government, Harvard University

Introduction by: Dr. Loren B. Thompson, Chief Operating Officer, The Lexington Institute

General John M. Keane, Vice Chief of Staff, United States Army

Ms. Susan Eisenhower, President and CEO, Eisenhower Institute

Summary

Dr. Loren B. Thompson, Chief Operating Officer, The Lexington Institute

• The global landscape has changed a great deal during the last two decades. The Cold War ended, the information revolution arrived. The delicate balance of terror gave way to a world of unpredictable and diverse dangers. Open markets and democratic processes gradually became globalized during that time although some people still resist the verdict of history. But, by most measures, today is the best moment in human history. It is a time of unparalleled freedom and prosperity and longevity.

• But one key feature of the global landscape that has not changed is the provisional quality of all of our successes. The same impulses that gave us the Dark Ages still reside in human nature waiting for an opportunity to reassert themselves. The hard-won freedoms of this new era can become tools in the hands of those who would seek to subvert them.

• Anticipating challenges, seizing opportunities, building capabilities—these are the three imperatives that decision makers must face in this transformed security environment: first, to see nascent dangers before they fully emerge; second, to channel global change into the path of peace and freedom; and, finally, to rethink the meaning of preparedness.

General John M. Keane, Vice Chief of Staff, United States Army

• Our strength as a nation is a product of the democratic, economic, cultural, and military accomplishments of past leaders who imparted great vision for this nation of ours.

• The September 11th attacks against our country were a horrific warning that the requirements for our nation's security have changed.

1. The Cold War environment offered a certain degree of stability and deliberations regarding national defense.

2. Today, leveraging the elements of a national power with the same precision as we did during the Cold War is much more difficult due to a wide variety of factors such as terrorism, narcotics trafficking, organized crime, and the proliferation of weapons of mass destruction.

3. That difficulty exponentially increases with the existence of state and nonstate actors who are determined to stop our influences and, in some cases, to destroy our way of life.

• As President Bush observes in his *National Security Strategy*, the gravest danger our nation faces lies at the crossroads of radicalism and technology.

Ms. Susan Eisenhower, President and CEO, Eisenhower Institute

• President Eisenhower presided as the informal Chairman of the Joint Chiefs of Staff and designed a unified budget and military command that really, truly constituted a different kind of revolution in military affairs. Securing the service chiefs' agreement, according to General Andrew Goodpaster, "required every bit of his unique military skills and persuasive abilities."

• His Cold War strategy set out a set of basic principles that remained literally unchanged for the next 45 years. The threat could be deterred by a secure retaliatory capacity, and Soviet expansion could be contained indefinitely until it was eroded by internal decay and deterioration. Coerced rollback of Soviet power was therefore rejected in favor of containment. The administration concluded that military forces and other means must be sustainable by the U.S. and its allies over the long haul of decades. Thus the economic vitality and political cohesion in support of the U.S. and its allies were critical components of this security.

• Understanding that the Cold War would be a long one, Eisenhower set out to ensure that U.S. government spending was consistent with the long struggle ahead. He feared that irresponsible fiscal policies could quite literally "destroy from within that which we were trying to protect from without." Contrary to NSC 68, and despite mutual distrust, the U.S. policy was to negotiate arms control measures to moderate the arms race and reduce the risks of war by miscalculation or accident.

• The allies and the United States worked aggressively to assist the post-colonial states to strengthen their governments and societies to become less vulnerable to subversion. He was confident that the Soviet Union had within it the seeds of its own destruction.

• In his 1964 memoirs, written 23 years before the tumultuous events of the late '80s that ended the Soviet Bloc and the U.S.S.R. itself, he wrote, "When the day comes that the Communist people are as well informed as those of free nations, then dissatisfaction, unrest, and resentment among hundreds of millions of people will eventually bring about either reforms in their governments or the violent destruction of Communist dictatorships."

• Among the most important legacies was really an extraordinarily close working relationship with Congress. He worked in remarkable harmony with the Democratic leaders in Congress: Congressman Sam Rayburn and Senator Lyndon Johnson. Today, these are, indeed, dangerous times, and we are challenged to think about America not only in the short term but in the long term as well.

• President Eisenhower believed it was important to bridge the gap between the civilian and military worlds. When he left his position as Army Chief of Staff, he said, "I cannot let this day pass without telling the fighting men, those who have left the ranks and those of you who still wear a uniform, that my fondest boast shall always be, I was their fellow soldier."

Mr. David Gergen, Editor-at-Large, *U.S. News & World Report*, and
    Professor, John F. Kennedy School of Government, Harvard
    University

• In the twentieth century, the American presidency became an office where many served but few succeeded. In an era of tumult, only two Republicans managed to serve as president for a full eight years. And those two men were the only presidents of either party who presided over eight years of peace and prosperity and also left office with a deep reservoir of respect and goodwill among their fellow citizens. Eighteen presidents in all, and only two kept us out of war overseas and tranquil here at home. One, of course, was Dwight David Eisenhower and the other was Ronald Wilson Reagan.

• Certainly there are clear parallels between Eisenhower's time after the war when he was a five-star general and then president and our own time. Then, as now, as World War II ended, an era of fateful conflict was concluded and the United States emerged not only triumphant but ascendant.

1. As World War II came to a close, the American economy accounted for more than half of the world's GDP, and we had a monopoly on the atomic bomb. Today, in a very similar fashion, we have barely 4 percent of the world's population and yet we account for about a third of the world's GDP. More than 40 percent of all Internet transactions originate in the United States, and our scientists here represent 70 percent of all the Nobel science winners alive today.

2. But then, as now, new threats appeared that cast a shadow across our national life and endangered our hopes for peace. An iron curtain descended and Berlin became a lonely outpost of freedom. The Soviets acquired atomic weapons of their own and vowed they would bury us. Today, we see an arc of terrorism and tyranny that extends from Osama bin Laden to Saddam Hussein and threatens America once again so that the American people no longer feel secure at home, in offices, or in airplanes.

3. Then, as now, we needed a new strategy to address new threats and we needed to reorganize major elements of our military establishment. Then, as now, we especially needed leadership that was strong, wise, moral, and uniting.

• Eisenhower's leadership was a model then, and it should remain so now. Indeed, his style of leadership seems even more relevant today than it was then. Today we look to leaders who empower others, who inspire them, who get them working together as a team, and that's what Eisenhower did so well. Every CEO, every president, every general, every coach can learn from him.

1. Eisenhower: "I believe that football, perhaps more than any other sport, tends to instill in men the feeling that victory comes through hard, almost slavish work, team play, self-confidence, and an enthusiasm that amounts to dedication." It was the approach that he learned playing with his teammates and then coaching that he brought to the military and political leadership—to insist upon close teamwork and to serve as coach to everyone in the organization.

2. Stephen Ambrose said that "Another element of leadership that he respected beyond the teamwork was that Eisenhower always made sure that others shared the credit."

3. Eisenhower wrote that "a good organization does not make a great leader, but a bad organization will kill you every time." He understood that management was essential to leadership. It is not leadership, but it's essential to leadership.

4. Eisenhower said: "I find myself, especially as I advance in years, tending to strip each problem down to its simplest possible form. Having gotten the issue well-defined in my mind, I try in the next step to determine what answer would best serve the long-term advantage and welfare of the United States and the free world. I then consider the immediate problem and what solutions we can get that will best conform to the long-term interests of the country, and at the same time, can command a sufficient approval in the country so as to secure the necessary congressional action." That is a model for decision-making in the White House.

• Now, beyond Eisenhower's analytical capacity were the personal qualities that were so important.

1. The Oracle Adelphia says, "Know thyself." We ought to add a second imperative—"Master thyself"—for leaders because only when you master

yourself can you serve others. Eisenhower was a man who knew and mastered himself.

    2. Time and again, he said "Only a leader who is optimistic, who believes and shows his troops and others that the job can be done, can inspire them to go ahead and do it." Even if you're pessimistic, he says, "I confide my pessimism, my fears. I confide to that pillow."

    • Eisenhower was of a generation that believed in duty, honor, country. Those ideas, critical at West Point, became a central part of his life.

    1. He used to talk about Robert E. Lee as a general. Lee once said that duty is the sweetest word in the English language. Eisenhower believed that.

    2. That sense of duty, which grew out of a sense not only that he serve his country, but also that he hold certain convictions, led Eisenhower to the presidency.

    • Eisenhower's principles, his convictions, challenge us today because the more you examine them, the more you realize that they are out of step with the temper of much of current thinking not only here in Washington but also across the country.

    1. He had fought in the war and he believed that the miracle of the allies working together in close harness was what won the war, so that he came out of the war believing that it's when the United States remains engaged overseas that we achieve the best results.

    2. In his April 1953 speech entitled, "The Chance for Peace," Eisenhower talked about his horror at the arms race that had broken out and how much it was costing us and at what sacrifice. Eisenhower went on to say, "This government, the United States government, is ready to ask its people to join with all nations in devoting a substantial percentage of the savings achieved by disarmament to a fund for world aid and reconstruction."

    3. Ringing through all of Eisenhower's letters, his work, his declarations, his speeches is his commitment to internationalism, to collective security, to solving problems through the United Nations. He was a great believer in the United Nations. He was committed to solving international problems, and he believed the way to solve international problems was through international agencies.

    4. Eisenhower felt that it was important to be fiscally responsible. He was in favor of lower taxes, no question about that, but he thought the way to get there was to tighten up, and he was willing to cut the Defense Department before he lowered taxes.

    5. The United States should extend the view of the rule of law across the world. Our best protection lies in a set of rules, norms, agencies, in which all nations join, which the United States, of course, provides the leadership and the moral vision, but that we recognize that others need to join and respect those laws too.

• Eisenhower was one of the most successful Chief Executives in our nation's history. He kept us out of war. He presided over 8 years of prosperity. No other president since him, until the war on terror, has come anywhere close to that kind of reservoir of support among the people. Eisenhower's legacy calls us to respect not only the man but also his principles and to ask ourselves, what application do they have in the world today?

Analysis

In his opening remarks, Mr. David Gergen focused on the relevance of President Eisenhower's legacy to today's national security environment. He commented both on the similarities in security environments between the late 1940s and 1950s and today and on the President's leadership style, principles, and personal convictions. Based on his experience as an adviser to four presidents, as a renowned author and journalist, and as a scholar and professor, Mr. Gergen believes Dwight Eisenhower is the ideal model for today's leaders as they face the challenge of the war on terrorism and the opportunity for globalization and the Information Age while building capabilities for the future.

As in Eisenhower's era, the United States has just successfully waged war against an enemy determined to end our way of life. Then it was World War II; today it is the Cold War. The United States enjoys unparalleled economic and military power today as it did in the late 1940s and, like then, that power continues to develop and grow. But the United States also faces a new enemy today. As with the Soviet Union in the early days of the Cold War, the United States faces a determined enemy in global terrorists who are determined to end American influence in parts of the world and to endanger our way of life. Mr. Gergen asserts that today's leaders can learn from Eisenhower's generation as they face these new threats while maintaining American power and prestige today and for the future.

Today's leaders can use Eisenhower's style of building a team, empowering its members, and then acting like a coach to encourage great performance and high standards. Today, information technology allows organizations to increase their spans of control and rely on individuals to act based on the current situation, not the last order or directive. To be successful, teams today must allow individuals more autonomy and independence, and leaders must provide clear direction and guidance to ensure collective success. Eisenhower exemplified this model as Supreme Allied Commander in Europe and in the White House. The lessons he learned on countless football fields made him a success throughout his career in public service. These same lessons and this same style will be successful today in business, government, or the military.

Eisenhower's principles and personal style also provide a great model for today's leaders. He was able to master his own emotions and approach decisions and situations analytically based on his experience and values. From an early age, he was committed to contributing his vast talents to the greater good of his country. His commitment to duty as an obligation to serve the American public should be an inspiration to this generation to serve the nation selflessly. His reluctant acceptance of the presidential nomination, his commitment to multilateralism and the United Nations, and his pursuit of fiscal responsibility demonstrate his continued effort to put his convictions first and to perform his duty while staying true to his beliefs. Eisenhower truly personifies the U.S. Military Academy's motto of "Duty, Honor, Country."

President Eisenhower was chosen as the namesake for this series of national security events because of his relevance to today's national security community. He successfully guided the nation through a time of tremendous challenge and danger with his inspirational leadership style while maintaining his convictions and beliefs. Today's leaders and policymakers can look to President Eisenhower for guidance as they face the security challenges of the twenty-first century.

Transcript

Note: The conference and each panel were preceded by a video introduction. While transcripts of these videos are not included in this document, the videos and their transcripts are available at the conference website: www.eisenhowerseries.com.

BACKSTAGE ANNOUNCER: Ladies and gentlemen, please welcome Dr. Loren B. Thompson, Chief Operating Officer, Lexington Institute.

DR. LOREN B. THOMPSON: Good morning, and welcome to the 2002 Eisenhower National Security Conference. This conference is the culmination of a yearlong dialogue on national security challenges and requirements sponsored by the U.S. Army, the Pentagon's Office of Net Assessment, the Woodrow Wilson International Center for Scholars, and three private organizations. The three private organizations are the Conference Board, one of the world's leading business forums since its founding over 80 years ago in 1916; the Peter F. Drucker Foundation, a seminal force for building better citizens and better communities; and my own organization, the Lexington Institute. As the junior partner in this coalition, Lexington would like to express its gratitude for the opportunity to participate and to thank all of the sponsors for the active role they've played in shaping today's and tomorrow's events.

Today's event is actually the latest in a series of annual national security conferences that trace their origins back two generations. During most of that time, the Army has been a major sponsor of the conferences. The global landscape has changed a great deal during that time. The Cold War ended. The information revolution arrived. The delicate balance of terror gave way to a world of unpredictable and diverse dangers. Open markets and democratic processes gradually became globalized during that time, although, as we know, some people still resist the verdict of history. But by most measures, today is the best moment in human history. It is a time of unparalleled freedom and prosperity and longevity.

But one key feature of the global landscape that has not changed is the provisional quality of all of our successes. The same impulses that gave us the Dark Ages and the Holocaust still reside in human nature, waiting for an opportunity to reassert themselves. As we all know now, the hard-won freedoms of this new era can become tools in the hands of those who would seek to subvert them. So it's fitting that the focus of this year's Eisenhower

Dr. Thompson

Conference is National Security in the Twenty-First Century—Anticipating Challenges, Seizing Opportunities, Building Capabilities.

That phrase defines the three imperatives that decision makers must face in this transformed security environment: first, to see nascent dangers before they fully emerge; second, to channel global change into the path of peace and freedom; and finally, to rethink the meaning of preparedness. We've tried to assemble the most thoughtful and influential thinkers from across America and around the world—legislators, policy makers, journalists, academics, entrepreneurs, and military leaders—to offer a spectrum of insights on what the new millennium demands of us. If we are successful, then the exchange of ideas that you hear over the next two days will contribute to the security policies of tomorrow.

In that regard, I want to emphasize that this conference is only one event in an ongoing process called the Eisenhower Series, a process that the Army and other participants have fashioned to inform their fellow citizens on the challenges that lie ahead. It is called the Eisenhower Conference and the Eisenhower Series because no individual more clearly exemplifies the qualities of patience, perception, patriotism, and leadership that will be required to secure freedom in the new millennium. On the eve of World War II, Dwight David Eisenhower was a remarkable man approaching the end of an unremarkable military career. Yet within a dozen years, he would become the

Supreme Allied Commander, the Army Chief of Staff, the President of Columbia University, the Commander in Chief of NATO, and finally, the President of the United States. It is encouraging to realize that America is able to find men and women of such qualities in its moments of greatest need.

Let me mention a few administrative matters here before I introduce our next welcoming speaker. First of all, one of the things the presence at this conference has purchased you is an opportunity to shape such future events. If you look in your packets, you'll find a questionnaire about the conference, and we would very much appreciate it if you would fill out that questionnaire and put your responses in the box outside the door, because we really do care what you think of this event.

Second, because the conference is part of the larger process, you're going to see a major report and a variety of subsidiary products coming out in the aftermath of the next two days' meetings. This year we're going to be offering streaming video and CD ROMs and all those other wonderful benefits of the Information Age as a way of giving the conference both more impact and more immediacy. But the success of efforts such as this depend on engaging the audience, so I hope all of you, to the extent that time allows, will take an opportunity to participate in the discussion by asking questions. If you have a question you'd like to put to the speakers up here, just raise your hand. A microphone will be passed to you. And then I'll call on you.

Third, don't forget to turn off all those pesky cell phones and pagers during the event. Or at least put them on vibrate. If you rely on incoming calls to keep you awake, we have a substitute in the form of coffee outside the door.

Finally, given the times in which we live, I suppose I should note that this is a very big and complex building. It's a good idea for you to identify the exit routes in advance, so that you know how you would leave the building if you needed to in any kind of an emergency. If you have any questions about how to get around the Reagan Building, there are staff people outside. You'll see them wearing badges. They can direct you to just about any destination. I've already asked them three questions and they were right each time. By the way, I'd recommend that when you do leave the room for any period of time, you take your personal belongings with you, just for security reasons.

Now, I'd like to turn to a person of considerably greater visibility and stature, the Vice Chief of Staff of the Army, and introduce him, to provide a welcome by the U.S. Army to all of you. He is General John M. Keane, as I said, the Vice Chief of Staff of the United States Army. Prior to assuming his current position in the late spring of 1999, General Keane performed a wide range of increasingly important roles at home and abroad in a military career that has spanned more than three decades. Among other things, he has been the Deputy Commander in Chief and Chief of Staff of the United States Atlantic Command, the Commanding General of the XVIII Airborne Corps, and the Commanding General of the 101st Airborne Division. His achievements have been acknowledged by many medals, including the Distinguished Service Medal, the Silver Star, the Legion of Merit, the Bronze Star, and the Meritorious Service Medal. He is widely recognized as one of the most perceptive, articulate, focused leaders in the U.S. military today. General Jack Keane.

GENERAL JOHN M. KEANE: Thank you. Good morning everybody and welcome. And thank you, Loren, for those kind words and that generous introduction. The Army is excited about its association with the Dwight David Eisenhower National Security Series, and we are just absolutely delighted to be one of the co-sponsors of this capstone event for the series, the Eisenhower Conference. Our many distinguished speakers and guests underline the importance of our discussions these next two days, so it's good to see all of you here, and frankly the numbers that will be here over the next two days have exceeded our expectations. General Shinseki was called away on short notice this morning and asked me to pass along his regrets that he could not be here this morning, but he will join us later today. We are indebted to each of the partners that Loren mentioned for their dedication to broadening our national security dialogue and helping to refine our understanding of the tremendous challenges we face as a nation. Our strength as a nation is a product of the democratic, economic, cultural, and military accomplishments of past leaders who imparted great vision for this nation of ours. Our charter in this series is to perpetuate President Eisenhower's enduring legacy of leadership. In his words, "Help promote a common knowledge and understanding of the critical issues of our time." Therefore, we are especially grateful to the Eisenhower family for their gracious support and appreciate their consent in naming this series, this conference, in honor of the thirty-fourth President of the United States, Dwight David Eisenhower.

Earlier this month, we commemorated the September 11th attacks against our country, and just six days ago, President Bush unveiled our National Security Strategy for these first years of the twenty-first century. So our discussions over the next two days could not be more relevant or timely. September 11th was more than just a beginning of our first—and I hope only—war of the twenty-first century. It was a horrific warning that the requirements for our nation's security have changed. The Cold War environment offered a certain degree of stability and deliberations regarding national defense. Today, leveraging the elements of a national power with the same precision as we did during the Cold War is much more difficult, as we all know, due to a wide variety of individual factors such as terrorism, narcotics trafficking, organized crime, and the proliferation of weapons of mass destruction. And that difficulty exponentially increases with the existence of state and non-state actors who are determined to stop our influences and, in some cases, to destroy our way of life.

As President Bush observes in his National Security Strategy, the gravest danger our nation faces lies at the crossroads of radicalism and technology.

General Keane

The implications of that observation are, in large part, the purpose of our discussions here. Over the next two days, I hope that we all make the most of this opportunity to engage in this national security dialogue, the profits of which will contribute to the preservation of our nation and the ideals of freedom that we American people hold so dear.

It is now my great pleasure and privilege to introduce Ms. Susan Eisenhower, a well recognized and widely consulted scholar of United States–Russian relations, a best-selling author, and a much sought after speaker for insights across many disciplines. Her expertise is well respected, and we are delighted that she could join us here today. Ladies and gentlemen, please join me in a warm welcome for Ms. Susan Eisenhower.

MS. SUSAN EISENHOWER: General Keane, Dr. Thompson, honored guests, it's a great privilege for me to be here today, and I must say that I was reminded on my way to this conference of one of my favorite stories related to me by my grandfather. In the early '50s when he was president, his younger brother, Milton Eisenhower, was president of Penn State University. Milton asked his brother, the president, to give a convocation speech at Penn State. Well, the weather was very much like it is this morning—off-and-on drizzle— and Milton was very worried about the fact that the event was planned to be outside, and there was some uncertainty about what it would mean if they had to move the gathering inside. So he called Ike in a bit of a panic and said, "What should I do? Should we move this thing inside or should we leave it outside?" And Ike replied, "Listen, Milton, that's your problem. I haven't worried about the weather since June 6, 1944." I think that does put the weather into perspective, and we're here today, actually, to have a very, very important dialogue about the national security challenges facing the United States.

I'd like to reflect, though, for a moment on my grandfather and his life and times. On June 12, 1945, a little more than a month after the end of hostilities in World War II, Dwight Eisenhower stood on the balcony of London's Guild Hall and accepted the Freedom Of The City and the London Sword. The killing had stopped, but the costs of the conflict had only begun to be measured.

Europe lay in utter ruins, and I think from a contemporary point of view, we can't even grasp the carnage and the destruction. Cities had been crushed, economies had collapsed, and the carnage was beyond contemporary comprehension. In the European theater, for instance, including Russia—these are among our allies alone—11 ? million allied soldiers were killed in action, and more than 7 million civilians perished from starvation, bombing, or butchery, and that's not counting those who were victims of the Holocaust. Nor do those figures reflect those of our enemies who died.

Ms. Eisenhower

I think that you can imagine that I'm justifiably proud of my grandfather's contribution to winning this terrible war in Europe, and I remember as a child he had been given as a gift a large photograph of the Normandy invasion. One of my most vivid elementary school memories was of him explaining a bit about the battle of Normandy to me and now, of course, as one has gotten older and read more on the subject, one is truly amazed, I think, at the talent and the fortitude and the commitment to forge the first integrated allied command in history. He made other contributions, however, as well, some of them less known to the general public.

As president of Columbia University, he was tasked by President Truman to come to Washington and do a number of important things. He presided as the informal chairman of the Joint Chiefs of Staff and designed a unified budget and military command that really, truly constituted a different kind of revolution in military affairs. Securing the Service chiefs' agreement, according to General Goodpaster, "required every bit of his unique military skills and persuasive abilities." His Cold War strategy, too, set out a set of basic principles that remained literally unchanged for the next 45 years. It was a coherent, winning strategy. As Bob Buyi and others from that administration have written, the strategy revised the Truman threat appraisal, objectives, and means embodied in NSC 68. It rejected the prospect of a Soviet attack by a date of maximum danger. The threat could be deterred by a secure retaliatory capacity, and Soviet expansion could be contained indefinitely until it was eroded by internal decay and deterioration. Coerced rollback of Soviet power was therefore rejected in favor of containment. The military forces and other means must be sustainable by the U.S. and its allies over the long haul of decades, the administration concluded. Thus, the economic vitality and political cohesion in support of the U.S. and its allies were critical components of this security.

Understanding that the Cold War would be a long one, Eisenhower also set out to ensure that U.S. government spending was consistent with the long struggle ahead. He feared that irresponsible fiscal policies could quite literally "destroy from within that which we were trying to protect from without." Contrary to NSC 68, and despite mutual distrust, U.S. policy was to negotiate arms control measures to moderate the arms race and reduce the risks of war by miscalculation or accident. And the allies and the United States worked aggressively to assist the post-colonial states to strengthen their governments and societies to become less vulnerable to subversion. Although Eisenhower hated the Soviet regime and everything it represented, he was confident that the seeds that it had within it were the seeds of its own destruction. In his 1964 memoirs, written literally twenty-five years before the tumultuous events during the late 80s that ended the Soviet Bloc and the U.S.S.R. itself, he wrote, "When the day comes that the Communist people are as well-informed as those of free nations, then dissatisfaction, unrest, and resentment among hundreds of millions of people will eventually bring about either reforms in their governments or the violent destruction of Communist dictatorships."

Many people may not realize that this fall is the fiftieth anniversary of the Stevenson-Eisenhower election. This November, of course, will be the fiftieth anniversary of the election itself. And as I described before, America was the only country left standing and was, indeed, the sole superpower after World War II. Many of my grandfather's ideas and policies today give us pause to think. Among the most important legacies that I have not mentioned so far was an extraordinarily close working relationship with Congress. He worked in remarkable harmony with the Democratic leadership in Congress— Representative Sam Rayburn, of course, and Senator Lyndon Johnson. Today, these are, indeed, dangerous times, and we are challenged to think about America not only in the short term but in the long term as well.

I would like to just add a personal note here. I think that every bit as important as the debate itself is how this debate is going to be conducted. The Eisenhower administration worked hard to remove the scourge of McCarthyism. *Who Killed Joe McCarthy?* by William B. Ewald is a wonderful book about the elaborate, behind-the-scenes administration effort to eliminate McCarthyism as a political force. I hope as we move forward in our national debate in the coming weeks and months, that we ourselves will be committed to a reasoned and respectful debate that should be the hallmark of this great nation.

I am personally absolutely delighted about the event here today. I think the Eisenhower Series is going to make an enormous contribution to the important dialogue that we have under way in our country today. I also think it presents a very special opportunity to bridge the gap between the civilian and military worlds. These are two worlds that Dwight Eisenhower traversed so comfortably. He, of course, in his White House years reached the pinnacle of civilian power and brought about peace, security, and prosperity. But, you know, he was an Army man at heart. And I think his simple words when he left his position as Chief of Staff of the Army are words that I think he would want to utter today, as we have troops deployed overseas. He said, "I cannot let this day pass without telling the fighting men, those who have left the ranks and those of you who still wear a uniform, that my fondest boast shall always be, I was their fellow soldier." On behalf of the Eisenhower family, we are honored that the United States Army has named this important series after Dwight Eisenhower, and I wish you all the very best in your deliberations in the coming hours and days. Thank you.

DR. THOMPSON: Thank you, Dr. Eisenhower, and General Keane. Susan, let me extend that thanks to your entire family for several generations of really extraordinary service to America. I think it's no coincidence that your family's chronicle of contributions parallels our nation's rise to greatness. Our opening address this morning draws lessons from General Eisenhower's tenure as president, a time, like today, of rapid political and technological change demanding new approaches to national security. That address will be delivered by David Gergen, one of America's most visible and valued commentators on global and domestic affairs. Mr. Gergen has been an adviser to four different presidents. He is one of the very few individuals in public life who has managed to cross the partisan divide in pursuit of higher principle.

Mr. Gergen entered his first White House position only a few years after graduating from Harvard Law School in 1967, serving first in the Nixon and then in the Ford administrations. He returned to the White House as President Reagan's communications director from 1981 to 1984, and then served one more time as domestic and foreign policy counselor to President Clinton during the mid-1990s. A remarkable aspect of Mr. Gergen's career is that he has managed to be as visible and as influential when he is out of government as when he is in it. For two and a half years, he was editor of *U.S. News & World Report*, during which time he drove that publication to record gains in both circulation and revenues. He was also a regular commentator on the *MacNeil/Lehrer News Hour*, providing a weekly source of insight and political sophistication on America's most respected news program. Today, he teaches at Harvard's Kennedy School of Government, while also serving as editor-at-large for *U.S. News* and as an analyst on ABC News' *Nightline*. There aren't many people who have managed to win praises in so many different facets of national life, politics, and academia. So we are very pleased that he is here to open the Eisenhower Conference today. David Gergen.

MR. DAVID GERGEN: Thank you, Dr. Thompson, for that very warm introduction, and let me say not everyone sees it in quite the same light. I had a fellow introduce me not long ago. He said, "Ladies and gentlemen, our speaker today worked in the White House for President Nixon, President Ford, and President Reagan. And then, if you can believe, went to work for a Democratic president, President Clinton." He then said, "Ladies and gentlemen, give a warm welcome, please, to the newest member of the world's oldest profession." So there are somewhat different views. But I'm delighted to be here.

I'm also a little surprised to have you invite someone down from the banks of the Charles for this august occasion. When I went to teach in Cambridge at Harvard, the best advice I got came from Allen Simpson. You may remember the Republican senator, a wise and witty fellow from Wyoming. He preceded me there on the faculty and he pulled me aside and said, "Don't let this go to your head, Gergen, coming here to teach at Harvard." He told me about a fellow in his part of the country who was out on his ranch one day when a young fellow drove up and jumped out. "Hey, old timer, if I tell you how many sheep you have on this ranch, will you give me one?" "Well, I reckon, son. How many do I have?" "You have 978." "That's very impressive. You're entitled to one of my sheep." The young man went over and picked up an animal and started to drive away. The old fellow yelled out, "Hey, young man, I've got a question for you." "Well, what's that, old timer?" "Young man, if I tell where you went to college, can I have my animal back?" "Well, fair's fair. Where did I to go school?" "You went to Harvard, didn't you?" "Well, how did you know that?" "It was easy, son. You just took my dog." So it takes all types.

And there are many compensating features in life. And today we have the wonderful pleasure of talking about the man from Abilene. Susan Eisenhower, General Keane, Dr. Thompson, ladies and gentlemen, and distinguished guests, in the twentieth century, the American presidency became an office where many served but few succeeded. In an era of tumult, only two Republicans managed to serve as president for a full eight years. Indeed, those two men were the only chief executives, the only presidents of either party, who presided over eight years of peace and prosperity and also left office with a deep reservoir of respect and goodwill among their fellow citizens. Think of it: eighteen presidents in all, and only two kept us out of war overseas and tranquil here at home. One, of course, was Dwight David Eisenhower. And the other was Ronald Wilson Reagan. Thus, it's entirely fitting this morning that we inaugurate this Eisenhower conference on national security at the Reagan Center here in Washington. Yet in convening us here in the name of Dwight Eisenhower, our sponsors call upon us to think more deeply about this man from Abilene. What is there about his life and his principles, as Susan Eisenhower underscored, that are meaningful to our own day? What parallels can we find? What significance? What differences that illuminate our own path? Not everything we learn from Eisenhower is comforting. Some of it scratches hard against our grain today. But we should think about him nonetheless. We know from experience that those who failed to know the past do not know the present either. So let us this morn-

ing begin with a few reflections—
adding to those that Susan has had,
and she's been a friend for many
years—on Eisenhower and his meaning for us today.

Certainly there are clear parallels
between his time after the war when
he was a five-star general and then
president and our own time. Then, as
now, as World War II ended, an era
of fateful conflict was concluded and
the United States emerged not only
triumphant but transcendent. As
World War II came to a close, the
American economy accounted for
more than half of the world's GDP,
and we had a monopoly on the atomic bomb. Today, in a very similar
fashion, we have barely 4 percent of
the world's population and yet we
account for about a third of the
world's GDP. More than 40 percent of

Mr. Gergen

all the Internet transactions originate here in the United States, and our scientists here in the United States represent 70 percent of all the Nobel science
winners alive today. We are transcendent now as we were then. But then, as
now, new threats appeared that cast a shadow across our national life and
endangered our hopes for peace. "An iron curtain descended," as Churchill
said, and Berlin became a lonely outpost of freedom. The Soviets acquired
atomic weapons of their own and vowed they would bury us. Today, we see an
arc of terrorism and tyranny that extends from Osama bin Laden to Saddam
Hussein and threatens America once again so that the American people no
longer feel secure at home, in our offices, or on airplanes. Then, as now, we
needed a new strategy to address new threats, and we needed to reorganize
major elements of our military establishment. Then, as now, we especially
needed leadership that was strong, wise, moral, and uniting. Fortunately,
Dwight David Eisenhower was exactly the right man at the right moments in
the right places. It's often been said that, "God looks after fools, drunkards,
and the United States of America." For those Americans of that time, there was
little doubt that with Eisenhower in command, Providence was smiling.

It is Eisenhower, the leader, that we most celebrate today, and properly so.
His leadership was a model then and it should remain so now. Indeed, his style
of leadership seems even more relevant today than it was then. In those days,
many of the leaders were top down— [like] Napoleon — I can do this, do that,

Today we look to leaders who empower others, who inspire them, who get them working together as a team, and that's what Eisenhower did so well. Every CEO, every president, every general, every coach can learn from him. I'd like to talk for a few minutes about his leadership qualities because I think they're so important. They're so important at places like West Point. They're so important in the normal training in the Army. They're important in training our diplomats. They're important in training us all as we deal with this period of uncertainty and transformation. "I like Ike," the campaign buttons read, but it was more than that. People trusted him with their lives. Everyone who met him came away talking of his candor, decency, and honor. Bernard Law Montgomery, not an easy man to inspire, said of Eisenhower, "He has the power of drawing the hearts of men toward him as a magnet attracts the bits of metal. He only has to smile at you and you trust him at once."

Ike loved football, played at West Point until he got hurt, and then became a coach; not only there at the Point but at post after post. There were times when he thought the only thing the Army cared about was his ability as a coach, not as a warrior, and he turned down coaching opportunities. But it has been said that the more time he spent with the game, the more he appreciated the importance of teamwork. And, in fact, he first discovered his talents as a leader and an organizer on the gridiron. Toward the end of his life he wrote, "I believe that football, perhaps more than any other sport, tends to instill in men the feeling that victory comes through hard, almost slavish, work, team play, self-confidence, and an enthusiasm that amounts to dedication." It was the approach that he learned in playing with his teammates, and then coaching, that he brought to the military and political leadership: to insist upon close teamwork and to serve as coach to everyone in the organization.

Think of him as coach, as a leader. It's a very different form of leadership than thou shalt do this. He helped people along. He forced, through his coaching, Montgomery and Patton to get along in Europe. He knocked heads together as Supreme Allied Commander and in the Joint Chiefs of Staff and then in NATO. His cabinet at the White House was the last that was a full working cabinet. Everyone around the table was expected to contribute, even outside his own area of expertise and management. And the president listened patiently to their views. There is a quality here, a similarity between Eisenhower and Lincoln. As David Herbert Donald has written, "Lincoln made everyone who worked for him feel that he or she was extraordinarily important to the overall effort." Everyone working for him had a contribution to make that was critical. And they were motivated to meet the high standards he set. That's exactly what Eisenhower did with everyone who worked for him.

I never had the privilege of meeting President Eisenhower. I did have the privilege, the honor, to go to Gettysburg and meet his widow, Mamie. And I did have the privilege of knowing some of those who had worked in his administration. They had been youngsters then and they stayed on, and they believed in public service. They came back to work for President Nixon, and they were highly respected figures around this city. One of them, Brice Harlow, was a mentor of mine, a man we all dearly loved. And they spoke with such reverence about working for Ike, what it was like, and how important they felt, and how he trusted them and they trusted him. I was struck then and have been struck ever since that somehow he inspired people in a different way, and it's something we need to remember today.

This past summer, I had the privilege of visiting Steven Ambrose, the historian, in his home in Mississippi, where he's fighting valiantly against an aggressive form of cancer. You may recall that, years ago, Eisenhower had read Steve's history of General Hallock and asked him to serve as his authorized biographer. The product was a superb two-volume biography to which I'm indebted for some of my remarks today, as well as a book about his role of command during the war. Well, there in Mississippi, Steve and I talked for two hours or more about leadership, about the various people he's written about over the years. Lewis and Clark, and Eisenhower, the various companies in World War II, and the men at D–Day. He loves Eisenhower, and he said another element of the leadership quality that he respected so much beyond the teamwork was that Eisenhower always made sure that others got the credit. Susan talked about D–Day, June 6, 1944, when Eisenhower gave the command, "Let's go." As Steve Ambrose points out, there was nothing more Eisenhower could do. He had made the big decisions. He had organized everything so well. And then he had to wait. And he had two statements drawn up. One was produced by his team, and it proclaimed victory by us, what we, the Allies, had done. Privately, Eisenhower sat, with no one else around, and wrote out another statement in the event of defeat. And it was not about we, it was about I: I take responsibility; I'm the one who made the mistakes. And he tucked that away in his wallet. And after the war, someone else found it and asked him if he'd thrown it away and that person asked him if he could keep it. And Eisenhower said yes, and that's how it found its way into history. Nobody knew that he had sat there quietly writing out a statement, taking full blame in the event of defeat.

I saw that again, by the way, in another leader, Ronald Wilson Reagan, when I was working in the White House with him, when we had our troops posted to Lebanon. As you may well remember, there was a terrorist attack there. We lost some 257 fine young men and women. And there was an investigation about what had gone wrong. Robert Long, who is no longer with us, ran that investigation and pinpointed blame within the military chain of command, and there were some who were singled out in the report. The report came over to the White House around noon that day. It was going to be published about 4 o'clock in the afternoon over at the Pentagon. And President Reagan read that report, looked through it with great interest. He was going off to Camp David that afternoon, and as he went, he stopped outside the helicopter and said, "Look, there's a report coming out here shortly about what happened in Lebanon. I want to make it clear: I'm the Commander in Chief. I take responsibility." That's what leaders do. And President Reagan wanted to make sure that the people in the Pentagon knew that he would be out front taking the arrows. And yet, they had discipline themselves inside, but the Commander in Chief takes responsibility when things go wrong.

That's the kind of leadership that we so long for in almost every institution, especially as we look at the kind of corporate scandals that have been occurring across the American landscape recently. And that's the kind of leadership that Dwight Eisenhower represented. He was also a superb organizer and diplomat. He wrote that "A good organization does not make a great leader, but a bad organization will kill you every time." He understood that management was essential to leadership. It is not leadership, but it's essential to leadership. And he pushed that very, very effectively. He rose up through the ranks of command not because of his command on the battlefield. In fact, he was frustrated that he couldn't get to the battlefield more than he did. He rose up through the ranks of command because he was such a good organizer. Alistair Cook has written that no one other than Eisenhower could have kept the Allied armies together during World War II the way he did. He had the best-organized White House in modern times. He had the best-organized government. And as I said, it was 360-degree leadership when he listened to everyone around him closely.

At the time, journalists and others criticized him because they thought he was indecisive, because they thought he let John Foster Dulles run the show over at the State Department, and because he sometimes seemed to mumble in his press conferences. And there was a view about him that perhaps he was a very nice man, a very decent man, but he may not be all that bright—that he was a bit of a bumbler. That was a common, widespread view among historians who did not rank him very highly when he first left office because they thought the team worked very well, but they couldn't figure out Eisenhower. They thought maybe he wasn't quite up to the quality of his own team and others were running it for him. We've heard the same about Reagan, of course. And one of the interesting things that happened after Eisenhower died, his papers were opened to historians in the early 1970s, and when they read his private papers, they found the man that he truly was: that he had intentionally put others out in front, that he had intentionally, at times at press conferences, talked in a way to fog up the issue because he wanted time to make a decision. He actually had a wonderful pen, and what they found was a man of keen intelligence, with a warm personality, but terribly rational and coldly analytical, who figured things out and then made his decisions from there. And from that experience, from opening up those papers, came a revision of people's views about who Eisenhower was.

There's a man at Princeton by the name of Fred Greenstein who had voted steadily as a Democrat. He was a Stevenson Democrat, and he started writing a book about Eisenhower thinking he was going to be very critical. And he was one of the first ones to get into the papers. And what he found so totally absorbed and impressed him that he reversed himself on what he thought Eisenhower was all about, and he wrote a book that has become a classic in the field. It's called *The Hidden-Hand Presidency: Eisenhower as Leader*, and it's a marvelously positive book because Fred Greenstein, this liberal Democrat from Princeton, found that in Dwight Eisenhower we had one of the most impressive men that he'd ever seen in public life. He was particularly impressed by his capacity for analysis and the way he made decisions.

There's a quote in here that I want to share with you that comes from a letter that was found in this collection that Ike sent to the NATO commander, Alfred Grunther, and it was about his decision-making process. And I think, again, this serves as a model at a time when we're trying to find our way through the thicket, and as Susan Eisenhower said, "We're trying to settle our differences here and figure out how we deal with this uncertain world that's around us in a way which keeps us together as a people. How do we conduct our debates?" And here's what Eisenhower said: "I find myself, especially as I advance in years, tending to strip each problem down to its simplest possible form. Having gotten the issue well-defined in my mind, I try in the next step to determine what answer would best serve the long-term advantage and welfare of the United States and the free world." The first thing he tries to figure out is the long term: Where are we going over the long haul? Let's set that as our goal. "I then consider the immediate problem and what solutions we can get that will best conform to the long-term interests of the country and, at the same time, can command a sufficient approval in the country so as to secure the necessary congressional action." That is a model for decision-making in the White House. Think long term, then consider your immediate problem, and figure out what you can do now. That not only helps you advance to your long-term goal but also can command support here at home and secure bipartisan congressional approval. This is a man who understands how to make a system work and understands that we live in a democracy, in which other branches of government share power and you must help bring them along. You need to have their support. And it's a model for decision making not only in the White House but, I must say, in the Pentagon as well. So I commend that to you. Now, beyond Eisenhower's analytical capacity, there were the personal qualities that were so, so important.

The Oracle Adelphia, says, "Know thyself." Sometimes we ought to add a second one for leaders: "Master thyself." Because only when you master yourself can you serve others. Eisenhower was a man who knew and mastered himself. He had a terrible temper. As Steve Ambrose relates, "Once when his younger brother Milton was given something from his parents and Ike was a kid, he was 10 years old or so, and he was and was so angry that he went outside to a tree and banged his fists against it until his hands were completely bloodied. When he came back inside, his mother read to him from the scriptures about the importance of patience and controlling one's temper. He said it was one of the best lectures he ever received. And he worked thereafter his whole life to control his temper.

Steve Ambrose said that when he was working on the biography, he and Eisenhower would be talking, and the name of someone or some unpleasant incident would come up in the conversation. He said that Eisenhower would get totally red in the face and would pause for a moment. He would get his temper under control, and then the sunny Eisenhower would resurface and they would continue their conversation. Eisenhower was a man who understood the importance of self-mastery. He used it so that he could present an optimistic face to others. Time and again he said, "Only a leader who is optimistic, who believes [in] and shows his troops and others that the job can be done, can inspire them to go ahead and do it." He said, "I confide my pessimism, my fears, I confide to that pillow." That is a wonderful example of what he was all about.

Finally, his leadership. Eisenhower was of a generation that believed in duty: duty, honor, country. Those ideas were critical at West Point, and they became a central part of his life. He used to talk about Robert E. Lee as a general. Lee once said that duty is the sweetest word in the English language. Eisenhower believed that. He really didn't want to become president. He was ready to retire. He wanted to go back to the farm. He wanted to put things down. But he agreed to become president—as he did in so many other things in his life—out of a sense of duty. As Steve Ambrose concluded, "He was a great and good man." His sense of duty led Eisenhower to the presidency. His sense of duty grew out of a desire not only to serve his country but also from certain convictions. He had principles, as related by Susan, about what the country should be like in a post–Cold War world. And that's what challenges us today. Eisenhower, the man, is the model for our times; the kind of leadership I believe we need in these times.

Eisenhower's principles, his convictions, challenge us today because the more you examine them, the more you realize that they are out of step with the temper of much of the current thinking, not only here in Washington but also across the country. And if we're going to deal with Eisenhower in this conference, we have to be willing to consider not only the man but also his beliefs, because they are different. He had a different approach from what is so popularly talked about today. And it's important to understand where he was coming from. He had fought in the war, and he believed that what won the war was the miracle of countries, the allies working together in close harness. So he came out of the war believing that when we work with other countries, and the United States remains engaged overseas, we achieve the best results.

When World War II ended, it appeared that the United States would be at peace with the Soviets. Then very quickly we went down two different roads and the U.S. had to reorganize its military operations. Eisenhower was right at the center of that reorganization. Susan Eisenhower said earlier that while he disagreed with some aspects of what Harry Truman represented, while serving under Truman, Eisenhower supported the president in most of his major initiatives, as a good soldier does. Eisenhower embraced as his own much of what Truman and the bipartisan consensus that formed right after the war was about. As Susan said, he believed in containment. He agreed with Truman on the airlift to Berlin. He agreed with Truman on the commitment to Korea. He agreed with Truman on limiting the war in Korea. He agreed with Truman on building the H–bomb. And, most importantly, he agreed with Truman on the formation of NATO and then went to serve there. From those experiences in the war and just after the war, Eisenhower became a committed, devoted internationalist who believed in collective security and that friendly nations coming together are the hope for peace. Eisenhower believed the United States does not act alone, but with others, and that those alliances and relationships are totally important to the future and the success of American foreign policy.

The following incident is striking: Eisenhower did not want to become president, but he was eventually drafted. Truman tried to draft him in 1948 to run as a Democrat, but Eisenhower didn't want to do that. Eisenhower at heart was much more conservative. He was conservative on domestic issues and was not in favor of the Democrats and said no to Truman. Even when the Republicans came to him—Tom Dewey and others wanted him to run—he was reluctant to do so. He thought it would be better if someone else ran. But then in January of 1951, he had a meeting at the Pentagon with Robert Taft. Robert Taft was the alternative in the Republican Party. He would have been the standard bearer. Robert Taft was a conservative senator from Ohio, and Dwight Eisenhower agreed with Taft on domestic issues. They were both conservatives at heart on domestic issues, but Eisenhower broke with Taft on the question of America's role in the world. Taft was more of an isolationist; Taft was more of a unilateralist. Taft wanted to withdraw from internationalism. Taft wanted to cut back on the United Nations. Taft wanted to cut back on foreign aid, to cut it to pieces. Those went against Eisenhower's principles. So, when he sat down with Taft in the Pentagon, he brought to the meeting a paper that included a joint statement from the two of them in which Taft would announce his devotion to internationalism and to the principles of internationalism, and Eisenhower would renounce any intention or willingness to serve and would give, in effect, a Shermanesque statement. Taft said no, he would not go back on his principles, and Eisenhower respected him for that. So when the meeting ended, Eisenhower decided to leave himself in a place where he could be drafted. He eventually went on to serve in the White

House and did so out of his conviction that America had to be an internationalist country that worked with others.

To read the kind of language that he then employed is so interesting today—and I will not take too much more of your time with this—but I think it's worth recalling some of the sentiments and what motivated Eisenhower as president and the convictions he held, because they are not what one hears today in much of the debate. One of the most important speeches he made after he became president was right here in Washington. Called "The Chance for Peace," it was given on April 16, 1953. He talked about his horror at the arms race that had broken out and how much it was costing us and at what sacrifice. "Every gun that is made, every warship launched, every rocket fired signifies in the final sense a theft from those who are hungry and are not fed, those who are cold and are not clothed. The world in arms is not spending money alone. It is spending the sweat of its laborers, the genius of its scientists, the hopes of its children. The cost of one modern heavy bomber is this: a modern brick school in more than 30 cities. It is two electric power plants. It is two finely equipped hospitals. It is some 50 miles of concrete highway. We pay for a single destroyer with new homes that could have housed more than 8,000 people."

He wanted to take a different road. "This is not a way of life at all in any true sense. Under the cloud of threatening war, it is humanity, hanging from a cross of iron." And of course in saying "a cross of iron," he was echoing William Jennings Bryan's famous speech about a cross of gold that had been given to Democrats at the turn of the twentieth century. Eisenhower went on to say, "This government is ready to ask its people to join with all nations in devoting a substantial percentage of the savings achieved by real disarmament to a fund for world aid and reconstruction. The purposes of this great work would be to help other people to develop the undeveloped areas of the world, to stimulate the profitability in world trade, to assist all peoples to know the blessings of productive freedom. The monuments to this new war would be roads and schools, hospitals and homes, food and health. We are ready, in short, to dedicate our strength to serving the needs, rather than the fears, of the world and we are ready by these and all such actions to make of a United Nations an institution that can effectively guard the peace and security of all peoples."

Ringing through all of Eisenhower's letters, his work, his declarations, his speeches is his commitment to internationalism, to collective security, to solving problems through the United Nations. He was a great believer in the United Nations. He was committed to solving international problems, and he believed the way to solve international problems was through international agencies.

His policy was to take it to the U.N. How strikingly different that is. Listen to this record: Eisenhower and the United Nations, 1953. A few months after he gave "The Chance for Peace" speech, he went to the United Nations and gave a speech that was called "Atoms for Peace." And he proposed that all nations contribute atomic materials to the United Nations, that the United Nations form an atoms-for-peace program. The program would promote the peaceful development of nuclear power under the umbrella of the United Nations. And it was only because of a Soviet veto that we failed to do that. But Eisenhower wanted to put it there at the U.N. Think of that.

That was 1953. In 1954 the Chinese shelled Quemoy and Matsu, the off-shore islands. Eisenhower took it to the United Nations. 1956, the Hungarian crisis: the Soviets march through Hungary. Ike immediately asks for a resolution through the U.N. to stop them. 1956: the Israelis join up with the British and the French in a surprise attack on Suez. The president of the United States says, "Unacceptable. Let's take it to the U.N.," and Eisenhower goes to the U.N. to force an end to it. 1958, Berlin: President Eisenhower proposes that Berlin— as long as it's all of Berlin—be placed under the United Nations. 1960, Uprising in the Belgian Congo: The Congolese president calls for the United States to intervene to stop the Soviet-led assault on his government. Eisenhower says we're not going in alone and goes to the U.N. to solve the problem.

This is a very different view that we are forced to consider today, that we have to think about carefully. It is a view that we have a threat out there—a mortal threat to this country. We live in uncertain times. And in order to solve that threat, the United States should not go it alone; the United States does not have the capacity and power to do that. We succeed best with allies and friends. It is a view that we must engage and be engaged internationally at all costs. It is a view that foreign aid matters. And Eisenhower insisted on funding foreign aid heavily. It is a view that the United Nations matters and we should work through the United Nations.

It was a view on Eisenhower's part that it was important to be fiscally responsible. He was horrified by the deficits he inherited from Harry Truman. At that time, the country, if you can believe, was only spending $80 billion a year, but we were $10 billion in hock each year. That was unacceptable to Eisenhower. He was a strong fiscal conservative. But Republicans came to him—the old guard—and said, "Let's cut taxes." His answer was, "We cannot cut taxes till we get the budget under control, and then we'll cut taxes." He was in favor of lower taxes, no question about that, but he thought the way to get there was to tighten up, and he was willing to cut the Defense Department before he lowered taxes. Interesting perspective.

And finally it was his view that the rule of law is something the United States believes in and that we should extend across the world; that our best protection lies in a set of rules, norms, agencies; that the United States provide the leadership and moral vision, but that we recognize that all nations need to join and respect those laws too. How different that sounds from where we are today. One can argue today with considerable persuasion that had Eisenhower then been a young man and lived to see what happened in the world, the failures at the United Nations for example—the way it has been captured by smaller countries, the irresponsibility of United Nations agencies, the failures we've experienced in foreign assistance over the years—it is quite possible that he would have changed his views over time and would have come to agree with the arguments that we hear today. I don't think one can discount that, but I think that's too easy a cop-out in terms of thinking about Eisenhower.

If we're going to be serious about what Eisenhower represented, not only as a model of leadership but also the principles that he represented, then we have to come to grips and ask ourselves, "Okay, they worked in his time. Will they work now? Should we give them serious consideration in our debates, in our deliberations? Are they not an honorable perspective—an honorable view that has served this country so well?" Remember that Eisenhower was one of the most successful chief executives ever. He kept us out of war, he presided over eight years of prosperity, he enjoyed over the course of his presidency a 64 percent approval rating in the Gallup Polls—an average for 8 years that is remarkable. No other president since, until the war on terror came, has come anywhere close to having that kind of support among the people. Given the fact that his views not only prevailed but also worked in the modern world, do they not deserve a respectful hearing? Don't we have to wrestle ourselves with the question, "Are we on the right track or do we need to consider, do we need to be thinking about these other alternatives that have served America well in the past?" Doesn't the Eisenhower legacy call us to respect not only the man but also his principles and to ask ourselves, not in a fawning way but in a serious way, "What application do they have in the world today?" Do we need to consider where we've come from, how that served us then, and how it might serve us now? Thank you very much for your attention.

DR. THOMPSON: Thank you very much, David. Mr. Gergen will be taking some questions from the floor now. We have about five minutes for questions. As I said to you earlier, if you'd like to pose a question, could you raise your hand? A microphone will be passed to you, and then David will call on you.

MR. GERGEN: Yes, please. Do you have a microphone? Who has the microphones? Are they hand-held? They'll come to you. I can repeat the question if you'd like. I can hear you. Please identify yourself, if you don't mind.

AUDIENCE MEMBER: My name is Paula Gordon, and I'm a freelance writer and have a web site on the homeland security issue. I'm remembering the interview that you had with Warren Bennis on organizing genius, and I'm thinking that the points that he made about the Manhattan Project might be an interesting point to bring up here concerning the exchange with Richard

Oppenheimer about the reasons they were there and what they were doing. And once they understood the purpose of why they were there and the importance of their actions, the entire tenor of their effort changed radically. And it seems from what you've said about the approach that President Eisenhower took on leadership that the kind of thing he was able to instill in people was the sense of mission, and I think that's so important today.

MR. GERGEN: Thank you for your comments, and you're absolutely right that President Eisenhower had, as he explained to Grunther, this notion that one thinks long term—a sense of mission about what you're trying to achieve. You make the short-term decisions, but you do that within the context of inspiring others with the mission, with the purpose of where you're trying to go. And the leadership requires you to engage others in a vision and get their buy-in—to persuade them through your words and through your deeds and through the trust they have in you. And that's why trust becomes so important to the person who is running the enterprise, the front of the enterprise, as Frances Hesselbein has demonstrated—not only with the Drucker organization but also with her time at the Girl Scouts. She became a person who understood and demonstrated how one leads to create a sense of mission and motivate others to buy into the vision. And that vision, in order to inspire others, has to be one in which others sense that there is equity and fairness to everyone. It is a mission in which all can share together.

What the United States needs now in the war on terrorism is to articulate to the rest of the world an alternative vision of what kind of world we can build together—even as we face the terrorists with our talons of war, as the American eagle reaches out with those talons. As we bristle with authority and prepare to retaliate, we must acknowledge that the other claw holds out an olive branch that represents a vision, and what we need to articulate. I think we are still struggling to articulate to the rest of the world an alternative vision of what kind of world we can build together. People in these other countries who could become terrorists, who are the feeding ground for terrorism, should have some sense that there is an alternative route, an alternative vision that they can buy into. Then one draws them into that vision and draws them away from the sense that all we want to do is retaliate. And that's why even as we are tough on terrorism, I think that the Eisenhower approach would have been to say, "We have to be tough on the Soviets. We can't let them expand." And he never let them do that, but at the same time, he held out this vision of peace. You know, the atoms for peace, a chance for peace. He was continually trying to build a structure in which everyone could share in prosperity, in which young children, hungry children in other countries, could share in that prosperity, and that's what I'm suggesting.

The Eisenhower vision today would be for us to hold out that alternative vision so that others could draw from that—a vision that includes the capacity for democracy in one's own country, the capacity for empowerment of women, the capacity to extend prosperity to others, so that in many of these countries where we're facing such hatred there is an alternative that we can work for constructively, together. That's what I mean by a vision that draws other people in. That's what Warren Bennis was talking about in the Manhattan Project in a very intense effort called *The Skunk Works at the Manhattan Project*, whereas what Eisenhower was trying to do is have this broader how do you form a vision for the world, how do you form a vision for the United States, in which people can join in and make constructive contributions and that's what he stood for. It's hard to see from up here, but I'll be happy to take another question, if you have one.

AUDIENCE MEMBER: You spoke eloquently of President Eisenhower's principles as they relate to America's role in the larger world and especially how those are relevant today. Are there any lessons to be learned from his principles in terms of organizing for homeland security? Especially given the partisanship that seems to be infecting the debate now about how best to protect America domestically?

MR. GERGEN: That's a useful question, and I'm not sure I can answer it well. Reasoning or by deduction from what he stood for and how he acted, he was obviously not afraid of creating large organizations. He believed that if you had a large organization, it was critically important that the person or the people on top shared responsibilities and had a shared sense of mission. I think he would be appalled by the degree to which the homeland security argument, and this is just speculation, has fallen into a partisan squabble and is delaying us. On this issue, I must say that I think the Democrats are wrong and that President Bush is right in asking for more flexibility in the way he organizes the workforce. I think Eisenhower would have been drawn to—or at least I am drawn to, and so maybe I can invoke his name—a perspective that is different, and that comes from two men who headed up a national commission that organized for homeland security: former Senators Gary Hart and Warren Rudman. They published a report before September 11. Senator Hart was with Condy Rice on September 6 urging her to move forward on the terrorist threat as rapidly as possible, and people were becoming aware of it, and the administration was becoming aware of it and was trying to act. They were trying to move when the terrorists struck. But Hart and Rudman both argued an alternative, and that is to think of people who are going to work. The question was what to do with the civil servants. Instead of treating them as if they worked at HHS or the Treasury Department, they should be treated as national security employees, and we have a different set of regulations that pertain to the Defense Department. People who work at the Defense Department as civilians and at the CIA and some of the other agencies are under a different set of civil service rules, which give the assistant secretaries and others much more flexibility in working with them. That is such an obvious way out of this impasse.

Why shouldn't the homeland security operation be treated just like the Pentagon in terms of people who work there? And after all, homeland security, while we talk about it being a large agency, 170,000 people, it is also true that the Pentagon dwarfs the size of homeland security, and we've learned how to make the Pentagon work in a way that's fair, and people like to work at the Pentagon. Large numbers of people apply every year for jobs there, and it's a place of honor whether you're a civilian or a military member there at the Pentagon. So there are answers to this, and I think that Eisenhower would find partisanship very irksome. He believed that America had a grander role to play in the world and that people should put down their petty concerns in order to serve this larger vision of what America could be and how to build a peaceful world. And that's what he called people to do.

He would favor and he would split with his own party. Some of the biggest problems he had were with the conservative wing of his own party. It was much more isolationist—the Taft wing of the party. He and Senator Taft, who were bitter foes for awhile in 1952, actually became very friendly once Eisenhower became president, and remained so until Taft died shortly thereafter. They worked well together. But Eisenhower had trouble with other parts of the Republican Party. He had trouble, as Susan Eisenhower said, with McCarthy. And he tried to transcend that. One of the wonderful things about Eisenhower was how he tried to transcend these partisan battles and was a father figure to the country. He understood that the presidency is a combination of head of government—you've got to play the prime minister role—and also head of state. And that the dignity and objective quality, and the fairness and decency and honor represented by leaders was totally important to the quality of life in our political life and in our public life altogether. As Susan said, he worked happily in a bipartisan way with the Congress, with Sam Rayburn, with Lyndon Johnson, and that's what produced results. We have departed in many significant ways from some of the virtues of American life in the past, and one of them was what America represents, and that is a spirit that when the chips are down, we are, first of all, Americans. Thank you, again.

DR. THOMPSON: Thank you very much, David Gergen. You know, it is said of Americans that one of their most appealing characteristics is their ability to quickly forget the grudges of the past, but I think that these remarks indicate how important it is to remember some of the key lessons of the past, and so thank you for reminding us not only who Dwight Eisenhower was but also what he believed and what it means for us today. Thank you very, very much. We will now be taking a break, and we will resume with our first panel in this room at 10:30.

PANEL 1

TODAY'S SECURITY ENVIRONMENT—THE NEW GLOBAL CONTEXT

Co-sponsor: The Conference Board

Chair: Ms. Gail D. Fosler, Senior Vice President and Chief Economist, The Conference Board

Congressional Perspective: The Honorable Jerry Lewis (R-Calif.), Chairman, Defense Appropriations Subcommittee

Historical Context: Professor Douglass C. North, Spencer T. Olin Professor of Arts and Sciences, Washington University, St. Louis

International Economic Perspective: Ms. Anne O. Krueger, First Deputy Managing Director, International Monetary Fund

Military and Security Perspective: Dr. Stephen J. Flanagan, Director, Institute for National Strategic Studies, National Defense University

Panel Charter

The events of September 11th introduced to the world scene a new form of national security threat, previously feared, now a reality. Nonstate actors with limited manpower and technology can create huge human and economic losses by attacking the economic-social infrastructure of modern society. The ability to strike anywhere, anytime, without amassing troops, equipment, and supplies has upended the rules of engagement in modern warfare. More alarming is the fact that the availability of nuclear and biological weapons suggests future attacks will be even more devastating.

This changing nature of the global security threat adds immeasurable complexity to an already complex global political environment. After 1989 and the end of the Cold War, what had been a standoff between two superpowers dissolved into regional, national, and sub-national disputes in almost every part of the world. These rising tensions are fed by growing social and economic problems, including poverty, a growing AIDS epidemic, small-arms proliferation, and narcotics trafficking.

Left to right: *Dr. Loren B. Thompson, Professor Douglass C. North,
Ms. Gail Fosler, Dr. Stephen J. Flanagan, Ms. Susan Eisenhower,
Mrs. Francis Hesselbein, Ms. Anne O. Krueger, General Eric K. Shinseki*

The purpose of this panel is to understand the broad economic, cultural, and historical context that has spawned this new global threat. The motivations behind today's threat are no longer modeled on nation-state conflict with the traditional goals of self-determination, expansion of land and influence, and/or the exercise of national power. Rather, the roots—irrespective of the specific motivations of the individuals involved—are cultural, religious, and economic. Indeed, any individual or group of individuals from any country of any race or national origin can be recruited because the goal is to destroy a way of life, not to move a national border.

This panel draws together four very different perspectives on the topic. The first is a global economic perspective that explains that role of widening differences in living standards and recent emerging-market economic crises in creating a growing pool of potentially disenfranchised poor around the world who believe the market system—and the United States as a leading proponent of the market system—has failed them. The second is a historical perspective that focuses on how tensions develop that create incentives for groups or states to take actions, often not rational by traditional standards, to alter, in dramatic ways, the existing balance of power. In the current case, these actions are clearly focused on the United States as the leading national power.

The third and fourth perspectives will come from the U.S. military and U.S. Congress. The United States is challenged to reformulate its traditional strategies at a pace unprecedented in its history. War is no longer a discrete event with a predefined time frame. War and peacekeeping are now intertwined such that both can and have been conducted simultaneously. At the same time, the Congress must review, comprehend, and legislate resources for this new, multidimensional threat.

Discussion Points

• What are the historical analogs to the current global threat and what can we learn from the outcomes?

• Do the demographic and cultural forces at work today inevitably lead to conflict or does the current threat have a unique character?

• Are the free-market solutions to emerging market economic problems limited?

• Do new institutional structures exist that would foster stability and growth?

• Is the relationship close between economic instability and military risk?

• Could nations where the economy is deteriorating badly become a spawning ground for terrorism—or do culture and religion trump economics as a focus for nonstate actions?

• How does Congress, which is structured to focus on specific jurisdictions of government interest, deal with the new complexity?

Summary

Ms. Gail D. Fosler, Senior Vice President and Chief Economist, The Conference Board

• We face an environment that has become enormously more complex. We face a series of weapons of various types of destruction—including our own domestic infrastructure—that provide huge diversity in terms of the combinations of threats and the complexity of understanding the possible responses.

Honorable Jerry Lewis (R-Calif.), Chairman, Defense Appropriations Subcommittee

• None of us will ever forget that scene last year when airplanes flew into those two huge buildings in New York. We had been attacked again, setting a stage for a challenge that President Bush has described as our "war on terrorism."

• The members of the Defense Appropriations Subcommittee know almost no partisan consideration. On both sides of the aisle, the members are committed to our national security, and it's that ability to work together in that environment that allows us to be as successful as we have been.

• At this moment, the challenges could not be more serious. The pressures upon us to set priorities for spending for national defense are reflective of the administration's posture.

• One of the most poignant moments of the last year was the scene shortly after 9/11. The President called together the entire House, Senate, and Supreme Court and the entire Cabinet except for one. During that speech, he captured the spirit of the American people. The American public did not want partisan politics; they were not interested in Republican against Democrat. They were sending a very clear message: You'd better be together because we believe this war and this challenge are serious.

• We will have disagreements in the weeks and the months ahead, but this team that's serving the administration is not there by accident, and they're doing their job with very serious purpose, and that advice and counsel is serving the country extremely well today.

Ms. Anne O. Krueger, First Deputy Managing Director, International
        Monetary Fund

• Globalization is the process of integration across nations through the spread of ideas, the sharing of technological advances, and trade in goods, services, and the movement of labor and capital across national boundaries.

    1. It is a process that has been going on almost throughout recorded history and has conferred huge benefits. It is not something that started recently.

    2. Globalization does, and always did, involve change, and people are typically afraid of change—even many of those who end up gaining from it. Some do lose in the short run when things change, but when change is going rapidly enough and in a positive direction, the short-term losers are few, and even they can become gainers over the longer term.

• Globalization has been subject to ebbs and flows.

    1. It gained impetus with the period of great discoveries in the fifteenth century and with dramatic falls in the cost of communication and transportation.

    2. After World War II, globalization got another big boost from the dramatic lowering of trade barriers among major industrialized nations under the important leadership of the United States.

    3. Over the last 50 years, the process of integration has accelerated and started to embrace many nations across the world with great success.

• Economic growth has been faster in the past 50 years than it was in earlier centuries.

1. We have created a world in which you can do more about poverty more quickly. Access to the buoyant international market has greatly facilitated faster growth for poor people in poor countries. It has permitted the degree of reliance on comparative advantage and a division of labor when things are going well that was simply not possible in the nineteenth century.

2. There has been rapid growth in international trade and in the supportive services that developed countries can provide that let developing countries do things right and do them quickly, without incurring the huge costs that would have prevented them from otherwise doing so.

• Technology transfer also helps to boost growth rates. Latecomers to the development already have the advantage of ready access to all the blueprints developed over several hundred years in the more advanced countries. Latecomers have also benefited from the falling costs of transport and communications. And in that, they've been able to transform their economies quickly.

• Population growth has accelerated not because people are having more children than ever before, but because more survive than ever before, and for longer periods of time. Growing incomes give people the ability to spend on things other than food and shelter—things such as education and health. And this ability has transformed life in many parts of the developed world.

• Economic growth has gone hand-in-hand with democracy and representation. Many more people around the world are now living free. People have also been given much more opportunity to vote with their feet; they go where there are more opportunities and where there are better chances for life.

Dr. Stephen J. Flanagan, Director, Institute for National Strategic Studies,
    National Defense University

• The terrorist attacks against the United States brought into sharp relief a security environment that has been evolving in recent years, heavily shaped by the end of the Cold War and very much influenced by the effects of globalization.

1. There's a whole new skill set that the national security community needs to bring to bear as it begins to tackle new security and defense problems.

2. Globalization is interacting with traditional geopolitical, ethnic, religious, and cultural rivalries to create a much more complex and dynamic security environment.

3. It has created a critical fault line between those benefiting from globalization and those buffeted by its effects. This divide cuts across various regions and even various segments of populations in the same countries.

4. Globalization is also leading to a new interdependence, and the divisions between foreign and domestic affairs have completely eroded.

• The key driver to globalization is the information revolution, which has also leveled the playing field in important ways, enabling certain medium powers and even small sub-national groups to be able to challenge and sometimes restrict the capabilities of major powers.

• In some regions, globalization, with its efficient but volatile markets and attendant financial shocks, is interacting with weak governance and unstable security affairs to exacerbate these economic disparities.

1. This is adding to the sense of hopelessness among certain groups in various countries and provides a fertile environment for recruiting terrorists and for spawning armed conflicts.

2. Globalization has also facilitated the expansion of international crime and the proliferation of sophisticated conventional weapons and weapons of mass destruction.

• These security and economic questions are intersecting in more pronounced ways that place more demands on our abilities. For example, there are the interlocking links and the organized crime activities of trafficking in drugs, people, and weapons, which are overlapping and sometimes creating alliances of convenience with terrorist groups that are an important part of this dark side of globalization.

• We also need to get at the sources of this rage and despair. We have to narrow the gap between prosperity and poverty; we have to work at ways to restore the sense of hope among many of these countries in the world.

• Defense planning these days is about a much broader set of issues than simply the movement of military forces around the world. In the last *National Security Strategy*, the Clinton administration recognized the importance of the implications of globalization, but most of the components of the U.S. government had not, and still have not, been very quick to adapt to these challenges and their structures and processes.

• Security, economics, science and technology, and law enforcement policies are essential to coping with these new security challenges of the global era, and they are still being developed largely in isolation from one another. These policy streams are generally integrated only at the very highest levels of our government and oftentimes only when necessitated by a crisis.

• We have to tell our story better, and there the administration has made great strides in the last year of enhancing our public diplomacy to better explain America's purpose in the world and to counter misinformation about what the purpose of our power is. But all of these elements of our strategy need to be much better integrated if we are to succeed in our efforts to promote global peace and security.

Professor Douglass C. North, Spencer T. Olin Professor of Arts and
Sciences, Washington University, St. Louis

• Two important aspects of today's security environment are the sources of the enormous variation in economic performance over time. Affecting those essential aspects are the belief systems that underlie the variations and the implications of those belief systems to the generation of violent behavior.

• We know a lot about the sources of productivity, and what makes countries rich or poor is very simple. They're rich if they're productive, and they're poor if they're not productive.

• Institutions are incentive structures; they're incentive systems. When we talk about institutions, we're talking about things like property rights, rules, the rule of law, etc.

• The rise of the Western world was really the development of what was a backward part of the world in the tenth century compared to the Muslim World, compared to China, compared to India. Its rise to dominating the world by the eighteenth century was an extraordinary development. It required fundamental institutional change that would move away from a personal exchange system of small-scale exchange to what Adam Smith long ago said was the source of the wealth of nations: specialization, division of labor, and large markets.

• So what evolved in the Western world was, in part, a belief system and, in part, good luck that together encouraged the development of impersonal exchange, large markets, productivity growth, and the technological miracles that made it such a significant part of the world.

• Contrast that very brief story with the Muslim world, which, in the twelfth century, was way ahead of the Western world. After the twelfth century, however, it literally decayed in the sense that institutional rigidities led to political and economic systems that failed to develop, that didn't encourage the growth of technology, the growth of markets, impersonal exchange, etc. Thus, no Muslim country in the world today is a high-income country except on the basis of oil, and oil was developed by Western technology.

• Human beings make choices about society, the structure they have, and the institutions. Underlying those choices are beliefs. And the belief system underlies not only choices that make us productive but also choices that lead equally to violence, to fanaticism, and to religious extremism.

• The belief system evolves in the context of the whole cultural environment—physical, political, economic, and social—and that environment accounts for enormous variety in the ways in which societies behave and also the ways in which fanaticism is generated. No neat relationship exists in the modern-day world between fanaticism and poverty.

Analysis

Ms. Gail D. Foster, Senior Vice President and Chief Economist, The Conference Board

The proliferation in sources and types of weapons of destruction—including those from the United States—has created a world very different from the one that existed just a decade ago. As the variety and frequency of possible security threats have increased, it has become ever more difficult to understand both the complexity of the threats and the form of possible responses. The world is no longer policed by containment and deterrence, but by a set of countervailing social, economic, and cultural values, some rational to us, others not. The collision of these values invites, indeed may sanction, acts of mass violence that will likely become more common before an effective response is found.

September 11 did not rewrite the global security threat. What it did was bring into sharp relief changes in the security environment that had been present for several years, including widespread weapons availability; the advent of rapid and cheap sources of communications, networking, and information; and a tandem rise in wealth and the speed at which wealth can be transferred around the globe. This "democratization" of assault capability permits small- and medium-size state and nonstate actors to challenge the major powers.

Globalization plays a peculiar and contradictory role in this process. While globalization, with the United States as its most prominent symbol, is the target of much of the rapidly evolving security threat, it is also, ironically, the source.

Globalization is the "process of integration across nations through the spread of ideas, the sharing of technological advances, the trade in goods and services, and the movement of labor and capital in ways that make that trade economically viable." What that means in practical terms is that globalization forces change in the direction of a new economic order dominated by American capitalism and backed by the global reach of American military power.

At the same time, globalization and the tremendous wealth associated with it have created much of the infrastructure, not to mention the resources, that make possible the escalating types and incidence of security challenges. People, goods, and funds move easily across borders. Most countries, especially in the West, are hugely diverse, with residents from every possible country and nationality. And the information technology that ties the vast global network together provides a ready communication channel for small groups dispersed in far-flung locations to plan and execute complex attacks.

Interestingly, it is not globalization itself but the accelerating pace of integration—supported by an explosion in cheap technology—that makes this "messy" security environment possible. We have long shown a tendency toward intense and, at times, technologically facile global integration. Likewise, globalization has been around for almost as long as history itself. What has changed is the pace—and along with it, the pace of economic development and change.

Over the course of the nineteenth century, per-capita incomes grew at about 1 1/2 percent per year. In the past 50 years, we have seen a number of countries catapult into the industrial world with 3 to 5 percent per-capita growth rates over 20-year time frames. This pace of change creates winners and losers, to be sure. But make no mistake; terrorism and the decline in global security are not driven by poverty. The leaders of these movements are often middle class and well educated.

That said, poverty does increase the pool of those who despair of ever participating in economic progress—indeed, may even reject it—and who can be trained to destroy its foundations. Unfortunate, too, is the large number of people living in countries that are fast slipping behind the more advanced world. Because the majority of these countries lack the democratic systems that are so closely associated with economic progress, they are vast breeding grounds for the anti-globalization sentiments that can be conveniently deployed to explain their poverty.

The National Defense University's Institute for National Strategic Studies recently published *Challenges of the Global Century*, an interdisciplinary study conducted over 18 months in which the Institute found that democratic countries have a combined GDP of $28 trillion—almost double the $14.5 trillion for the rest of the world. But democratic countries account for only 1.7 billion of the world's 6 billion people. The per-capita income gaps are even larger, with the richer countries enjoying per-capita incomes of $17,000, while the poorer countries average $3,400.

Almost three-quarters of the world's population live in countries that are not only poor but also dominated by centralized regimes of one form or another. The scope of these often-authoritarian governments underscores the geographic and demographic sweep of the crisis of public governance—a crisis that only exacerbates the institutional and cultural norms that already prevent countries from realizing their full potential.

To some extent, in fact, the recent economic successes of many emerging markets have helped to drive a deeper wedge between rich and poor. Unfortunately, this gap is widening. Despite the overall increase in global income and wealth, the gap between the richer democratic countries and other nations in the past decade has widened from $15.2 trillion to $17.7 trillion—an increase of $2.5 trillion in this already substantial gap.

Regional differences within countries can be as great or greater than the other differences between them. Key Indian and Chinese cities that are closely linked to the global economy may have per-capita income levels that are 10 or 20—or more—times higher than in the interior regions that communications, technology, and modern global markets have yet to reach.

These huge income gaps, decentralized power, and the rise of strong subnational groups—often along ethnic or cultural lines—are now linking to form new, movable frontiers of violence. Aided by this spreading geography of conflict, a host of other organizations—regional and international public institutions, transnational corporations, nongovernmental organizations, and terrorist and other criminal organizations—are using the instruments of globalization to challenge the power of the nation-state.

The Asian financial crisis, triggered by an exodus of foreign capital from Asian financial markets, eroded government legitimacy, exacerbated ethnic tensions, and catalyzed East Timor's struggle for independence. The Kosovo Liberation Army used the Internet to traffic drugs and other criminal activities, raise funds, and reach the diaspora. Meanwhile, Serb reformers used the same technology to get the word out to the world as to what was really happening in Serbia. Sierra Leone's Revolutionary United Front Party financed terrorist activities with global diamond sales, while local and international terrorist groups in and around Colombia have financed theirs through narcotics trade.

In sum, local groups' ability to organize and affiliate through the global transportation and information infrastructure has never been greater. Moreover, growing political instability and the increasing technical sophistication of these insurgent groups have weakened the counter-ability of many national governments to curb this activity. Globalization is thus both a target of rising violence and political and cultural unrest and an instrument for supporting and promulgating the resulting violence around the world.

Indeed, the darker side of globalization is the rapid growth in organized crime vis-à-vis the trafficking of drugs, people, and weapons. With the same transactions, criminal organizations not only finance terror and other organized violence but also transmit the means for carrying out such violence. These links are important from the national security policy perspective. We must avoid diverting important domestic security resources aimed at curbing drug trafficking in, for instance, the Coast Guard, to antiterrorism initiatives. The two may be, and likely are, linked.

The growing global infrastructure for terrorism and other violence is made much more dangerous by weapons proliferation. Clearly, a major concern is the proliferation of weapons of mass destruction that is driving the present U.S. policy toward Iraq. Globalization is most damaging in this arena not only because it accelerates the pace of proliferation but also because it makes the negative consequences more damaging. However, the increased threat comes not solely from weapons of mass destruction but also from the proliferation of advanced conventional arms and communications capabilities. Smart munitions, countermeasures, and new doctrines are making lesser conventional forces more formidable. Even small sub-national groups are now able to use global positioning system (GPS) transponders and other communications links to target conventional military forces, deny access to key areas, or disrupt operations.

Complicating the problem of weapons proliferation is the expanding number of geographies where regional conflicts could escalate into a strategic-level problem with possible global consequences. The Middle East; East Asia—particularly cross-straits issues between the People's Republic of China and

Taiwan; India and Pakistan; and the Korean peninsula are all areas of extreme concern. Added to these visible and well-known conflicts is the growing instability of weak states arising from ethnic conflicts or, in the case of Africa, the debilitating effects of AIDS, environmental degradation, and new conflicts over water. The instability on so many fronts makes much of the emerging world a potential source of global security threats, ranging from Southeast Asia, though Africa and the Middle East, all the way to the Balkans. This analysis helped drive last year's strategic review—which included, interestingly, the southern border of Afghanistan.

This turmoil in the "southern arc of instability" has acquired greater strategic importance lately because of its close relationship to global economic stability. Consequently, the United States has shifted its defense strategy focus from continental Eurasia to the southern and eastern regions of the Eurasian landmass: North Africa, the Middle East, Southeast Asia, and Oceania.

The scope of this involvement will require joint military capabilities, a flexible posture to facilitate quick-response deployments of power, continued forward presence, access to new locations, and extensive cooperation. To implement this strategy, the United States must widen its scope of partners and friends while sustaining partnerships with long-time allies—a policy that the Defense Department has identified as our new strategic framework for defense. The goal of the strategy is to assure friends and allies and to dissuade others from future military competition.

This places the security-planning framework in a whole new context. Rather than preparing for victory in two major theaters, the object now is decisive victory against an adversary in one theater, the defeat of a major aggressor in a second, overlapping theater, and the ability to simultaneously conduct a limited number of smaller-scale contingent actions. This approach means a major change in how the United States structures its defense forces, including integrating these forces with homeland security and rethinking the European Command.

Make no mistake; the United States does not want to remain the world's military hegemon. But neither does it want to see other powers rise to threaten the forces of freedom and liberty in the world.

Indeed, the scope and complexity of the new threat require building ties with nongovernmental, nonmilitary agencies. The need to get at the sources of hate and despair adds urgency to new initiatives like the President's challenge of $5 billion in development assistance to countries that improve their governance. The gap between prosperity and poverty must narrow, and financial measures may be required to offset some of the negative effects of globalization.

The most difficult aspect of the security challenge is in understanding how to bring prosperity and, hopefully, active engagement to countries that are, today, relatively poor. Government and international development programs and other sorts of well-meaning efforts have mostly failed because economic growth depends on incentives, and incentives—though often administered through a range of market and nonmarket institutions—arise from the political system. Just what makes some countries successful in developing incentives is the great puzzle of economics. Economists understand a great deal about how economic systems work once they are created, but they know surprisingly little about what makes some regions and countries develop systems—in some cases, very successful systems—in the first place and why others fail completely.

Once the West, including Europe and North America, was a backwater. In the tenth century, China and the Islamic Empire defined the frontier of technology, science, and culture. Over the next thousand years, however, these relationships reversed. Not only did the West develop a wide range of institutional structures, including property rights and the rule of law, that set the stage for the tremendous advances of the eighteenth and nineteenth centuries, but both China and the Islamic Empire stopped advancing and slipped backward. No major Muslim country today is a high-income country, and whatever gains have been achieved are the result of the sharp rise in the value of oil—not the result of their economic advances.

Economics is a theory of choice. Individuals and cultures decide how they wish to organize their societies and with what institutions. But where do these choices come from? It is too simple to assume that democratic political institutions will automatically lead a people to develop the incentive structures that create prosperity. India and the Philippines are good examples.

What underlies choice is belief, and this cuts two ways. Belief systems underlie the choices that make us productive; but they also underlie the choices that make us violent and fanatical and can lead to religious and political extremism. Without understanding the sources of fanaticism and violence and doing something to undermine those beliefs, the future will be very bleak, indeed.

Where to begin? At the beginning. The root of any belief is moral consciousness. This is what separates human beings from other primates and what unites us as a species. Moral consciousness is the source of creativity, productivity, great art and literature, economic growth. It is also the source of fanaticism and violence. The question is, what produces one rather than the other?

The physical, social, political, and economic structure of any people evolves from its belief system. Economists traditionally ignore this whole area of inquiry. Yet it is quite clear that the reason why even the advanced economies operate very differently from one another is that the belief systems that drive their cultures and the psychologies that underlie their economies are quite different.

This just underscores the point that it is not poverty per se that drives violence. It is fanaticism occasioned by a belief system that conjures or encourages violence. And that can develop in any country, no matter the level of economic development.

Tackling these belief systems is very difficult. All societies have non-rational beliefs, religion being the best example. The antidote for fanaticism and violence that has so far proved successful is counterviolence, otherwise known as national defense. It works.

But an alternative—or, more likely, complementary—approach is to try to understand the sources of these belief systems and create institutional structures that change them. For example, instead of escalating the conflict in the Middle East over the Palestinian question, why not provide huge resources to the region to be used only to develop institutions that would help the Palestinian people create a modern state with strong ties to the rest of the world? In other words, why not create mechanisms that would spawn a global culture with varying belief systems that tend toward resolution by negotiation rather than violence? This approach might require military and civilian institutions to cooperate more closely to redefine the intersection between peace and war in a way that involves everyone in the process of peace. This is a very different way of thinking. But the escalating rise in global violence suggests that a common global culture of peace, one that involves a much wider range of institutions than in the past, may be the only truly effective solution.

Transcript

DR. LOREN B. THOMPSON: Our first panel today provides a foundation for all of the discussions that follow by assessing the emerging global security environment. Science-fiction writer Arthur C. Clarke said some time ago that the future isn't what it used to be. Certainly, that is true in the case of security policy. The world that many of us were trained to work in simply doesn't exist anymore. Concepts, like containment and deterrence, that seemed timeless twenty years ago, now have considerably less currency. A new global order is emerging that demands different strategies and capabilities. Happily for us, the chairperson of this morning's panel was trained in a field that is, if anything, growing in importance since the end of the Cold War, due, in no small part, to the contributions that she and her organization have made. She is Gail D. Fosler, senior vice president and chief economist of the Conference Board.

The Conference Board is approaching its 86th anniversary as the world's leading business forum—a hugely respected and hugely influential organization. One reason for its continued success is Ms. Fosler herself. The *Wall Street Journal* has repeatedly named her as "the most accurate economic forecaster in America." In her capacity as chief economist, Ms. Fosler directs the Conference Board's worldwide economic research program, a source of such well-known metrics as the leading economic indicators and the consumer confidence index. Before joining the Conference Board, Ms. Fosler was chief economist and deputy staff director of the Senate Budget Committee. She is a director of the Unisys Corporation, H.B. Fuller, Baxter International, and DBS Holdings, and she's a

trustee of John Hancock Mutual
Funds. Her projections of future economic performance are closely followed in financial markets around the
world, and they are reported in all of
the major media. Please join me in
welcoming Gail D. Fosler.

MS. GAIL D. FOSLER: Thank
you, Dr. Thompson. It's rare that you
hear anyone say good things about
economists, and I am very much in
your debt. I think that our conference
organizers' choice of timing for this
event could not have been more timely. Certainly, we have tensions rising
in the Middle East, and we also face
the IMF meetings tomorrow, which
actually join what are going to be two
very important themes on our panel.
We face an environment that has
become enormously more complex.

Ms. Fosler

We face a series of weapons of various types of destruction, including our own
domestic infrastructure that provides huge diversity in terms of the combinations of threats and, I think, the complexity of understanding the responses.

We have an extraordinary panel, and I want to thank my panelists in
advance for taking the time for this event because each of them faces very special pressures in terms of their own commitments and their own roles. What I
will do is just briefly introduce them as they come on stage, and then we will
begin the panel discussions and go to questions and answers.

So if I can introduce, in the beginning, Congressman Jerry Lewis.
Congressman Lewis is the Chairman of the Defense Appropriations
Committee in the House of Representatives. He has been a long-standing
member of Congress. We are hoping very much that he will give us a congressional perspective on how an institution that is really devoted to highly
focused—in some ways very compartmentalized—responsibilities deals with
what is a very multidimensioned environment; and one that requires committees and probably members that are not accustomed to working together to be
able to work together in a more committed, more focused, and, in some ways,
more expeditious way.

Our second panelist is Professor Douglass North. Douglass North is the
Spenser T. Olin Professor in Arts and Sciences at the University of
Washington. He received a Nobel Prize for his work in economic history,

Professor North is an advocate and, indeed, a leading intellectual in the field of what we economists call *institutional economics*. Institutional economics is not just the standard concepts of economics that you all are familiar with thinking about—income, how the stock market is doing, whether the consumer is spending, whether interest rates are going up or down—but rather determining some of the most important turning points and long-term projections of economic growth for an individual society. It is the institutions that they have in place and how effective those institutions are in terms of regulating and providing incentives to the key economic actors in an economy.

And third, we have Dr. Anne Krueger. Anne is the first deputy managing director of the International Monetary Fund, and I think given what is on her plate this week, we owe a very special note of thanks to her for taking the time to join us. Anne, I think, has been very much at the fulcrum of dealing with some changing policy prescriptions as to how we might deal with a world in which we have often thought of the center as the key industrial countries and the periphery, emerging markets. Anne is very much a leader intellectually in sort of breaking down that barrier and helping us all come to realize that there is no center and there is no periphery; that there is a much more holistic globe and we may need to make some changes in our policies as we deal with what is not a new reality but, I think, a new recognition on our part.

Our final panelist is Dr. Steven Flanagan. Dr. Flanagan is the vice president for research and director for the Institute for Strategic Studies. Dr. Flanagan has just completed a project looking at globalization and the national security threat. He brings us a unique interdisciplinary look at the issues that we have on our panel this morning, both from an economic and globalization standpoint, and also from the standpoint of one who is a leading thinker and writer in the field of national security policy.

Each panelist will speak for approximately fifteen minutes. I will begin with a question for the panelists so that you can organize your thoughts. Then we will go to a question-answer period for the rest of our time. Unfortunately, Congressman Lewis will have to leave us after his remarks because of the press of business on Capitol Hill, but we will conduct the rest of the panel and then welcome time for discussion. I hope we will have some spirited discussion, because we do not have a group of people here with a monolithic view as to what the challenges and responses are, and I hope that we will be able to articulate some of their areas of difference, as well as their areas of agreement. Thank you.

CONGRESSMAN JERRY LEWIS: First let me apologize to the audience for having to leave. The Appropriations Committee is meeting as we are meeting, and I must return. But in the meantime, I want to share with the audience the fact that it is my privilege to chair the subcommittee that appropriates all the funds for national security. At this moment in our history, I cannot imagine a job that is more stimulating and challenging, as well as exciting. In the meantime, the subcommittee handles only about $370 billion of our money available this year, a minor piece of the national budget, well over half of the discretionary dollars that are available.

I'd like to begin my remarks by perhaps giving some impressions of our responsibility, but starting first with, in my mind's eye, one of the most important impressions of my life. I was raised in southern California. I remember very clearly my mother coming to the front door yelling to the boys who were down the street to come home, for something was of great importance that day. It seems the Japanese had bombed Pearl Harbor. Today, in this subcommittee on national security

Congressman Lewis

that appropriates these funds, are few members who remember that event—our country being attacked in its homeland. Impressions are very important as we carry forward our work. None of us will ever forget that scene a year ago, when airplanes flew into two huge buildings in New York. We had been attacked again, setting the stage for a challenge that President Bush has described as *our war against terrorism*.

One of the points about my subcommittee's work that I'd especially like to mention is that thirteen members are on the subcommittee. But our subcommittee knows almost no partisan consideration. We take on very serious, very difficult issues. On both sides of the aisle, the members are committed to our national security. Moreover, it's our being able to work together in that environment that I think allows us to be as successful as we have been.

At this moment, the challenges could not be more serious. The pressures upon us to give priority to national spending for national defense are reflective of the administration's posture, and I want to share a bit of that with this audience. Only a few months ago, most of Washington was suggesting that perhaps the president was on the wrong track. Indeed, shortly before that, many of us had wondered how he'd gone about selecting this rather incredible committee of advisers. One way or another, he selected a vice president who had had some experience in national security. Dick Cheney had spent four years as secretary of defense—an immensely talented fellow who seemed to be carrying forward discussion that was somewhere on the right side of those conversations about national security. On the other hand, the current secretary of defense, a part of the team, had had some experience as well. He'd served before as secretary of defense; he'd served in the House of Representatives. People wondered for some time about Colin Powell. What role is he going to play, the new Secretary of State? Not everybody remembers that it was Richard Cheney who reached down into the bowels of the Defense Department, picked out a one-star, and made him his chief of staff. I think the secretary ruffled a lot of feathers by having the audacity to bypass so many who were ahead of Colin Powell. Colin Powell, as you know, is now secretary of state. The role he plays, people wonder about. Condoleeza Rice, just down the hall from the president, is the person who probably gives him the most frequent advice and counsel. Nonetheless, not long ago, Washington was just amazed that such a panel could be put together. Yet recently, we've had more than one conversation suggesting that maybe it's by accident that the president got to where he has today. Isn't it strange that Washington can't figure out that maybe this immensely talented panel of people and advisers might have been thinking about what their jobs were about? And indeed, this same panel happens to be involved and employed by the same boss. They all work for the Commander in Chief. Colin Powell didn't become the secretary of state by accident; he's a team player. Condoleeza Rice, some people suggest, has not nearly the experience that would allow her to do these things well—a brilliant woman who is making a very significant contribution to the president's program.

The president declared war on terrorism. One of the most poignant moments for me, while serving in the Congress, was the scene shortly after 9/11. The president called us all together—the entire House, the Senate, the Supreme Court, his entire Cabinet except for one. And during that speech, he essentially captured the spirit of the American people that reacted to the fact that we had been attacked upon our homeland for the first time in many a generation and reacted to this one central theme: The American public did not want partisan politics. They were not interested in Republican against Democrat. They were sending a very clear message: You'd better be together because we believe this war and this challenge are serious. A scene that I'll never forget—there was the President of the United States, the Commander in Chief, coming down to the well of the House following his speech. Tom Daschle walked across the well of the House. They embraced before God and everybody, in friendship, in recognition of the challenge ahead of them, but ever more important in my mind's eye, in understanding that they were in this together.

We will have disagreements in the weeks and the months ahead, but I believe most intently that this team that's serving the administration is not there by accident, and they're doing their job with very serious purpose, and their advice and counsel are, I believe, serving the country extremely well today.

MS. FOSLER: Thank you, Congressman Lewis. May I ask you just one question? I think it would be interesting for you to give a few comments on how the events of 9/11 have changed the way that you and your committee do your work.

CONGRESSMAN LEWIS: As I indicated in my opening remarks, the wonderful thing about our subcommittee is that there is almost no party in the room when we talk about serious issues. I have this job by grace of the fact that I happened to be elected to Congress, but it couldn't come for me at a more challenging time. And if it weren't for my partner, Jack Murtha from Pennsylvania—a fabulous guy who understands that there should not be partisan consideration when we look at national security—the work would be an awful lot tougher.

There's great pressure on the Congress right now about what we do with our dollars. The Defense Appropriations Bill is before us at this very moment. We'll very likely meet next week to put together with the Senate the closing key decisions regarding our bill. It will probably be one of two appropriations bills that get to the president's desk—this bill and military construction, which is a relatively small piece of the entire package. But, indeed, the tone will be set by our work. As a result of 9/11, the public's message, "We expect you not to show partisan difference; we expect you to be working together," has been heard loud and clear by the committee. But I must say, to my satisfaction, that has been the instinct of the committee from the first. Therefore, the work is going forward very well. Significant decisions are being made as we speak. And, indeed, I believe that our national security is much better off because of the way the committee handles its work.

MS. FOSLER: Thank you. And thank you for being with us.

CONGRESSMAN LEWIS: I appreciate your having me. My privilege.

MS. FOSLER: Now, I think in terms of the order, I would like to turn to Anne and then Steve Flanagan and then round up with Professor North, because I think we can focus on where we are, and then Professor North can give us an idea of where we are in a fairly broad historical context.

MS. ANNE O. KRUEGER: Thank you. It's a pleasure to be here and to be discussing the whole international economic perspective with regard to security issues. I thought what I might do is focus on several aspects of the phenomenon that surrounds us all that is called *globalization*. It's an interesting word that has come into our vocabulary. As you know, there are some protesters out there and others who think they're going to say something about that tomorrow. We think we have something to say too. I think it's an inter-

esting concept, in a way, around
which to try and organize our thinking as to what's going on.

I'll say a few words at the end
about how I think globalization
relates directly to security threats, but
I am no expert on security. As close
as I ever came was once doing a book
review on export controls for the
arms industry, and after having written that, I got a few phone calls saying, "Since you're an expert on
defense..." I quickly gave that up and
went back to what I knew about.

In any event, we hear a lot about
globalization and yet it's very seldom
defined, and different people can pick
different definitions. I like to think of
it as the process of integration across
nations through the spread of ideas;
the sharing of technological
advances; and trade in goods, servic-

Dr. Krueger

es, and the movement of labor and capital across national boundaries. In other
words, it's almost everything that's going on. But what's more interesting—and
I'm sure Doug North will say more later, and I will try not to tread on his territory—it is a process that has been going on almost throughout recorded history and has conferred huge benefits. It's not something that started recently,
and I'll come back to some arguments about that in a moment.

Globalization does, and always did, involve change, and people are typically afraid of change—even many of those who end up gaining from it. And,
of course, some do lose in the short run when things change. But when change
is going rapidly enough and in a positive direction, the short-term losers are
few, and even they can become gainers over the longer term, which doesn't
mean they like the interim. To argue as the protesters will—or some of them
will tomorrow or Saturday—that globalization is a bad thing is like arguing
that the air isn't quite as pure as we'd like, therefore, breathing is a bad thing.
On the other hand, I think the thing to do is to see if we can clean up the air;
the policy prescription is not to stop breathing. And in exactly the same way,
the world we live in is a world in which this process has been going on, and
any effort to think realistically at all about going back on that is a nonstarter.

A couple of countries have pretty much cut themselves off from the international economy; tried to go it alone. I think of Myanmar, which was the
third richest country in Asia in 1950, and which has pretty systematically and

deliberately cut itself off and is now beginning to look at some of the costs it's paid and beginning, perhaps, to try and do something about it. We have other countries that have tried it for a while, learned it won't work, and gotten about their business of integrating with the world economy.

Globalization has, of course, been subject to ebbs and flows. It gained impetus with the period of great discoveries in the fifteenth century and in later centuries with dramatic falls in the cost of communication and transportation. One of the incidents I like to tell to fix people's minds on how far we've come is that the House of Rothschild basically began its fortune by discovering that they could use carrier pigeons to bring news from Brussels to London, thereby beating everybody else by several hours, which gave them a huge advantage of knowledge in the European markets. Carrier pigeons were a huge technological step forward, which seems somewhat funny now but at the time was pretty serious. And the invention of the telegraph and the laying of the transatlantic cable cut settlement times between New York and London from 10 to 3 days, which was a huge step forward in terms of the efficiency of international financial markets. And think what it must have been like when the first telegraph wire went through. We think now of globalization as all these remarkable changes. But think what it must have been like when you could get news of what was happening across the Atlantic almost instantaneously, instead of when the ship got in a week and a half later.

Now, all that said, after World War II, globalization got another big boost from the dramatic lowering of trade barriers among major industrialized nations under the leadership—the important leadership—of the United States. And over the past 50 years, trends have continued, and with that, liberalization by the process of integration has accelerated and started to embrace many nations throughout the world with, as I will argue, great success.

Economic growth has been faster in the past 50 years than it was in earlier centuries, which, of course, increases the pace of change with some of the tensions involved there. In the nineteenth century, the most rapidly growing country in the world was the United Kingdom. The economic historians estimate that the average rate of growth per capita income over the entire century was about 1/2 percent per year. We have a very different situation now. The rapidly growing countries that got it right early in the 1960s—Korea and so forth—have achieved per-capita growth rates many times that, so much so that in the heyday of Korea's growth—1963 to 1973—it experienced more growth in per-capita income than the United Kingdom did based on our current estimates in the entire nineteenth century.

Change, in that sense, can come faster. We've created a world in which you can do more about poverty more quickly. Access to the buoyant international market has greatly facilitated faster growth for poor people in poor countries, and that's where I will come into my theme of the relationship with security later. It's permitted the degree of reliance on comparative advantage and a division of labor when things are going well that were simply not possible in the nineteenth century. There's been rapid growth of international trade and there's been rapid growth in the supportive services that developed countries can provide that let developing countries, when they get their act together, do things right and do it quickly, without incurring the huge costs that would have prevented them from otherwise doing so. Communications, wholesalers, finance, insurance—all of these things would be terribly expensive for poor countries to provide for themselves and would put them at a cost disadvantage.

Technology transfer also helps boost growth rates. Latecomers to the development have the advantage of ready access to all the blueprints developed over several hundred years in the more advanced countries. Some of those blueprints are relevant partly because their processes are more adaptable for countries abundant in unskilled labor, partly because they are goods that are more in demand, relatively at least, in developing countries. They don't have to reinvent the wheel, so they can just start to learn as they go and then move up, if they like the value-added chain. Latecomers have also gotten lots of benefit from the falling costs of transport and communications. And in that, they've been able to transform their economies quickly. People now forget that Korea was 70 to 80 percent agriculture in 1960. Eighty-eight percent of its exports in 1960 were primary commodities. It was the third poorest country in Asia, with the heaviest density of people on land of any country in the world at that time. And think where it is now.

Over the last decade, joining the international economy has helped some other countries, such as some regions in India, to help make transition in India. I have in mind those parts of the country where the information-based economy and the impact of faster growth on living standards has been phenomenal, and don't let anti-globalizers ever tell you otherwise. Population growth has accelerated not because people are having more children than ever before but because more survive than ever before and for longer periods of time. Growing incomes give people the ability to spend on things other than food and shelter—things such as education and health. This ability has transformed life in many parts of the developed world. Infant mortality has declined from 180-per-thousand births in 1950 to 60-per-thousand births currently throughout the developing world—not worldwide, because it's even lower if you consider industrialized countries.

The average literacy rate, as best we could estimate it in the 1930s at a very generous assumption—people were asked if they could sign their name, and if they said yes, they were literate—has risen from over 40 percent then to an estimated 70 percent today. Even with population growth, the number of poor people, defined as those living on less than a dollar a day, has fallen by about 200 million, much of it due to the rapid growth in China and India. If there's one measure that can summarize all this, it's life expectancy. Only 50 years ago, life in much of the developing world was pretty much what it used to be in the rich nations a couple of centuries ago: nasty, brutish, and short. But today, life expectancy in the developing world averages 65 years, up from 40 in 1950, and that's huge. Life expectancy was increasing even in sub-Saharan Africa until the effects of the regional conflicts and the AIDS epidemic brought about a reversal. The gap between life expectancy in the developed and the developing world has narrowed somewhat with all of that, although of course our life expectancies have gone up too with improved health care, better access for more of our population to improved nutrition, and other benefits.

Economic growth has gone hand-in-hand with democracy and representation. It's not a separate issue. Many more people around the world are now living free. According to Freedom House, the proportion of countries with some degree of democratic government rose from 28 percent in 1974 to 62 percent in 2000, and electoral democracies now represent 120 of 192 or so countries that constitute nearly 60 percent of the world's population. People have also been given much more opportunity to vote with their feet. They go where there are more opportunities and where there are chances to build a better life. They do not vote by going back to rural areas and conditions of life such as they were. They like and want globalization and the things that it brings.

Now, there's a clear contradiction between these manifest benefits of growth and globalization and the outcry against them. The protests are particularly bewildering to those of us who have followed this progress, because the gains have come about without many—or indeed any—of the feared side effects coming to pass. Take for example the perennial concern that rapid growth depletes our fuel resources and, once that happens, growth will come to a dead stop. Let me remind you, in the middle of the nineteenth century it was thought that the world would shortly run out of whale oil and that would be the end of civilization because no one could read at night, but that's passed. World oil reserves, estimated in years that you could go on at your current rate of consumption without depleting them, are now 40 years. They were estimated at 20 years in 1970. There's no doubt that by the time 2040 rolls around, we'll find either some other new energy sources if the price of oil rises, or something else.

Nor have we done irreparable harm to the environment. The evidence quite convincingly shows that economic growth does bring an initial phase of deterioration in some aspects, and I stress some of the environment, but it's followed even in those by a subsequent phase of improvement. People choose to spend more of their income, when they get more income, on cleaning up around them. They don't like living in dirty places with unclean air and all that, and the estimate is that something between $4,000 and $6,000 per-capita income is when that happens. And even in countries that are much poorer than that, people no longer throw their sewage out the second-floor window or do many other things that were very harmful, public-health-wise, several centuries ago.

Even in poor countries, we haven't seen a major outbreak of black plague or any of the things that were a feature of life several centuries ago.

What about labor and social conditions in the developing world? Conditions in the so-called sweatshop factories in developing countries should be compared, I think, to the other choices available to people in those countries. For instance, the growth of the footwear industry in Vietnam has translated into a fivefold increase in monthly wages, from $9 a month to $45 a month. Still nothing by our standards, but that amount can completely transform the lives of workers and their families. Insisting that such workers be given a decent wage would, by our standards, completely erode any competitive advantages of businesses using unskilled labor, and that's, of course, where those workers are learning so they can move up the value-added chain later. Likewise, child labor is sometimes prevalent in developing countries because the alternatives are so much worse: starvation for the whole family or letting someone go to work with malnutrition. And I point out that it's especially beneficial for the girls to have opportunities because their alternatives are very frequently forced early marriages, prostitution, or life on the streets as beggars. Child labor doesn't look so bad if you think about those alternatives. And there's ample evidence the parents are the same throughout the world. Nobody wants to treat his or her children that way. When life is grim, you make hard choices, and it isn't a choice between pleasant things.

There's also an argument that globalization is associated with the loss of control of nations. I would argue that, in fact, the real loss of control and the real lack of power is poverty. Poverty is living in a permanent state of crisis, and that's what most people in most developing countries do. There are also concerns about inequality. I think it's important to distinguish, first off, between increases in inequality by which is meant what percentage of the total income is gained by what percentage of the people and increases in poverty or reductions in poverty. In most countries, in fact, the evidence is that when you get a rate of economic growth per capita of 2 percent, virtually every income group's income goes up by approximately 2 percent. Some people who are poor get rich faster, some who are rich don't, but on average, you do not get very much change in the income distribution in the short run.

It's very hard to go back through the rapidly growing countries such as Korea and identify groups of people whose living standards actually fell. By the way, it's also impossible to prove that the inequality got worse in Korea during its years of rapid growth. The evidence just doesn't support it. On the other hand, there are losers who do come about, but even they often get compensated by the gainers. In Korea, it's true there are older people living on small farms who weren't doing any better than they had been, but they had sons and daughters in the cities earning three or four times what their parents earned and sending remittances back. So even there, they had social mechanisms that did it. Unless you're worried about inequality per se, as contrasted with increasing poverty, much, if not most, of the concern about globalization on that score does not seem appropriate. Countries that have experienced faster growth by opening up the world economy, in fact, have opened up opportunities for unskilled workers faster, and, in general, that group has been a group of big gainers in the whole process. If you look not at within-country equality but worldwide inequality, the news is good. The poor have grown richer more rapidly than the rich, and it's due in part to the increasingly rapid growth in China and India, where there were very many poor people.

The only thing we can figure out at the IMF is that protesters aren't really against growth or globalization, but they're against change or fear the impact of change, and since change benefits so many of the poor, their fear seems to us to be somewhat misplaced. In the nineteenth century, Governor Clinton, then governor of New York, received petitions saying that it was dangerous to health, and especially to the health of women, to have trains running at 15 miles an hour; it was bad for the body. I suspect that some of the allegations today about what's happening in globalization may be that same kind. There are, of course, losers, and they're people who lose relatively. But as we get richer, we can afford better protection and insurance for them. In poor countries, even, we are making great progress in finding ways that, with their limited resources, there can be some minimal social safety nets that really help.

So to conclude, I think that the world is on a good path and that on that path, we are more and more effective in reducing the incidence of poverty. How does that relate to security? Well, I already said that I think that there is a link. You can't grow very rapidly without developing a big middle class. You can't get a big middle class and keep it happy without giving it increasing say in the political process. People who are middle class have something to lose, and they are the people who basically, in a democracy, will *not* vote to do other things. Those who seem to be the ones who are threatening security are not the ones who are gaining. People who have enough opportunity to improve their lives and have a say in their government don't protest. Nor do they focus on attacks. The ones who attack are the losers—the ones who, for whatever reason, have chosen sets of economic policies that offer no hope for their people. Interestingly enough, they do not even seem to be the poor in those societies, but they are the ones in those societies who are frustrated because their countries aren't doing better.

We in the international financial institutions believe that supporting the legitimate efforts of legitimate governments to increase the livelihood and give opportunities for most of the populations contributes greatly to security because as people find their ways to modern, industrial, democratic societies with opportunities within the economic arena and see their own countries as being able to stand with pride on the world stage, we will see less threat to the security issue. Thank you very much.

MS. FOSLER: Thank you, Anne.
I think that we may even be able to
open up some disagreements earlier
in the panel session than not, but I
think this presents a wonderful
opportunity, Steve, for you to look at
the economics and see if you agree
with the security outcome.

DR. STEPHEN J. FLANAGAN:
Thank you very much. It's a pleasure
to join you today. I think this panel
has a good cross-section of the skill
sets that we need to address security
affairs, and I'll do my part to hold up
the end of looking at security while
very much cognizant of some of the
comments that Ms. Krueger has just
made and Dr. Fosler made earlier
about the need to look at security in a
much more holistic way than we ever
have in the past.

Dr. Flanagan

It's a pleasure to join you today. I note a number of my colleagues are joining you later in the program from the National Defense University, a university with strong links to President Eisenhower because of his role in founding
first what was the Army Industrial College, later to become the Industrial
College of the Armed Forces at Fort McNair. So it's very appropriate, and I
think my colleagues will add some valuable perspectives on a number of issues
that I'm going to touch on very quickly today.

I am going to look at globalization and its impact on U.S. defense policy,
but very much building on and agreeing with some of the foundation that Ms.
Krueger has provided. While I'm not an economist, I will put up a few slides
drawing on some economic analysis. It's daunting to be sitting at this table
with Anne Krueger and Gail Fosler, to put forward any economic judgments,
but I will say that I think some important economic judgments undergird the
emerging security environment that we are now living through.

I'll start by saying that the events of September 11 last year didn't change
everything, but they did bring into sharp relief a security environment that has
been evolving in recent years, heavily shaped by the end of the Cold War policy and very much influenced by the effects of globalization. As I said, I agree
very much with Anne Krueger. From our perspective and the analysis that
we've done—working with a number of economists who were part of a study
that Gail Fosler mentioned completing last summer—I think globalization got

a bad name partly because it was oversold by the initial prophets. It has both very positive and very negative effects, and I'll touch on some of those, because they are some of the effects that we've been dealing with in the security domain, particularly over the last year. But it is important that we understand it. A year ago, I never would have thought, running a Defense Department think tank, that I would have been looking to the judgments of a criminologist on our staff for assessments of how we could do better in tracking terrorist finances. So there's a whole new skill set that the national security community needs to bring to bear as it begins to tackle new security and defense problems, and I'm going to try to elaborate on some of those points. But it was very much evident in the setup piece to this panel.

Globalization is interacting with traditional geopolitical, ethnic, religious, and cultural rivalries to create a much more complex and dynamic security environment. And it has created a critical fault line between those benefiting from globalization and those buffeted by its effects. This divide cuts across various regions and even various segments of populations in the same countries. These divisions are economic, they're political, but they're also cultural. But I would argue—and I think this is implicit in something that Anne Krueger just said—that the most important divisions are really not economic ones but divisions between hope and despair—those divisions between those people who feel that they have some control over their destiny and those who feel overwhelmed by powerful external forces. Now, globalization has become a popular focal point of that anger, and sometimes globalization equates with the United States and McDonald's imperialism. I agree very much, what was implicit in Ms. Krueger's comments, that it is also a crisis of governance; it's a crisis of bad governance exacerbating poverty, cultural norms that hold back countries from realizing their full potential. So it's a much more complicated picture than just simply saying the rich are getting richer and the poor are getting poorer as a result of globalization. There are many other reasons and factors for that, and not simply the American military hegemony that advances American capitalist ventures around the world. Nonetheless, as we know quite well, that was indeed the target. The implicit message of the applauders of September 11, 2001, was to attack two of the great symbols of what they feel is the new world order, the American capitalists dominated by and backed up by the global reach of American military power.

Now, globalization is also leading, though, to a new interdependence, and this is almost second nature to everyone now. Everyone completely understands, after last year, how these divisions between foreign and domestic affairs have completely eroded. We just had a major symposium last week at NDU discussing the new domestic preparedness agenda on homeland security. Who would have ever thought that we'd be inviting people from the National Governors Association, the National League of Cities, and the American Red Cross to a symposium at National Defense University on security issues? Again, another reflection of the changing security environment and the changing world.

The key driver, of course, to globalization is the information revolution, which has also leveled the playing field in important ways, enabling both certain medium powers—but even small subnational groups, as we've seen—to be able to challenge and sometimes restrict the capabilities of major powers. And this adds up overall to a very messy strategic situation that demands changes in our national security strategy and future military operations.

Now, what I would like to do very quickly is to touch on, again, some of these key security challenges, particularly how globalization is exacerbating some of them, and then highlight some of the changes in U.S. strategy and defense posture that are being taken to meet these challenges. I'll move quickly and I have a few slides. I promise not to subject you to death by PowerPoint. I would also say just before I continue that while I am a Department of Defense employee, my remarks are my own and do not reflect the views of the Department or the National Defense University. So with that out of the way, let me talk first a bit about globalization's impact and looking, again, from the security perspective, at globalization and then go on to talk about its interaction with some of these key security challenges.

Many troubled and undemocratic regions of the world—the greater Middle East, much of Southwest Asia, Africa, and a large part of East Asia—are overwhelmed with the challenges of globalization. In these regions, globalization, with its efficient but volatile markets and attendant financial shocks, is interacting with weak governance and unstable security affairs to exacerbate these economic disparities that we talked about a little bit earlier—some of the social problems and, indeed, regional tensions. This is adding to the sense of hopelessness among certain groups in various countries, and it provides a fertile environment for recruiting terrorists and for spawning armed conflicts. Globalization has created anger toward the United States and other industrial democracies, and it has also provided, as I said, this fertile ground for the growth of terrorism—not only terrorism of global reach, such as we've been focused on, but also local terrorist groups who direct their anger at what they see as this power system stacked against them. Globalization has also facilitated the expansion of international crime and the proliferation of sophisticated conventional weapons and weapons of mass destruction, and terrorists have availed themselves of both of these developments, a source of continuing concern.

Now, I'm going to talk a little bit about the economic divide, if I could have the second slide on the bifurcated world economy. As I said, with two distinguished economists sitting at the table, this is a cartoonish bit of economic analysis. But it is designed to show an overall trend and the main point I made, that the world is increasingly divided between the winners and losers in globalization. And that's greatly affecting the perspectives of the citizens of those countries as they look at their political and security situations. During the last decade we've seen enormous growth, 30 percent growth, in the total world economy, $30 to $40 trillion. But globalization, particularly in the short term, has created a widening gap between rich and poor, and it has continued to cause these painful social upheavals and financial shocks in many places.

Some people could say that this chart behind me is the *why they hate us* chart, but this would really be overly simple. Poverty didn't lead to 9/11. As we all well now know, the 9/11 plotters did not come from poor families. But they did see themselves disenfranchised by this economic structure. They did see their hopes and opportunities boxed in by the economic array that they saw before them and the situation in some of their home countries. So, it is important that we look at this as part of the puzzle of addressing and trying to improve our overall security situation. What you see there, in gross figures to show you what this means, are the countries that are largely democratic and therefore have governance that is enabling them to benefit better from globalization. They have seen an average GDP of about $17,000 per year, with about 1.7 billion people in the total population. In comparison, these other regions, the regions in the pale blue and green, have a 4.3 billion population and a $3,400 average GDP. So in other words, the shorthand is 70 percent of the world's wealth is earned by 28 percent of the population, and the per-capita wealth is four to seven times greater on average than the vast number of poor countries that house nearly three-quarters of the world's people. That is the gap of globalization. That is part of the thing that the people on the streets the next several days are pointing toward. And I think we in the security community can't fail to be cognizant of that.

While all boats have been rising in this growing global economy, the rich *are* getting richer a bit faster because of a larger base upon which they are building, and many of the other countries at the bottom end of that chart are paddling furiously upstream in their canoes just to keep up. The gap has widened; it grew by almost $2.7 trillion between the most affluent countries at the top of that chart and the countries at the bottom; and the regional differences are even greater within certain countries. This promotes a number of factors. It promotes both fragmentation and integration. In fact, one of our contributors coined the word *fragmentation* because why does it seem that the world is coming together in the European Union, for example, but we are also seeing this fragmentation of the growth of subnational and separatist groups throughout Europe and other parts of Latin America? Again, it's a confusing world picture, and these trends are countervailing and sometimes contradicting one another, but they are ones that influence the overall security picture. One of the key questions is how will some of the countries that are both positively influenced by and adversely impacted by globalization— India, China, for example, who have pockets where they benefit tremendously, particularly in coastal areas, from being plugged into the global economy, yet their interior regions remain very much untouched by some of the positive effects of the communications revolution and the revolution in global markets.

Now, let me turn to the national security implications of all this because I'm clearly out of my league here on economics. And that's really what I was asked to focus my remarks on. But it is in this context that this regional and international situation is being conducted, and it's important that we understand that basis. Local governments, nonstate activities, but traditionally large transnational corporations, terrorists, and some nongovernmental organizations are all making use of the instruments of globalization, and this is manifested in a number of different ways. Let me just cite a few examples, because we sometimes don't think about it as we watch some of these regional and local crises evolve, and think about the threads that connect these dots. The Asian financial crisis in 1997–1998, which eroded the government's legitimacy in Indonesia and other parts of Southeast Asia exacerbated economic tensions there, catalyzed in the East Timor independence movement, and led with a multinational peacekeeping force with the U.S. looking to Australia to help manage the post-crisis stability.

In Kosovo in 1997–1999, the Kosovo Liberation Army used the Internet, drug trafficking, and other criminal activities to raise funds to reach the Albanian Diaspora. Yet at the same time, Serbian reformers, using the Internet, got the word out to the world as to what was really happening inside Serbia; what Milosevic was doing. In Sierra Leone recently, and again another crisis in the news today, the rebels financed many of its activities with the sale of diamonds on the international diamond market. And in Columbia, very close to home here over the last several months as debate goes on about our policy there, we've seen the links between the narcos and the terrorists and the insurgents with certain international terrorist groups and the implications of having a vast swath of ungovernable space right in our own hemisphere. So, these security and economic questions are intersecting in more and more pronounced ways, in ways that place new demands on our defense and security capabilities.

Let me touch on a few of those although in such a brief time, I can't possibly do anything but highlight some of the issues that you're going to touch on later in this symposium. But beyond terrorism, there are a number of other key global security challenges that we are grappling with that present a new series of challenges to defense and security planners in our government. As part of terror are the interlocking links and activities of organized crime, of trafficking in drugs, people, and weapons, which overlap and sometimes create alliances of convenience with terrorist groups that are an important part of this dimension of this so-called dark side of globalization, the actors and the countries that are using some of globalization's tools to conduct nefarious activities that suborn our security. And so we are very much seized with these and looking at trade-offs as to what impact, for example, as the Coast Guard increases its counterterrorism activities, it has on its efforts to counter drugs. Ed Malloy has spoken out very clearly about this, that it's not an *either-or* proposition, because some of the terrorists are using drug running to support their activities. Therefore, we need an integrated strategy that addresses both dimensions of this problem.

The other big threat looming, which has been of major importance as we discuss the next steps on Iraq, is the proliferation of weapons of mass destruction and long-range delivery systems. And in this area, globalization has had mostly damaging effects, for it both accelerates the pace of WMD proliferation and makes its negative consequences much more contagious. We can come back to some of that in the discussion. But it's not just weapons of mass destruction. Proliferation of advanced conventional arms and advanced conventional capabilities, even communications sets, are an important part of the new security challenge that defense planners confront today. Smart munitions, countermeasures, new doctrines are making lesser conventional military forces much more formidable and even small subnational groups are able to use GPS transponders and other communications links to pinpoint where they are and, sometimes perhaps, where our forces are. This gives potential aggressors asymmetric capabilities and forces that can deny U.S. armed forces access to key areas or disrupt our operations, which again, create new challenges. There are many regional crises with potential to escalate to strategic-level problems or have global consequences. Daily we're reminded in the Middle East with the crisis in the peace process and the problems in the Gulf, problems in East Asia, particularly between the PRC and Taiwan over cross-straits issues. In South Asia is the always lingering potential that the tensions between India and Pakistan could escalate to new levels, and there are still concerns and uncertainty about the Korean peninsula. Those are some of the major regional crises that we in the defense planning community are looking at.

Beyond that is the instability of weak states—the ethnic crises, the violence that could spill over in Africa and Asia and the Balkans; the crisis that Ms. Krueger mentioned in Africa with AIDS and how that is going to disrupt the future stability and security and prosperity of countries throughout Africa and their ability to protect themselves as the ranks of draft-eligible males are depleted by that horrible scourge. Environmental degradation, new struggles over water, and the lingering concerns about access to energy are all important problems.

Where we come to in all of this—and this is, again, a bit of a cartoon, but it does reflect—is to the conclusion in our study. This had some influence on the Quadrennial Defense Review last year—that what the U.S. defense planning community confronts is increasing turmoil in the red zone that you see up above you on that chart in what we call the southern arc of instability. This arc is the overlay between lingering ethnic, regional, and other tensions and the disadvantaged in globalization, bringing together the two parts of my comments. The map is a bit unclear as to the countries' borders, but I think we caught the southern edge of Afghanistan in that swath. Who would have ever expected that we would be asked to deploy long range into Central Asia, particularly those who derided Partnership-for-Peace exercises that were taking place in Central Asia a few years ago as we built our cooperation with some of those countries along Afghanistan's periphery.

That is the new focus of our strategic planning and where much of our attention is being devoted. It is the area where our forces are increasingly being called to deploy. Again, in our very simplistic map, we were trying to call attention to—and as I mentioned in my comments about long-range deployments—the fact that our forces, if you look at them, are maldeployed to address that particular focal point of future security activity. We are not located in those regions in large numbers. The revolution in military affairs, the effects of transformation, are making it such that we don't necessarily have to be located in those areas permanently to have basing to address some of the security problems, but it is an important part of sustained operations in some of these areas. It is something that creates new challenges for our military operations. Increasingly, this security challenge, this arc of crisis, is going to require the maintenance of joint military capabilities. For those of you not familiar with military speak, that means multiservice capabilities and a flexible, adaptive defense posture that's able to project power rapidly into the outlying world; a continued foreign presence that ideally is somewhat diminished so as not to exacerbate some of the regional tensions and resentments that we see, particularly in the Persian Gulf; and access to new locations and new facilities. We need new partners and friends to be able to work with a widening circle of countries, as we've seen in joining this new coalition against terrorism, and we need to continue to sustain our partnership and relationships with longtime allies and friends.

This then leads to what we and the Department of Defense have identified as the new strategic framework for defense. Again, the main goals of our defense effort are assuring our friends and allies and dissuading future military competition, and that is much more than a military mission. It is a mission of trying to convince any potential challenger that it's not worth the effort; that the United States does not want to remain a world hegemon, that it does not want to see powers rise that would threaten the overall forces of freedom and the liberties of the countries that are a part of this wider coalition against terrorism—countries that are broadly committed and hold dear the democratic principles and freedom. You may have heard Dr. Rice, speaking last night on the news hour, make this point very, very clearly, that it's not an issue of maintaining American dominance; it's a question of the use of American power for good, and how our approach is designed to deter any potential regional or global hegemon from even trying it—an approach that, in a sense, worked quite effectively with the Soviet Union.

We also seek to deter threats and coercion, and this will be a good topic for discussion. The National Security Strategy Document issued last week amplified and added an important perspective on this that was addressed first in the President's speech at West Point this summer: the question of preemption of certain imminent threats where deterrence won't work, particularly in the case of terrorist action and use of weapons of mass destruction. Finally, the principle that if deterrence fails, U.S. military forces and defense capabilities should be capable of moving quickly to defeat an adversary decisively.

Now, to take this down to yet another level of operations, which our military colleagues in the audience will be all too familiar with, but I wanted to lay this out for some of the others in the audience. As some of you may know, the long-time defense planning under the previous Quadrennial Defense Review was for two major theater wars, two canonical wars—crises in Northeast Asia and the Persian Gulf. It became clear, partly because of that arc of crisis that I pointed out, as the QDR planners reviewed it, that this framework was too rigid and not flexible enough to deal with the need for action on the global scale; that we needed forces that were flexible and capable of working in a much more diverse environment. And we needed to shift more from regionally focused planning to capabilities planning, that we needed certain kinds of capabilities, and they're articulated there in terms of what the defense priorities are. But again, rather than thinking of winning and achieving complete victory in two major theater wars, the defense planning guidelines now call for the capacity to defeat a major aggressor in a second overlapping theater, but not to win decisive victory, that is to say, regime change, as is articulated in No. 3.

Another key challenge as we go ahead with the implementation of this defense planning framework is to balance the demands of the war on terrorism and homeland security with the requirements of defense transformation of adapting both practices and procedures and technological capabilities of our armed forces to these revolutions in military affairs and the revolutions in information and technology and the revolution in business affairs; all those buzzwords that I'm sure you'll hear more about over the next several days. The secretary of defense has also moved to reshape the way in which the forces are structured, beginning with the reshaping of the new North End Command for Homeland Security, changes in the European Command, other changes. Another important development in recent months is that the military commands, the unified commands, regional and functional, have developed important new dimensions to factor in nonmilitary capabilities in their defense planning and operation by developing joint/interagency coordinating groups to build ties with civilian agencies in addressing terrorism and other transnational threats. I'm sure as time goes on, they'll find that these connectivities, these links to nondefense agencies, will become increasingly important.

Let me just make a few points about state actors, because as I said, defense planning these days is about a much broader set of issues than simply movement of military forces around the world. In the last National Security Strategy, the Clinton administration recognized the importance of the implications of globalization, but most of the components of the U.S. government, frankly, had not and still have not been very quick to adapt to these challenges and their structures and processes. Security, economics, science and technology, and law enforcement policies are essential to coping with these new security challenges of the global era, and they are still being developed largely in isolation from one another. These policy streams are generally only integrated at the very highest levels of our government and oftentimes only when necessitated by a crisis. Many of you know some of the scrambling that went on after September 11 to build the ties between strange bedfellows in our government—the Treasury Department, the Defense Department, the DEA, and other agencies in the health sector—who don't have a regular habit of talking to one another, particularly at the working level. So the war on terrorism has given us a stark reminder of the need to have a much more integrated approach to security.

Let me just make one other important point, and I think you might find it odd coming from a defense planner, but we need to also get at the sources of this rage and despair. And here, the President's initiative and millennium challenge of a $5 billion expansion in foreign assistance and foreign development assistance for those states who make improvements in their governance is an important, and I think, much-neglected and powerful tool in this struggle and one that I hope will get more attention as this campaign against terrorism goes on. We have to narrow the gap between prosperity; we have to work at ways to restore the sense of hope among many of these countries in the world. They have to do their part, and that's implicit in the president's millennium challenge. But we also need to take the financial measures and other steps to buffer these weak states from the more brutal effects of globalization. Finally, we have to tell our story better, and I think the administration has made great strides in the last year toward enhancing our public diplomacy to better explain America's purpose in the world and to counter disinformation about what the purpose of our power is. But all of these elements of our strategy need to be much better integrated if we are to succeed in our efforts to promote global peace and security. Thank you very much.

MS. FOSLER: Thank you, Steve. Professor North, what do you think about all this?

PROFESSOR DOUGLASS C. NORTH: Well, I think it's very nice that I'm last. It gives me a chance to build on, perhaps disagree with, what's gone on before. You'll get both.

Professor North

I'm going to concentrate on two issues. One is, I want to explore the sources of the enormous variation in economic performance of economies over time. And second, I want to explore the belief systems that underlie the variations and the implications of those belief systems to the generation of violent behavior. Let me start with the first one.

We know a lot about the sources of productivity, and after all, what makes countries rich or what makes countries poor is very simple. They're rich if they're productive and they're poor if they're not productive. One of the world's great authorities on productivity, and one who has done more to teach us more about economic growth than anybody else, is the person sitting on my left here. Anne has been a pioneer in our learning much more about productivity and the way in which it impacts on various parts of the world. So we know a lot about productivity growth. In fact, what's called the *new growth economics* has laid it out in some detail, but there's something missing. Anne and I argue about this all the time, so it's not a new one. And what's missing is that we've got to ask ourselves, if we know what makes for economic growth, why isn't all the world rich?

It's not all rich because the incentive structure that underlies productivity growth differs all over the world. Now, incentive structures are what make it worthwhile for people to engage in productive activity, to develop new technology, to develop human capital, and its skills and knowledge. All those things require that it be worth your while to get them. On the other hand, if you look at poor countries around the world, you will find that the incentive structure is simply missing. In fact, the incentive structure is more often than not to take it from your neighbor or steal from somebody else rather than be productive yourself. Incentive structures are institutions. That's what institutions are; they're incentive systems. When we talk about institutions, we're talking about things like property rights, rules, the rule of law—all the kinds of things that Anne has already mentioned in the course of her talk. So we know a lot about them. What we don't know, and what we do very poorly, is how to get them, and that's very crucial. Now, the reason we don't is that some big hole is missing in economics.

Economics and so-called *neoclassic economics*, of which Anne is one of the leading figures, tells us a lot about economies and particularly tells us a lot about economies that are developed. Where you have developed markets, you look at how markets work. However, as an economic historian who has explored 10,000 years of economic history—a lot of time—I'm interested in why there's such enormous variation in the degree to which human beings have been able to take advantage of opportunities. So what's missing in all of our discussion is, we don't have a good understanding about the underlying process of economic growth. That underlying process is one in which we evolve and develop institutions, if we do it right, that make us more productive. Now the problem with that is that we know a lot about the economic institutions that will make you productive, but those have to be put in place by political systems. Let me say that again because, while we economists think that we're the source of understanding about economies, really politics are more important because you have to have a political system that's going to put in place political rules of the game, credible commitment that, in turn, is going to put in place economic rules of the game, property rights and rules, and the rule of law that's going to make that work. We don't know how to do that. We have some clues about it and we've been learning a lot, but we're far from understanding what goes on.

Now, let me turn to my next point, just to illustrate this. The rise of the western world, which Anne talked very eloquently about already, was really the development of what was a backward part of the world in the tenth century. The western world compared to the Muslim world, compared to China, compared to India. It was its rise to dominating the world by the eighteenth century. It was an extraordinary development. It required fundamental institutional change that would move us away from a personal exchange system of small-scale exchange to the kind of thing that Adam Smith long ago said was the source of the wealth of nations, which is specialization, division of labor, and, indeed, large markets, which enable you to do that. But moving from personal exchange to impersonal exchange required fundamental changes not only in the economic rules of the game—those were tough enough—but also you had to create political systems, polities, if you will, that would put in place rules of the game and enforce them. We don't know how to do that yet.

We have many clues about it, and indeed my own university created a center in political economy because we're so interested in trying to learn more about it, but we still don't know how to do it. So what we see evolving in the western world is, in part true judgment, in part a belief system that encouraged what I'm going to come back to in a minute, and in part good luck that, together, made it so that the western world evolved, developed impersonal exchange, large markets, productivity growth, and the technological miracles that Anne mentioned that made possible our becoming such a significant part of the world and coming today to run the world, which we do economically.

Now, contrast that very brief story with the Muslim world. The Muslim world in the twelfth century was way ahead of the western world. In fact, most of the development of science and technology and mathematics that we have was far more advanced in the Muslim world than it was at that time in the western world. But what happened to the Muslim world after the twelfth century was that it literally decayed in the sense that institutional rigidities maintained themselves and led to political systems and economic systems that didn't develop, that didn't encourage the growth of technology, the growth of markets, impersonal exchange, and all the things that I'm talking about. I don't have time here to explain why that's so or why they didn't do that, but suffice to say that enormous variation has been crucial and is still crucial today. There is no Muslim country in the world today that's a high-income country except on the basis of oil, and oil was developed by western things and therefore they don't deserve any credit for what happened at all. I'm going to come back to this contrast because it has a lot to do with where we want to go.

What lies behind creating the proper institutions? Economics, rightly, we say, is a theory of choice. That is, we believe that human beings make choices about society, the structure they have, the institutions, and rightly we want to ask where choices come from. Here economists have failed us because they have not seriously looked at what underlies choice. What underlies choice are beliefs, and the belief system that evolves, therefore, underlies not only choices that make us productive, it also underlies choices that lead to violence, to fanaticism, to religious extremism equally. So we better start to understand it, because if we don't, we will never get a handle on being able to make sense out of the world that induces this violence, and if we don't, in the world that has just been described here we face a future that is very uncertain because if, in fact, we cannot learn to find out the sources of fanaticism and violence and, in turn, be able to do something to undermine those beliefs, we have deep trouble down the road.

Again, I don't have time to go into the details on this. There's still an enormous amount about it that we don't know. You start, however, with one of the great mysteries. There are two great mysteries, in my view, in the world. One is the origin of the universe, and the physicists say the explanation of the big bang is a cop-out. And the other one is consciousness.

Consciousness is what distinguishes us from everybody else. Consciousness is our self-awareness about ourselves in time and space, and that self-awareness is not only the source of genius, the source of creativity, the source of all the wonders that have made human beings different from other animals and primates. It's all that and more. And if you want to explore great music, art, literature, or if you want to explore the successes that we've evolved, including the things that Anne described about the growth in productivity, the growth in health and sanitation and welfare that's made us rich, all those have come from consciousness.

Consciousness also is a source of violence, fanaticism, extremism of all kinds. They come from the same source. What produces one rather than the other is that you have to combine the way consciousness works with the cultural heritage of different societies. It's the belief system that evolves in the context of the whole cultural environment—physical, political, economic, and social—that, together, produces the variations that make for enormous variety in the way in which societies behave and in the way in which you generate fanaticism and so on. Let me be clear. There is no neat relationship in the modern-day world of fanaticism between fanaticism and poverty—none at all. In fact, most of the people in 9/11 were educated, and they certainly didn't come from poor families. So even though we're interested in these things, we don't look to poor countries in the world as a source of violence. What we look for is the kind of mixture of beliefs that evolve with the frustrations that have characterized parts of the world that you haven't been able to develop or where you limit opportunities in such ways that you induce a belief structure of that kind.

Now, there's lots about this we don't know, and indeed one of the things that makes me extremely unhappy with much of what I see in terms of policy, including American policy today, which I happen to disagree with quite strongly, is that we don't pay enough attention to the sources of the way in which belief systems evolve, how they relate both to consciousness and to the cultural heritage of different societies in order to be able to try to understand the origins and, therefore, to learn down the road to do something about them. So what I'm hoping that we'll do somewhere along the way is, we'll devote resources to try and understand much more than we currently know about consciousness, about belief systems, about how belief systems get integrated with the cultural pattern of evolution of different societies—political, economic, and social—and then I think we'll begin to get at attempting to confront the origins of the kind of fanaticism and things that were characterized in 9/11. Thank you.

MS. FOSLER: We have about a half-hour left for questions. We have microphones in the aisles, and I invite you to raise your hand. We'll pass a microphone to you. Please say who you are and address your question to an individual on the panel or to the panel as a whole.

AUDIENCE MEMBER: I was very fascinated by your thoughts here because I'm running up against that consciousness issue constantly teaching democracy in the Third World, and I was wondering, do you have any theories of how we could work on the consciousness and make the consciousness be a proper belief that leads to peace and prosperity as opposed to destruction?

PROFESSOR NORTH: Well, we're just beginning to seriously explore what is becoming perhaps the most exciting field, I think, today in the world—

cognitive science. Most of the work I do these days is with cognitive scientists, who are neural scientists in medical schools as well as psychologists and philosophers. What we're trying to find out is how the mind and brain work, and something else that is very interesting—one of the universals in all societies is that supernatural explanations exist. There are no exceptions to that anywhere in the world. Now, as soon as you know that something is universal, then you have to say—and rightly so—that the basis of this is something innate in the way in which the mind and brain work. While I disagree with some of the evolutionary psychologists who carry this further than I would, nevertheless they have called our attention to the genetic adaptations that appear to have worked. Part of our answer, therefore, lies in the innate characteristic that nonrational explanations are universal. Religions, of course, are a classic of it; not just religions but superstitions and so on, everywhere. What is not explained at all is that you can have religious beliefs or supernatural beliefs, but why do you insist on others conforming to it? Now, that is the neat trick. Because I don't mind if Anne has crazy religious views, but I object to the fact that she's going to try to impose them on me. And, in fact, what we find, of course, is that it's the mixture of having beliefs that are nonrational combined with the fact that you insist upon other people having those beliefs and are intolerant of people not having those beliefs, and that's why we're a long way from there but we're beginning to start to see it. As I said, it's not related to poverty and it's not related to lack of education. It's related to, in my view, fundamental obstacles in the cultural heritage that produce this combination. That's not a good answer because we have a long way to go.

MS. FOSLER: Let me just follow up and ask if there's an antidote to these fanatical beliefs.

PROFESSOR NORTH: Well, you have the antidote we've used so far, which is violence. I mean, we want to kill them, which is a good thing to do, I might add, but I do not think that's an answer. This is where I find myself at odds with Mr. Sharon and Israel and, indeed, with President Bush at times. It's because they don't seem to be concerned with trying to get at the root cause. I think we have to start to understand the root cause if we're going to minimize or reduce that. You're never going to eliminate a world in which people are going to be violent with each other. That's an innate feature of the world. We can, however, make it so that the kinds of cultural patterns and developments we have in the world don't encourage that kind of belief.

MS. FOSLER: I think we have another question?

AUDIENCE MEMBER: I guess this is a follow-up on what Ms. Fosler is asking. If it is something that is innate, if there is a consciousness issue that creates this cultural violence, then isn't the answer rather than understanding it, changing it? It seems to me that the reason France and Germany no longer fight each other is because they're basically on the same sheet of music; they have similar value systems, basically similar viewpoints on things that are worth fighting for. We don't fight poor countries that are democratic and Christian and have similar capitalistic outlooks on things. Isn't the thing to essentially force change on these people rather than understanding the differences?

PROFESSOR NORTH: I think you have a good point. I do not believe that there will ever be a time in which we won't get all kinds of crazy wild ideas permeating people in the world or, to be more generous with them, superstitions, beliefs, or extremist religions. I think what we have to try to do is see that such beliefs are not widely adopted by people. It's one thing if we have people who have such beliefs. As I said, I don't care what beliefs people have. I want to see, however, that you do not have a fertile field for those belief systems and fanatics to be able to attract support from people around the world to produce this on a mass scale. And clearly, we have this. You only have to look at what's happened in the last year to see that this fanaticism has been encouraged and has support in areas. That's what we want to try to reduce, not individual fanatics. We've had them from the beginning of history, including a lot in the history of Christianity itself. What we're trying to do is see that they do not attract the kind of attention that will produce fanatic mass murder.

MS. FOSLER: It seems to me that if you think of the security issue, especially the U.S. position, we are sort of this global police force. Obviously, you would want to create some institutional structures, which means that the police force is used less, rather than more. We have the U.N., but we haven't made much change in what I would call the kind of global culture, the institutions that try to bring some of these different cultures together so that the cultures agree on some basic rules of behavior and push to the more extreme some of these fanaticists. Do we have the institutional structure that we need to be sure that the police force is not used more rather than less?

DR. FLANAGAN: There's a sense that the American people don't want to be global cops; they don't want to be the force of first resort for all regional problems and international crises. Therefore, a lot of U.S. government policy over the last decade has been about widening the circle of partners with whom we can cooperate. We had a symbol of one of those steps yesterday in Warsaw, where seven new members of NATO who previously had been partners in our Partnership for Peace at NATO were given the expectation that they would receive an invitation to join the alliance. We've had, as I mentioned earlier, a widening circle of cooperation with a number of those governments in Central Asia as a result of the Partnership for Peace.

Admiral Blair spent a lot of time talking about building a security community in the Asia-Pacific region, and by that he meant building some of the synapses, the connectivities between the militaries and the civilian governments of that region to be able to work more effectively on common interests. In building the coalition on the war on terrorism, we've had this same effort of trying to build a widening circle of countries, some of whom, quite frankly, we have to hold our nose in the process of cooperating with because they don't necessarily share our belief systems or our values. But we do have certain common interests. And so I think a lot of the focus of our policy has been on both building this wider coalition of partners and also building capacity in those countries, and that's certainly a major focus of our counterterrorism assistance and of building capacity to help not only the military but the civilian agencies of various governments around the world to work with us more effectively.

The issue of wider U.N. capabilities is a contentious one, and I don't want to get into that, or the whole question of a standing U.N. military force or other kinds of capacity. One of the big gaps that we continue to see in post-conflict situations is the gap between military and police in the conflict aftermath. What are oftentimes needed are police functions that the military is quite justifiably reluctant to perform. And so the gap of military and police in post-conflict settlement is being played out again in Afghanistan. We saw it and continue to see it played out in the Balkans. It remains an important challenge that the international community as a whole really hasn't bridged because there are only so many retired police officers out there that you can cobble together to deal with these problems.

MS. FOSLER: Anne?

MS. KRUEGER: I'm a little bit out of my field in the sense that I think we'd stick more to the economics. I'll say what I said before, that as much as I think that all the cognitive science stuff is very worthwhile, I think there's a lot of evidence on two fronts. One, in the countries where economic growth is reasonably satisfactory and living standards are rising and things are improving for people, energy is concentrated on those things. And in that sense, there is less of a temptation. I see the terrorists as coming from societies in which there's tremendous frustration because they know they have the glorious past; they've somehow hinged onto this. They don't see a way forward for their countries, given the inappropriate policies. And in that regard, I think that the IMF, the World Bank, and others already play a role. I think that role can and should be strengthened. I think there are other mechanisms that could go to supporting more rapid opening of opportunities for hope.

The second part is that any reasonable economic growth is going to have to be predicated, I believe, on increasing education in terms of the number of people who have access to it, the length of time they are able to be educated, and the quality of education. Doug talked a lot about superstition and irrational beliefs. It seems to me the assent of man has come precisely because we have learned in modern industrial societies that there is such a thing as cause and effect, and we do have standards of proof. We look at something that happened, and we say why did that happen? It's the things that are not yet understood about which one is more likely to go into the realm that he's worried about. Well, the thing about that is, that as one has moved away from the peasant society where things are done like they were always done, and the thunderstorm or whatever is already outside something that we understand, the scope in which you're likely to get the kinds of things that I think you're worried about is likely to be less. So, in a sense, I think I'm willing to stand with our development processes as we have done them, insofar as more people are brought into the system, enabled to have opportunities and empowered to improve their own lot through education and other things.

There are amazing studies of things like, how do farmers who have 200 or whatever acres adapt to changes? And one finds that with even one more year of primary schooling, on average, the farmers will be considerably more successful in these regards. We've all had the benefit of all of this, and so we tend to assume that if you like something everybody has to, and that's simply not true. And I think that if there were an area where I think we, as a people, could pay more attention, it would be provision of mechanisms by which there could be much more rapid increase in the scope for education and educational opportunities in all parts of the world, including our own.

MS. FOSLER: You get to be last again.

PROFESSOR NORTH: I don't altogether agree with Anne about her optimistic view about cognition and the way it will evolve with education somehow, even with higher income, but I do want to directly address myself to your question, and I'm going to be very controversial.

I want to talk about the Arab-Israeli conflict, which I think we've made a horrible mess of. Now, I have a view that you may not share, but the Palestinians are second-class citizens in the world and, indeed, the Israelis treat the Palestinians very much as we Caucasians did the Jews for eight centuries in Europe. Now, I don't mean that too strong, because I think the Israelis have been a lot better at it in many respects than we were, but I do think that if we're going to solve the Arab-Israeli conflict, we have to make it worthwhile for both parties to engage in a dialogue that is going to produce results. I don't think Mr. Sharon understands that at all. I think he only has one answer, which is to simply use more violence against violence. I think what you have to do, down the road, is to provide a structure in terms of offering incentives to Palestinians and Israelis alike that's going to encourage them to have cooperative behavior with each other.

I would frankly give the Israelis $4 billion and tell them they had to spend half of it developing Palestine into being a complementary integrated political-economic system with Israel, and I think that is the beginning of intelligence. We are the only country in the world that can see that that happens, and I don't see Mr. Bush devoting any attention to attempting to do that. Don't misunderstand me; that doesn't solve many problems. But I think it's the beginning of being able to reduce the amount of conflict, the amount of violence, and the beginning of developing something that everywhere in the world we've got to do if we're going to survive in this world, and that is to develop ways by which we can get along with each other. And you don't do that without having something more than just violence and opposition.

MS. FOSLER: Well, that ought to stir up some questions. There's one in the back.

AUDIENCE MEMBER: This is for the panel as a whole and hopefully to the Chair. Businesses in a microeconomic sense confront very low hurdle rates for investment based on the cost of capital worldwide, yet in a macroeconomic sense, we still don't see investment cycles picking up. And investment is an engine of economic growth that is vital and important for enhancing security. What policies—kind of piggybacking on Professor North's $4 billion comment—could start investment on a global basis and what are the prospects that those policies will be pursued?

MS. KRUEGER: Investment can be an engine of economic growth; there are investments that are not. Doug and I both believe in incentives, whatever our other differences, and when you have a framework in a country where the incentives are not for doing the things that will yield high returns, you get a very different outcome and investment is not an engine for economic growth. Now, some countries have the wrong incentives, and they are invested in the wrong things, so they don't grow. In other cases, there's just a very low rate of return on everything because—again, I would come back and agree with Doug—there's going to be too much stolen or the rule of law isn't there, so even if you make it, the chances are they'll take it away from you.

So, much of what's going on in the world and the high cost of capital is the uncertainty, because we all know that there's sort of a basic return, but then there's a risk premium, and the risks in many countries are very high. So, there are two challenges for economic growth, one of which is to get whatever there is invested in reasonably rewarding uses, and that does not always happen. So when people tell me investment is *the* engine of growth, I kind of worry because there are a lot of countries—and I remind you of the former

Soviet Union—that had very high real rates of investment, 40 percent of GDP, and they basically were unable to grow because they had in place other policies and so on that prevented that investment from having the productivity it might have had.

MS. FOSLER: I might get myself in trouble with Anne, but I'm not so sure it's the absolute level of investment that is a problem. I think it is the distribution of investment. You mentioned the low hurdle rates, and I think one of the reasons that there are low hurdle rates is because, as opposed to what we feared at the end of the 1980s, that we would have an inadequate level of savings to fund investment; we actually found ourselves in a very sort of capital-rich world in the 1990s. Moreover, we actually created such momentum that I would argue that much of what we saw at the end of the 1990s, 1990 and 2000, in terms of the tremendous capital coming into the United States, was not a problem of the overall level of the availability of capital, but the fact that the risk parameters and returns that were at least perceived really concentrated that investment in part of the world that I think as a mature industrialized country doesn't necessarily have the opportunities that yield long term the highest rates of return.

When we look at investment—and this sort of plays into some of our other discussion—as it is distributed around the world, it is increasingly focused on China, Mexico, and then we have to see going forward Brazil, which has now been a member over the last few years in that arena and is going to continue to be a member. But if you look at potential growth rates, just in terms of population and entrance to the labor force and potential productivity, there are a lot of locations around the world that investment, in some sense, could be productively generated. But the risks associated with entering those markets—and exchange-rate risk is a very important part of those risks—are, I think, disproportionately high.

Anne talked about the expansion of the role of the IMF, but we made enormous progress, not as a historian myself but having read the history of the immediate post-war period. I always thought of it, as a baby boomer, as this kind of economic nirvana where we came up with these institutions and we got some exchange rate stability and everybody grew and lived happily ever after, but it was really a period that was fraught with a lot of currency crisis and instability. We have gone a long way, through swap arrangements, through banking policies and the like, to create an environment where maybe there are 20 countries now that have relatively low risk parameters, but I think that there are these other countries, in what we think of as the periphery, that are managing. They are exporting more than they're importing, they're struggling to stabilize their exchange rates, and I think we need some policies that help to lessen the risks that those countries face, or investors face, in investing in those countries so that we get a much more balanced kind of portfolio of global investment and maybe, to some extent, that would create a more level playing field that would ease some of this anxiety about the differential between the growth rates of the *haves* and the *have nots*.

MS. KRUEGER: I don't think we're disagreeing at all. I think what I said was there was low investment in countries because their policy framework provided the inappropriate incentives and the reason why you get very low investment there is precisely because those policies are inappropriate. And I think that, there again, the fund mandate has been more and more to work with them on getting exactly the risks you're describing by getting appropriate policies, including governance and all that Doug talks about in place.

MS. FOSLER: You have the last word, because you are the panelists, but I think that when I look at what happened to Mexico, for example, in the peso crisis, as a Catholic, I referred to it as Mexico creating a venial sin and they paid a mortal penalty. The notion that a country would have an over-expansion of its monetary policy, it's done all the time, and yet the value of their currency was cut by two-thirds. There was over-investment and somewhat excessive stimulus in the high-growth Asian countries, and their currencies went down by 60 percent. Most of these countries now have balanced budgets and they're increasing their foreign exchange reserves, which are all in some ways sort of restrictive policies, and I just feel that it's like sending your kids off to school—yes, we would like them to be independent and always conduct themselves in a manner that they will as adults, but occasionally they need some help. You have actually suggested a bankruptcy proceeding, and maybe you'd like to say something about that, but I think those kinds of policies need to be discussed more.

MS. KRUEGER: Well, let's go back to Mexico, since it's in the past and therefore we're not getting into current arguments. The Mexicans had had 100 percent inflation in 1987. They had had a debt crisis before that, because they had over-borrowed. They then decided to try to cure their inflation by holding their exchange rate. So they fixed their exchange rate and adjusted it much less than the rate of inflation for, I think, 8 years running. So there was real appreciation in the peso. The way they covered their current account and fiscal deficits was by borrowing. Now, unless the United States is willing to lend increasingly large amounts of money to those countries that want to borrow the most, at some point those kinds of parties have to stop.

In the world as it then was, that party stopped and, by the way, I think the international community did fairly well in the Mexico crisis. Although Mexico resumed economic growth within a year, the governor of the Bank of Mexico himself would tell you that a major change was that they moved to floating exchange rates by 1996, which has given them much more flexibility in their economy. But the more fundamental point, I think, is that if a country wants to have a fixed exchange rate, then it's going to have to adapt its monetary and fiscal policies to keep that exchange rate realistic relative to the rest of the world.

In East Asia, Thailand had had 25 baht to the dollar from 1960 something or other until 1990 whatever, and in that period of time, Thailand had averaged something like 7 percent per year inflation against a U.S. 3 percent. Four percent per year real appreciation over that period of time is going to end somehow. And as I said, unless you want to keep on lending indefinitely, not well. Once a country has reached its borrowing capacity, it doesn't have a choice but to adjust. It's not a question of, "Is this unfair and how do you help them?" In fact, the evidence is that the inflation is what hurts; the fiscal deficits are what hurt. And getting that part of the body politic in order is part of what Doug is talking about in institutions. I don't think Doug is advocating high rates of inflation or huge fiscal deficits or any of this stuff. So I guess my problem is that, yes, you have a teenager who goes out and crashes the car, and you immediately give him another car to crash again?

MS. FOSLER: Well, you see, economists disagree. This man here.

AUDIENCE MEMBER: I just have a comment. The industrial strength of this country is in the small businesses. They hire most of the employees in this country and they're the stabilizing force of this country. Just an observation, and I'm not an expert in this field, but the commonality in the relative success of all countries, including this hemisphere, has to do with the relative size of their small business infrastructure, and the rise and fall of these countries will be small businesses. If you look at what's happening in this country right now, it's caused a major economic dent because of the large companies and what they recently did, and if you look at the profile and at Department of Defense, three or four large companies control all of the Department of Defense acquisitions as compared to where they were three years ago. So I'm suggesting that maybe you ought to look at another area, and that would be small businesses. And by the way, I represent small businesses in the Department of Defense.

MS. FOSLER: Well, this group is getting really contentious. Maybe we will take one more question before we can get to fisticuffs at lunch. Back in the back.

AUDIENCE MEMBER: I'm Dr. Nicholas Rigg, economist, Department of State, currently teaching at the U.S. Army Command and General Staff College. National security for the twenty-first century, anticipating challenges, we're all looking at Iraq right now. I'm wondering about the institutions in Iraq. If we go in, will there be an alternative to either a Baathist party or a fundamentalist regime ala Iran taking over in Iraq? Are there institutions and pulls of political power that can give some sort of alternative between those two extremes?

DR. FLANAGAN: Well, it's a huge question, but certainly one that has to be thought through as we move ahead in the next steps with regard to Iraq policy. The whole question of de-Baathization, if you will, of Iraq and the capacity of some of the existing parties, the various émigré groups that don't seem to really have much traction internally and, historically, that's usually the case. They've been out of Iraq for a long time. They're not in touch with that many of the current population, so there's a big unknown. We don't know what the political culture of the current population really is, but I think people are making a concerted effort to try to figure it out, much more so in recent months.

There are concerns about the potential for Balkanization of Iraq—three separate Iraqs that could emerge from a post-conflict situation—a Kurdish Iraq, a Shiite in the South, and the Arab center. But it's not even that simple because the populations are somewhat interspersed, so I think there's an enormous set of questions there related to how to rebuild, and that's why I think that the discussion has been that this is a long-term commitment that we and the international community would be embarked upon of rebuilding Iraq and reshaping its political system, culture, and the whole question of the security forces, which would be an immediate concern.

You have the special Republican Guard, the elite around Saddam himself, who have nowhere to go, so they will be the most intense and the most recalcitrant. Many people suggest that the regular army is easily turned, and in fact, already signaling to Kuwaitis and others that they're maybe ready to join in the fight. So there are enormous uncertainties about what will actually happen when and if the time comes that it comes to force. But long term, the whole question of political change in Iraq, and again, what if there is a military coup before the actual action of the international community or the U.S. alone against Iraq begins? That group of colonels or generals out there may be waiting for the moment they think is right; what price will they demand? So there are many different scenarios that one could spin out and it's really premature, I think, to get into, but obviously an important set of questions and ones that need much further study.

MS. KRUEGER: I don't have any particular comment except to say that quite obviously, looking at what would be the successor situation, both in Iraq and in the region relative to ahead of time is clearly a major concern, which extends certainly northwestward through Turkey and especially with the Kurdish situation there, so I think it's more than just a question of institutions in Iraq.

PROFESSOR NORTH: I think one of the things that should make economists humble, and we don't tend to be very humble I have to point out, is that our success record, and particularly in transition economies in the former

Soviet Union, has been very, very poor. We've had some modest successes in the countries that have been taken over by Russia and Central Europe. In the countries that formed the Soviet Union, the success has been very poor and that's because we simply don't understand enough about the sources of productivity and growth. We don't know how to get them. Getting them means you understand the way in which institutions evolve over time, how they intermix with culture heritage, with your history; and how in turn you produce a policy that will put in place political and economic rules of the game. We don't know how to do that. We've learned a lot, and again, Anne has done some very important work on this in various parts of the world, and I've done a little bit here and there around the world, but that's not to say that that's a reason not to try to restructure Iraq. It's to say that if you're going to go into Iraq, you ought to be very, very aware that you're getting yourself into a mess; that at least now you're way over your head with respect to our understanding and knowledge that could go in and restructure it effectively in even any moderately short run.

MS. FOSLER: Thank you. Thank you all. You had a lot of questions. They were spirited questions, a wonderful panel, and I hope that we've set the tone because, obviously, part of the uniqueness of this conference is the focus on the nongovernmental organizations and this kind of knitting together some of this institutional discussion that we've begun with today. So I think we now will adjourn and go directly to lunch. So thank you very much.

LUNCHEON ADDRESS

ECONOMICS AND NATIONAL SECURITY

Mr. Dick Grasso, Chairman, New York Stock Exchange

Introduction by: Ms. Gail D. Fosler, Senior Vice President and Chief Economist, The Conference Board

Summary

• Economic growth and development and strong national security are mutually dependent and would not exist without the other.

  1. The U.S. economy could not function and the global economy would be in grave trouble without strong national security and strong partners around the world who share the belief that those who perpetrate an attack against America are not simply attacking America, they are attacking the free world—those who value the choice of political and economic freedom.

  2. There is no private economy without a great military; there is no private economy without great national defense.

  3. The policy is not one of sheer military brute force; it is a partnership between private and public sector initiatives.

  4. The Cold War was won by the twin forces of Ronald Reagan's commitment to the Strategic Defense Initiative and forcing the Soviets to spend themselves into economic oblivion and Margaret Thatcher's unwavering commitment to privatization.

• The September 11th attacks literally brought the world economy to a standstill for the next five and a half days.

  1. A group of rogue murderers, not some super military force, brought global economic performance to a standstill.

  2. This is a critical time to strategize a very different response to a very different enemy—the enemy not only of freedom around the world but also the enemy of economic global interconnectivity.

  3. The attacks underscore why we need a powerful response to those who would attempt to terrorize.

4. In the most comprehensive of public/private partnerships ever, the military, the political leadership, and those in the financial markets put aside traditional rivalries and differences to come together for one very simple and common objective.

5. The Treasury Department has seized or blocked more than $100 million and identified more than 3,000 individuals with terror organizations, blocking financial institutions from doing business with them.

6. Economic growth, investment growth, job growth, and rising standards of living cannot continue here or around the world without a defense mechanism that declares to those who thought 9/11 was the fulfillment of their call, "We will find you, we will prosecute you, and we will melt you before you're ever able to do it again."

7. We best honor those lost in the attacks by creating a defense mechanism in this country and linked with our partners around the world that says it is unacceptable to do what you did last September, and you will pay the ultimate price if ever you try it again. Those who believe they should continue the philosophy of hate and murder will be found and dealt with.

• To avoid market standstills in the future, the United States must invest more in defense. The current 3.8 percent of GDP invested in defense must be increased dramatically to sustain the inextricable link between economic performance and national defense.

1. The nation cannot have a great economy without a great military. And no great economy can survive if that military and that national defense mechanism are not nurtured and stimulated and invested in, relative to both economic capital and human capital.

2. A man or woman spends 25, 30, 35 years serving this country and in mid-40s, perhaps even early 50s, returns to civilian life and faces a very different economic environment, a very different task of finding employment. That person should never be in that position. That person should, for the rest of his or her life, be supported by the nation he or she defended.

• Today, we are locked arm-in-arm with our partners around the world in a very singular and unambiguous challenge to never let September 11th happen again. We do that with investment in infrastructure, investment in our military, and investment in prosperity for those nations yet to achieve the American dream.

• The U.S. economy is still the strongest the world has ever known, albeit having some indicators that are not as vibrant today.

1. The market is struggling because of two issues: trust and the war on terrorism.

2. Deficit spending in times of war, in times of conflict like today, is not only desirable but also absolutely essential.

• The challenge of reestablishing trust in the markets and in corporate leaders also requires a public-private partnership. No single entity, either in the public or private sector, can deal with it.

1. The New York Stock Exchange impaneled a special blue ribbon committee on corporate accountability. It created a brand new platform of listing requirements and corporate governance standards, which fundamentally say to American investors, to consumers, and to employees of the Enrons, the WorldComs, the Adelphias, and the Tycos: "This is unacceptable to us as owners and employees and to the overwhelming majority of corporate America."

2. The Securities and Exchange Commission needed to institute tough new requirements, vigorously pursuing those who breach their responsibilities to the public markets.

3. What you can and must do is prosecute dishonesty. So you have to pursue, prosecute, and incarcerate those who have broken their responsibilities with the owners. The system is not broken; there are only people within the system whose morals and ethics are broken.

Analysis

As Chairman of the New York Stock Exchange, Mr. Grasso provides a unique perspective of the link between strong national security and economic growth and defense. He was clear in his position that both elements of national power are mutually dependent and inseparable. His remarks focused on two central themes: trust and confidence.

As Mr. Grasso described the relationship, a strong economy depends on strong national security both directly and indirectly. The direct investment in defense industries and collateral investment in support technologies and services that are necessary for a strong military contributes to a strong and growing economy. But, more importantly, a strong military provides the security and stability that are essential for investors and consumers to have the confidence in their personal financial situation and in the nation's economy.

Inversely, in today's global environment, a state cannot be stable and secure without a strong military, and that military strength requires significant investment. Mr. Grasso repeated his belief that, while the United States invests far more in its military than any other state, it also has the world's largest economy and must not only continue this significant investment but also increase it. Additionally, Mr. Grasso twice iterated his belief that the United States must invest more in its military personnel, both in active duty pay and benefits in retirement. By increasing the financial incentives for military service, the U.S. will continue to attract and retain the most qualified and talented service members to sustain our military and support our national security. These soldiers, sailors, airmen, and marines will have the confidence to know that they can serve their country for a career while providing fully for their families and their future.

Mr. Grasso highlighted the impact of the terrorist attacks in 2001 on New York City and Washington, D.C. While the New York Stock Exchange was closed for five and half days, it reopened without flaw and continues to support trading through the war on terrorism. These facts are a testament to the confidence of the American consumers and investors in their security and their economy. As Mr. Grasso states, this resilience would not have been possible without a remarkable partnership of public and private institutions representing all elements of our national power.

Mr. Grasso's comments regarding the current corporate scandals reinforced this theme of trust and confidence. While the government, the security exchanges, and private institutions have taken steps to address the scandals systematically, the solutions lie in corporate leaders maintaining fidelity to their investors. Leaders who breach that trust must be personally punished to reinforce to other executives and to investors that the trust between a corporation and its stockholders must be inviolate.

Mr. Grasso provided an exceptional analysis of the link between national security and economics that built on the Panel I discussion of the global security environment and set the tone for following discussions on building capabilities for the future.

Transcript

MS. GAIL D. FOSLER: Thank you all. You were a wonderful group at this morning's panel, and I have an even bigger treat for you in the form of Dick Grasso. Introducing Dick is a great honor. He is the Chairman and CEO of the New York Stock Exchange, and before that, he was the CEO and President of the Stock Exchange. He has spent all of his professional career over the past 30 years at the Stock Exchange. But he has a very special link with this group because he was also a member of the Army. He is going to speak today on the topic of Economics and National Security. I'm going to say something that will probably embarrass him. However, I think there is no one better in these times that can address this topic. Dick used his background at the Stock Exchange and his background in the Army to create what I think will remain one of the great system's feats in modern history, and that was restoring the operation of the financial markets after 9/11.

At the Conference Board, we have many technology firm members, and I saw from behind the scenes, as well as from reading the newspaper, what was presented to the public. During those difficult days, Dick Grasso was told that what he wanted to achieve was impossible. Just as many of you in the military, he used his military fortitude and determination and said, "Just do it!" As a result, the week after that devastating attack, we had the world's largest financial market open for business. In fact, after some initial instability, they came back to doing what we trust them to do best, which is bring all of our deci-

Mr. Grasso

sions together with options and opportunities. We had stability not only in the U.S. but also in the global financial system. Therefore, it is with great pleasure and great honor that I introduce Dick Grasso to you. Thank you.

MR. DICK GRASSO: Thank you very much, Gail, for those very kind remarks. Ladies and gentlemen, it is truly an honor and a pleasure to be with you today. But I must tell you in all candor, when I received the invitation from General Shinseki, I paused for a moment because I know that when the Chief of Staff invites an E–5 to address a conference like this, the E–5 is going to be in a lot of trouble. While Gail very graciously portrays the very proud time I spent in the United States Army, those of you in the Army will recognize very quickly my service, as distinguished by my prefix, which was US, rather than RA.

I served very proudly in our nation's military and was equally proud when I met General Shinseki last year on Veterans Day. Since the 1918 Armistice Day, each year at the New York Stock Exchange, at the 11th hour of the 11th day of the 11th month, we stop the market for two minutes of reflection. Last year, we were privileged to have General Shinseki, General Jumper, and the commandant, General Jones. It was a very moving observation to recognize those 2.6 million men and women who served both on active and reserve duty to keep our nation the shining star of freedom that it is today.

I'm so privileged and honored that General Shinseki would invite me to address this group. Each year—equally important to the New York Stock Exchange calendar—in commemoration of Memorial Day, we have a very special observance. This past year, General Myers graced us with his presence to recognize the 1.1 million men and women who have made the ultimate sacrifice on behalf of our nation. So, when I got General Shinseki's letter reflecting on the last 12 months, it was a very easy yes—both from the point of view of being able to thank the men and women in the world's greatest military who are here and those who will watch these proceedings from around the globe. Equally important is to be able to thank each of you, because the ability to do what we do would not be possible without those of you who serve our nation today in uniform. So when I've been asked to talk about the linkage between national security and economic performance, it is perhaps an opportunity to go on for hours, or to simply end your agony by telling you that one would not exist without the other.

If in any way we need to be reminded of the inextricable link between economic performance and national security, think back to that painful day, September 11, 2001, as we saw first the north tower and then the south tower hit, and then the two coming down. For the next 5? days, literally, our economy and the economy of the world was brought to a standstill. We reflected in the great hope that many of those 2,801 who ultimately lost their lives were to be, in fact, saved. We watched, literally, worldwide economic performance come to a standstill. If one needs to understand the importance of a strong national security, we need only remember that second day of infamy this country faced a year ago. Therefore, it was for me a very easy job to accept, when the general extended this very gracious invitation, because our economy, and, certainly my market, which produces almost $50 billion in commerce every day, could not function, the U.S. economy could not function, the global economy would be in grave trouble without strong national security and strong partners around the world who share the belief that those who perpetrate and attack America are not simply attacking America; they are attacking the free world, those who value the choice of political and economic freedom.

Today, how very special it is to be able to be with President Eisenhower's granddaughter, because today I have the opportunity, from the financial market standpoint, to thank her and the entire Eisenhower family for the renaming of this series. Who better to reflect upon in terms of the need to link a strong investment in security with strong economic performance? What better name than President Eisenhower? As he took office upon his first election, we look back at the times and we compare them to the times we face today. Then, slightly more than 14 percent of our GDP was spent on defense; today, less than 4 percent—less than 4 percent of the $16 trillion economy. It was poignantly pointed out on September 11, that that will never be enough.

Secondly, as we look at these wonderful men and women who wear our nation's uniform for 20, 25, 30, 35 years, what can we do as a nation to assist while they serve and to support them when they have completed their service? I'm going to come back to that, because as General Shinseki knows, being in the private sector, I'm immune from political pressure. (laughter) I say that tongue in cheek, but it is a favorite of mine, because I believe that when a man or woman spends the better part of their professional life serving their nation, the country has an obligation to them that is unfulfilled when they leave military service, and something needs to be done about that. However, I will close on that point, because it's something that I care about deeply.

As I look at economic performance today and I link it to the question of national security, what do we think about? We look at the U.S. economy, a $16 trillion GDP. We look at our trading partners around the world. We remember that it was not some super military force that brought global economic performance to a standstill, it was a group of rogue murderers. For those who find the war against terror to be difficult, for those who believe it may in some way limit one's freedoms in a free society, I encourage you to visit ground zero, to stand as I have on many occasions and look into that cavern and ask a very simple question. Why were the freedoms of those 2801 taken that day? Why were they taken away? The 200 here in Washington at the Pentagon? The almost 50 in the fields of western Pennsylvania?

This is not a typical time for building defense. This is a critical time to strategize a very different response to a very different enemy—the enemy not just of the freedom of citizens around the nation and around the world, but the enemy of economic global interconnectivity.

Our economy, the U.S. economy, is challenged some may think. Let me remind them, it is the strongest the world has ever known, albeit with some indicators that are not, perhaps, as vibrant as we would like them to be today. Our nation will grow its GDP between 3 and 4 percent this year, with no visible signs of the return of inflation, with cost of money at a 40-year low. Those are traditionally the recipes for a very strong stock market performance. But every day, when I'm in audiences such as this around the country, people say, "Why, Dick, is the market struggling as it is?" The market is struggling because of two discounts: one being the trust discount and the other being the issue of terrorism. Can we win a war and can we pursue that conflict to its ultimate conclusion so that we will be able to say to our children and to our neighbors: "There will not be another September 11"?

Economic activity, as I look at the inextricable link between national and global security and the performance of economies—ours and our trading partner nations—when one thinks about what happened in a 5½-day period, it is an extraordinary underscore of why we need a powerful response to those who would attempt to terrorize. As powerful as the response was last September, in 5½ days, in perhaps the most comprehensive of public-private partnerships ever put together, the military, the leadership from the political ranks, and those in my industry all came together. We stripped one another of rank, and we basically put aside traditional rivalries and differences, and we had a very simple and common objective.

On September 17, 2001, at 9:30, we rang a bell, and when we rang that bell, it said to the murdering perpetrators of that heinous act: "You've taken innocent lives; you've destroyed billions in property. You've brought the economy, at least on a global scale over these last five and one-half days to a standstill, but you have failed miserably. You not only failed in your ultimate goal, which was, in addition to destroying lives and property, bringing the economies, both the national economy here and its trading partners around the world, literally to their knees, if not to conclusion. You have failed bitterly." When that bell rang at 9:30 that morning, it was a powerful message that no one who is an enemy of freedom can ever succeed.

If you need to look at the elements that drive why I feel as strongly as I do, look at the need to size the economic damage done on September the 11. The airline industry, in just the United States, last year lost $7 billion and will lose perhaps as much as $7 billion again this year. The flow of goods just over our northern borders, which averaged roughly $1.4 billion a day, came to a halt. Literally, every major point of commerce as measured by goods and services came to a standstill. How do you deal with that? Very simply: by not investing 3.8 percent of GDP in defense, but by taking that number up dramatically; by continuing what President Eisenhower understood and so well articulated, the inextricable link between economic performance and national defense. You cannot have a great economy without a great military, and no great economy can survive if that military and that national defense mechanism aren't nurtured and stimulated and invested in, both as to capital and human capital.

I look at the last 50 years and I compare those two investment numbers, and it's really quite hard to understand why people have difficulty comprehending why that budget needs to grow. I understand the difficulties right now as we look at the national level. We are facing what once was a surplus perhaps becoming a deficit. However, let us never forget, deficit spending in times of war, in times of the conflict we face today, is not only desirable, it is absolutely essential. I think we have to rally behind the realities that September 11th brought upon us. If we don't, the economic costs will be enormous. I look at my market as a certain microcosm of what one might consider.

We were a $17 trillion equities market not too long ago. Today we are a $14 trillion equities market. That shrinkage is pale in comparison to other markets both here in the U.S. and around the world. However, it wasn't too long ago, actually 15 years almost to the date, that the totality of the American market was only a $3 trillion market, and in 5 days, between October 14–20, 1987, we lost one-third of that value. We didn't lose it to a terrorist enemy. We lost it to a confluence and a return to rationality of the fundamental principles of valuation.

Today, the stakes are five times the level they were 15 years ago. September 11 taught us so many lessons. We in financial markets are the linkage not just among and between markets here in the United States but also among and between markets around the world. The fact is that financial markets can be a conduit for both job creation and economic activity, but they can also be a conduit for those who would bring harm to peoples around the world. I applaud what Secretary [Paul] O'Neill has done with his colleagues at Treasury to create a worldwide network to stop the flow of terrorist funds. More than $100 million has either been seized or blocked. More than 3,000 individuals have been identified as known to be of terror organizations, and financial institutions are blocked from doing business with them.

These are the types of strategies that we wage today in this war on terrorism. In the financial markets, at the big board itself, we learned many painful lessons last September. I had 135 of my colleagues in the south tower. I learned how blessed we are in this country that we have people in uniform, be it military uniform or the uniforms of our fire and policing agencies, people who are willing to be running up the stairs as my colleagues were coming down the stairs. The most successful rescue in the history of our nation—26,000 people came out of those two towers because 343 firefighters, 27 New York City police officers, and 37 Port Authority police officers gave their lives that day. Those 401 people blessed 26,000 with life and the privilege of living in this great society of ours.

As we look at this question about national defense and economic performance, they're one and the same, ladies and gentlemen. We cannot possibly have economic growth, investment, stimulation of job creation, and raise the standards of living here in the U.S. or around the world unless we have a defense mechanism that says, without ambiguity, to those who thought 9/11 was the fulfillment of their call: "We will find you, we will prosecute you, and we will melt you before you're ever able to do it again." Unless you're willing to embrace that thesis, this economy and the economies of our partner nations around the world are in terrible jeopardy. It is not a policy I'm advocating of sheer military brute force. It is a partnership between public and private. It is a partnership between private sector initiative and public initiative. As President Eisenhower talked about the balance, one of his very first actions after taking office was to appoint the Treasury Secretary to the National Security Council. It is a balance.

Think of it in the context of the war we won in the 1980s—not a hot war, but a cold war, won by the twin forces of Ronald Reagan and Margaret Thatcher. President Reagan, God love him, whether he was to achieve it or not, his articulation of SDI forced the Soviets to spend themselves into economic oblivion. Lady Thatcher, then Prime Minister, with her unwavering commitment to privatization, took the inefficient entities of governmental ownership and returned them to the disciplines of the free-market process. Those that would prosper and use their capital efficiently would grow and their owners would thrive. Those that didn't would go the way of the 5-cent subway ride. Those twin forces won us that war and changed the world forevermore. We thought, up until September 11, that we were living almost in a Disneyesque society.

In this country, terrorism didn't exist. It was a phenomenon to be experienced in Europe, in Latin America, in the Pak rim. Yes, we had our own American terrorists in Oklahoma City, but we only read about the heinous acts of terrorist groups outside of the United States until September 11. September 11 was a wakeup call for this country and for the world. When those two towers came down, 83 nations lost men and women. Today, we are locked arm-in-arm with our partners around the world in a very singular and unambiguous challenge to never let September 11 happen again. We do that with investment in infrastructure, investment in our military, and investment, if you will, in prosperity for those nations yet to achieve the American dream.

Raising standards of living in some of the poorest nations around the world is perhaps one of the most important tasks we have, just as we faced the tasks following rebuilding in World War II. As we face the tasks each time an enemy is confronted and defeated by this country, this country goes back and helps, as we will today in Afghanistan and in Iraq, to make certain that the beauty and dream we have all lived can be lived by more in all parts of the world. September 11th was a wake-up call. This country took a blow. My city, in particular, literally now faces a $5 billion budget deficit. If it had to happen, New York City was the place that could rise as it is doing now. We will never be able to do enough to honor those we lost in New York, in Washington, and in the fields in western Pennsylvania. However, we honor them most by rebuilding economically and militarily. We honor them best by creating a defense mechanism here in this country that is linked with our partners around the world and says, "It's unacceptable to do what you did last September, and you will pay the ultimate price, if ever you try it again." Those who believe that they should continue the philosophy of hate and murder will be found and dealt with.

Lastly, and General Shinseki asked that I specifically take some questions, but I should say not on the performance of individual equity securities. (laughter) That would get me in even deeper trouble than perhaps I might be in these days. Let me close with a reflection as to where I started. A man or woman spends 25, 30, 35 years serving this country, and at an age of late 30s, mid 40s, perhaps even early 50s, returns to civilian life—a very difficult economic environment, a very difficult, challenging, and daunting task of trying to find employment. That person should never be in that position. That person should, for the rest of his or her life, be supported by the nation. I'll conclude where I started. There is no private economy without a great military. There is no private economy without great national defense. That cost—that sacrifice one makes of 25, 30, 35 years is not being rewarded today. I know that this great president will reward our wonderful men and women going forward, and I support his efforts. Thank you very much, General, for the invitation to be with you today.

AUDIENCE MEMBER: I'm Larry Wood, a retired Army colonel. Thank you very much for those kind remarks. My question is that you said there were two factors that were influencing the market, most recently, but your follow-on comments only address the latter, the war on terrorism or the boding ward with Iraq. What can we do as a nation, what can we do as a national security community—this partnership with the private sector you alluded to—to address the issue of trust?

MR. GRASSO: It's as much a public-private partnership to deal with the trust discount, as there was a public-private partnership to deal with the aftermath of 9/11. No single entity, either in the public or private sector, can deal with it. It is, in essence, this wonderful collage of initiatives, starting with the Stock Exchange itself. In February of this year, we asked the question, "What must we do to deal with the misdeeds that are being reported almost daily?" More importantly, what must others do that we can support? So we impaneled a special blue-ribbon committee on corporate accountability and created a brand new platform of listing requirements, corporate governance standards, which fundamentally say to the governing mechanisms of publicly held corporations: "You must have a majority of your board comprised of independent directors, people not associated with management in any way or conflicted in their responsibilities. You must have committees on the board of audit, nominating and governance, and compensation comprised entirely of independent directors. Those independent directors must meet periodically without the presence of management, and must report to the shareholders those meetings and, in essence, the name of the presiding director." What are we trying to do here? We are trying to create a cultural change in the board room to remind the managements and the governing mechanisms of publicly held corporations that I, as an independent director, serve not for the private entertainment of management or to simply rubber-stamp what management strategies may be, but rather to be a collaborator with, and at times be in confrontation with, the direction of the company, the direction of management, with the hope that by recognizing my role, my role in the final analysis is to serve those hundreds of thousands of shareholders who are not invited into the boardroom.

I serve as a fiduciary for those shareholders, and I'm there, hopefully, to accrete value to the entity by giving guidance and wisdom and perspective. The Securities and Exchange Commission needed to do what it has done in terms of reaffirmation of financial statements, in terms of tough new requirements and prosecutorial vigor to go after those who breached their responsibilities to the public markets. Through the legislative process, with the leadership of the president, we now have the Sarbane-Oxley Act. This legislation sets standards in place. In the collective, it is a collaboration of public-private partnerships to say to the American investor, to consumers, and to employees of the Enrons, the WorldComs, the Adelphias, and the Tycos that those who breach their responsibilities are unacceptable as owners and employees to the overwhelming majority of corporate America. For every Enron, there are thousands of Exxons—companies who do it right each and every day for the benefit of their employees, their shareholders, and the communities and customers they serve. You wouldn't know that by reading the daily press. I'm certainly not one to say it's only a hand-

ful. It happens to be only a handful in relation to the 15,000 publicly-held companies in America, but if the number were one, it would be one too many.
Because of the trust and confidence that have driven the American capital markets to be the shining star that the world aspires to, it rose over these last 50
years from fewer than 4 million investors to more than 85 million investors. The
absolute crude oil to the process was the public's belief that they could trust the
integrity of what they were reading, and that's been breached.

The final part to my solution is one that people often don't like to hear.
You can neither legislate nor, by Stock Exchange standard, mandate integrity
and honesty. What you can and must do is prosecute dishonesty. You have got
to pursue, prosecute, and put in jail those who have breached their responsibilities to the owners. The system is not broken. There are people within the
system whose morals and ethics are broken. When the American public understands that we are serious, that second discount that I talked about will come
out of this market. For all of the darkness that forecasters like to offer, let us
not forget, as I said in my brief comments, this is the strongest nation on earth.
This is the strongest economy on earth. It's growing at a rate of between 3 and
4 percent, with money costs at 40-year lows, with inflation nonexistent. If I
were to tell you that 5 years ago, or 10 years ago, you would have said, "Where
do I sign up? Where do I invest?" Not today, because three things govern performance in the market: fundamentals, and ours are strong; technicals, and
they oscillate with the mood of the moment; and the psychological, and right
now the psychological doesn't feel good, but it will.

The twentieth century has proven that for any period greater than six
years, equity investment in quality, real companies—as distinguished from the
thesis of the late 1990s when people forgot that you could not calculate a
price-earnings ratio (a PE multiple) if there were no E. (laughter) Where that
was the case, they said, "Well, let's look at top-line growth." Well, when you
didn't have revenues, you couldn't have top-line growth. Then they said,
"Well, let's look at share of eyeballs. Let's look at burn rates." These are all
phenomena of a mania. They are not, by the way, unique, just as the scandals
that we read about each day are not unique. The valuation based on crowd
mentality goes all the way back to Holland, when people were trading tulips
for homes (1624); to the late 1920s, when some of the best and brightest wrote
the innovations coming out of those wonderful laboratories that Radio
Corporation of America would change the way we live and work forevermore.
It was a paradigm shift. Sound familiar? They were right. They were absolutely right. Radio Corporation of America's laboratories produced things that
today we still benefit from. The only thing they got wrong was valuation—
proven by the fact that 50-plus years later, General Electric bought RCA for 10
cents on the 1928-dollar. In 1928, the stock sold for almost $700. General
Electric bought it for $61 50-plus years later. In the second half of the 1990s,
historians will look back and say: "What were they thinking?" But then again,

we need to do a better job in my business of making sure people think twice. If it sounds too good to be true, it is.

The trust discount is going to come out of this market, because when people start going to jail, consumers and investors will understand we're serious. The country is serious. This is not just about Wall Street. There is no such thing as the historical separation of Wall Street from Main Street. Wall Street and Main Street are one and the same today—85 million Americans directly and more than 200 million indirectly are in the equities market. Everyone in this audience is an owner, directly or indirectly, both of equities and of my institution. My institution is a private institution, but it's a private institution with a public purpose, to serve every one of you here and every one out there. The only way we do that well is by never forgetting that it's the public's trust, the public's belief that they are guaranteed fairness. They are never guaranteed a profit, I'll never do that, but I will pursue until the day when we can guarantee them fairness. Then the market will take care of itself.

AUDIENCE MEMBER: I'm Nick Rigg from the U.S. Army Command and General Staff College. Question: Just as surely as the military provides the necessary security for economic prosperity in the United States, the military would be very sorry if it did not have the economic base to give us precision-guided weapons, computerized communications, and so forth. We rely tremendously upon the economic base. Your industry in particular has provided the financial wherewithal to fund all of these new technologies and indeed you contribute over the years to "paradigm shifts" to use your words. Today we are faced with a crisis in the Middle East, a crisis of asymmetric warfare, and so forth. I'm just wondering, and I don't have the answer, can your industry also contribute to affecting the paradigms, which our adversaries hold? Are you engaging or can you engage more the institutions and cultures, which are currently our adversaries, to help us in this war against terrorism?

MR. GRASSO: The question is an excellent one. Certainly, we play two roles in trying, in a small way, to help the military pursue this war. The collaboration we in Treasury have is to block asset movement so that we can, to the extent that one can be air tight, prevent funding from the activities of those organizations of terrorist pursuit. Secondly, I would say that we play a collateral, or positive, role in trying to help emerging nations raise standards of living through capital markets and privatization opportunities. If you were to ask me to pursue that a bit, I would tell you to look at the experiences we have had with the People's Republic of China. A dozen years ago not a single Chinese company was traded at the big board; today, there are more than twenty-two.

There are partnerships, opportunities to go into places like the former Soviet Bloc countries, to go into places in Latin America, where there are activities that are clearly terrorist in background, and to work with those who believe, as we do—that economic and political freedom can be raised and standards can be raised through the free-market process, working with countries around the world who want to bring their infrastructure companies to levels of modern application through capital investment, through funding that would come from the U.S. capital markets. Therefore, I would say there is a positive role we can play, because the more we contribute to raising standards of living and to creating better information, better understanding of the fruits of a free society, the less we will have that small group out there who can so mislead a large population in the wrong direction. It's a very narrow-based answer; however, from personal experience, having worked with the former president of Colombia, some of the people in these terrorist organizations understand that one of their greatest opponents, beyond the military opponent, is the free-market process. This is why many believe that while the targets in New York were the two towers, the real target was the market that sits six floors below my office, because that is the embodiment of the American economic dream and the global economic dream. I'm told I have time for one more. Yes, sir?

AUDIENCE MEMBER: I'm Jim. I wonder if you can tell your views on what you think should be done with the real estate of the World Trade Center.

MR. GRASSO: I have the privilege and the honor of serving on the Lower Manhattan Development Corporation, which is that public entity that will channel the $20 billion of federal money into redevelopment. I also have the deep honor of serving at the request of former Mayor Guiliani on the Twin Towers Fund, which is a fund to support the families of firefighters and police officers lost, and therein is the polarity. There are many who believe that the entirety of those 16 acres, be it the resting ground of 2,801 men and women, should nevermore be built upon. The commercial application of many in my business realize of the 2,801 lost in New York, many were from the financial services business. I lost Herman Sandler, a dear friend of mine from Sandler and O'Neill. If he were standing here, he would say, "You honor us best by rebuilding, by coming back larger and more potent than ever before." That is the best monument we can give.

We have to be respectful, and we will do that. A large part of those 16 acres will be dedicated to a memorial that will be world-class and, in the view of many, will perhaps become the most visited spot on earth. We must be certain, 50, 100, and 200 years from now, that those who come to visit that spot never lose the perspective that we have today, of what happened that day, and those wonderful men and women. Therefore, it's going to be a balance. It's going to be a restoration of commercial, residential, and cultural, and there will be a monument that I know Herman would smile down on and say, "Dick, you did a good job." Thank you very much for having me today.

PANEL 2

SECURITY COOPERATION—WORKING WITH OTHERS IN A GLOBALIZED WORLD

Co-sponsor: Woodrow Wilson International Center for Scholars

Chair: Dr. Robert S. Litwak, Director, International Studies, Woodrow Wilson International Center for Scholars

Perspectives on Multilateralism: Dr. G. John Ikenberry, Peter F. Krogh Professor of Geopolitics and Justice in World Affairs, School of Foreign Service, Georgetown University

Perspectives on Unilateralism: Dr. Charles Krauthammer, Syndicated Columnist, The *Washington Post*

International Perspective: Dr. Thérèse Delpech, Director of Strategic Affairs, Commissariat de l'Energie Atomique, France

International Perspective: Dr. Yoichi Funabashi, Chief Diplomatic Correspondent and Columnist, *Asahi Shimbun*, Japan

Panel Charter

This panel will examine perceptions of and responses to the challenges of the post–9/11 international environment. Discussion will focus on how the United States defines its interests and the threats to those interests, as well as the strategies and policy instruments the U.S. administration should employ, either multilaterally or unilaterally, to meet those threats. The non-American panelists will offer their perspectives on America's emerging international role following 9/11 and assess the extent to which the views of key allies will converge or diverge with those of the United States on the central issues of interests, threats, strategies, and policy instruments.

Since the end of the Cold War, the United States has been called "the sole remaining superpower" and the "indispensable nation." Former French Foreign Minister Hubert Vedrine even coined a new term—hyper-power—to convey the magnitude of the United States' unrivalled international status. But though American power has never been greater, so too has there never been greater uncertainty and contention about what to do with it.

Left to right: *Dr. Loren B. Thompson, Dr. Robert S. Litwak, Dr. Charles Krauthammer (seated), Dr. Thérèse Delpech, Dr. G. John Ikenberry, Dr. Yoichi Funabashi, Mrs. Francis Hesselbein, General Eric K. Shinseki*

The current U.S. foreign-policy debate—typically framed across a broad range of issues as the choice between unilateralism (going it alone) and multilateralism (working in concert with others states)—reflects a persisting tension between America's dual identities in world politics. The United States is the paramount power with a unique responsibility for the maintenance of international order, while at the same time, it is an "ordinary" country with its own national interests existing within a system of sovereign states equal under international law. Reconciling or managing the competing pulls of these twin identities is one of the major challenges facing the U.S. administration.

The tension between these twin roles, now playing out in the transformed international environment of the post–9/11 period, is not new. Since the end of the Cold War, the standard formulation of American declaratory policy has been that the United States would act multilaterally when possible and unilaterally when necessary. The 9/11 attacks exposed the new vulnerability of the American homeland to a mass casualty assault by a terrorist group with a global reach. That the al Qaeda terrorists were able to mount their operation from Afghanistan, widely regarded as a "failed state," has recast the pre–9/11 debate about failed states and "nation building." In the aftermath of September 11, the Bush administration warned of the danger to international security posed by the "axis of evil"—Iraq, Iran, and North Korea—and of possible links between these "rogue states" and terrorist groups. Because of the horrific consequences of an attack with a weapon of mass destruction and the inability to deter a transnational terrorist group, like al Qaeda, the administration has declared a willingness to use force preemptively and unilaterally if circumstances necessitate doing so. With reports of al Qaeda activity in over 60 countries, U.S. national security officials acknowledge the need to engage in security cooperation with other states, but maintain that the mission will determine the coalition and not the other way around. They argue that the exigencies of the new era may require unilateral U.S. action without the legitimizing cloak of multilateralism. Proponents of multilateralism hold that the pursuit of what is perceived as an American national agenda will erode international support for what the Bush administration has cast as a global war on terrorism.

Discussion Points

• Did the 9/11 terrorist attacks lead to the transformation of international relations or the affirmation of existing norms and institutions?

• Were these terrorist acts perceived as an attack on the United States or the West more generally? Is there a gap in perceptions between elite and public opinion?

• What are the appropriate strategies for dealing with transnational terrorist groups and with "rogue states" that challenge international norms with respect to proliferation and terrorism?

• What are the respective roles of force and nonmilitary policy instruments in these strategies?

• Under what conditions, if any, should the United States use force preemptively and unilaterally? If the United States asserts its right to do so, what will be the consequences for international order?

• Can we bridge the gap between the United States and its key allies on these issues of threat perception and strategy formulation?

• Is a new division of labor possible between the United States and its allies in Europe and Asia who possess less military capability? Can guidelines be worked out in advance of a crisis?

Summary

Dr. G. John Ikenberry, Peter F. Krogh Professor of Geopolitics and Justice in World Affairs, School of Foreign Service, Georgetown University

• A year after the 9/11 terrorist attacks, how much has the world changed? The existing international order is neither falling apart nor even in upheaval. Indeed, the crisis creates opportunities (1) to renew alliance partnerships and strengthen multilateral cooperation and (2) to continue the process of integrating Russia and China into the international system. The United States discovered a new threat, and it isn't China, contrary to the views widely expressed prior to 9/11.

• The United States has largely dissipated the international goodwill it engendered after the terrorist attacks. America is debating how to deal with terrorism and "rogue states," while the rest of the world is debating how to deal with America. The most important task facing policymakers is to ensure that American power is viewed as legitimate and morally acceptable to U.S. allies and the wider world. To accomplish this goal, the United States should continue its post–World War II strategy of wrapping, and thereby institutionalizing, its power in multilateral arrangements.

• Since the end of World War II, the United States has built international order by using two grand strategies. The first is the *realist* grand strategy forged during the Cold War, organized around deterrence, containment, bipolarity, and great power alliances. The second is the *liberal* grand strategy organized around the promotion of democratic political systems and market economies, multilateral institutions, and cooperative security. These twin strategies built a remarkably successful, unprecedented international order—a stable, legitimate order that connects Europe, Japan, and the United States. The bargain was that the United States would provide its European and Japanese partners security and access to American markets and technology in return for their diplomatic and logistical support of the U.S.-led Western international order.

• U.S. actions in the post–9/11 period could undermine this strategic bargain. The profound disparity between the United States and other powers makes it easier for America to say no and to act alone. Multilateralism and American strategic restraint are not the enemies of American primacy. In the past, the United States has exercised its unilateral power, but it been used as a tool toward building an international community that serves American interests. The post–World War II period—the most institutionally creative period in world history—created a foundation for American power. It has made American power more legitimate and therefore less likely to be contested by other powers.

Dr. Charles Krauthammer, Syndicated Columnist, The *Washington Post*

• Unilateralism predates September 11th. It was evident in the Bush administration's attitude toward the Kyoto Protocol on Climate Change and the Biological Weapons Convention. The Bush administration would not allow itself to be restrained and diminished by multilateral arrangements.

• Unilateralism does not necessarily mean that the United States will or wants to act alone. Unilateralism means that the United States will not be held hostage to the preferences, policies, and interests of others, particularly when supreme U.S. national interests are at stake.

• For the last quarter century, the U.S. foreign policy establishment has been obsessively preoccupied with other countries' opinions and international legality. Post-Vietnam internationalism, steeped in a distrust of American power and purpose, sought legitimacy and validation for any U.S. action from the outside. Thus, in the current debate on Iraq, some in the Senate have argued that U.S. military intervention should be contingent on U.N. approval to provide it legitimacy.

• But the U.N. Security Council is essentially a committee of the great powers, each pursuing its own interests. How does the consent of Russia and France confer legitimacy to American actions and why is it necessary to obtain it? The argument is made that the United States should sign multilateral treaties, such as the land mine treaty, so that it is in sync with world opinion and not isolated. Yet as the sole superpower and guarantor of peace in unstable regions, the United States may need to act unilaterally and exempt itself from the fashionable opinion of the day.

• The contemporary international system has two unique features. The first is America's preeminent position of power, which has created a unipolar moment in world history. This status creates an opportunity for the United States but has also made it uniquely vulnerable, as evidenced in the September 11th terrorist attacks. The second unprecedented characteristic is the advent of weapons of mass destruction and, in particular, their proliferation to small powers and even nonstate actors.

• The profound threat posed by the increased availability of weapons of mass destruction to rogue states and terrorist groups means that the United States cannot base its security on outdated concepts, even if compelled to act unilaterally, without the legitimizing cloak of multilateralism.

• The most important task is to rekindle the sense of urgency evidenced after the September 11th attacks. The United States was bound to lose international sympathy after it was no longer the victim and acted in Afghanistan and elsewhere to defend its supreme national interest.

Dr. Thérèse Delpech, Director of Strategic Affairs, French Atomic Energy Commission

• Three superficial ways of assessing the current state of trans-Atlantic relations should be avoided. The first is to focus on the usual litany of specific issues on which views differ, for example, the Middle East conflict, the International Criminal Court, and the Kyoto Protocol. A second counterproductive way is to rehash the old burden-sharing debate. The third is the misleading dichotomy between unilateralism and multilateralism—because Europe does not always act multilaterally nor does the United States uniformly go it alone. For example, in the recent German parliamentary campaign, there was discussion of "the German way."

• President Bush's decision to take the issue of Iraq back to the United Nations was important. His September 12, 2002 speech put the political onus on the United Nations to enforce its own Security Council resolutions that were passed at the end of the 1991 Gulf War.

• Three important psychological factors are shaping policies on both sides of the Atlantic. The first is that Americans are discovering vulnerability at a time when Europeans, who have known major wars since the seventeenth century, no longer want to focus on it. The second is diverging views on the key issue of sovereignty: the United States is insisting on a complete and unprecedented freedom of action at a time when the Europeans are ceding their state sovereignty to a supranational entity—the European Union (EU). In Europe, this process is, if anything, accelerating with the prospective incorporation of new East European members into the EU. The third psychological factor relates to time: America is focused on the present and future, and that is a source of its dynamism; by contrast, in Europe, the present remains the past because of the continuing legacy of World Wars I and II.

• Three strategic factors also shape trans-Atlantic policies. The first is the declining centrality of Europe in Washington's security perspective. The Balkan wars in the 1990s maintained that illusion for the decade after the Cold War. The second geostrategic factor is America's increased focus on security in Asia and, of course, global terrorism. The third geostrategic factor is that the centers of gravity of European and American security are moving in opposite directions: Europe is moving east with the enlargement of the EU, whereas the United States in increasingly focused on the Middle East and Asia.

• Terrorism is a common threat. Even if one acknowledges that the United States is uniquely at risk, so too is Europe, where terrorist networks are located. A number of potentially horrific terrorist attacks have been foiled in Europe, but experts agree that the worst is yet to come. There is a chilling new conjunction of technology and violence—in particular, the privatization of extreme violence to individuals and nonstate actors.

• All of the major powers are preoccupied with their own problems: America is obsessed with homeland security, Europe with enlargement, Russia with domestic political and economic problems, and China with events only within its regional sphere. This trend is not conducive to multilateralism.

Dr. Yoichi Funabashi, Chief Diplomatic Correspondent and Columnist,
      The *Asahi Shimbun*, Japan

• U.S. allies are increasingly worried about aspects of the American war on terrorism. The German parliamentary campaign did cynically exploit anti-Americanism, but one should still ask why the German people responded to that rhetoric. This political phenomenon is a remarkable turnabout only a year after the September 11th terrorist attacks. Moreover, it is not confined to Europe; in Japan, more than three-quarters of the public oppose a war on Iraq.

- The Bush Doctrine has three elements. The first is that "the mission determines the coalition." The second aspect is the "axis-of-evil" formulation grouping Iran, Iraq, and North Korea. The third is the new doctrine of military preemption that was elevated to official U.S. policy in the Bush administration's September 2002 *National Security Strategy* document.

- To meet the challenge of global terrorism and the axis of evil, the United States has attempted to forge an "axis of good"—America, China, Russia, India, Europe, and Japan. Notwithstanding their current cooperation over terrorism, the long-term national interests of these various states do not change, thereby calling into question the durability of these new relationships.

- America and China, in particular, share neither common values nor a common vision of international order. Their differences over Taiwan and human rights will also limit the extent of their cooperative relationship.

- The administration's preemption doctrine is a radical and fundamental departure from past policy. If this military posture were to be adopted by other countries, it could undermine the rules of international conduct and lead to chaos. America's allies agree that terrorism poses a major threat, but question whether this new military doctrine is the appropriate response.

- Rather than a single, all-encompassing military strategy, the United States should adopt specific policies to differentiate among the diverse security challenges posed by the axis-of-evil countries. Terrorism poses a diffused, elusive threat that can be contained but never totally eliminated. It might better be addressed as a law enforcement rather than a military problem.

- A U.S. policy of deterrence may not work against terrorists, but it could be effective against a "rogue state" such as Saddam's Iraq. The Iraqi dictator is homicidal, but there is no evidence that he is suicidal.

- In discussions of a possible conflict and postwar reconstruction in Iraq, some observers have proposed a "MacArthur Doctrine" based on America's post–World War II occupation experience in Japan. During World War II, U.S. officials consulted with the best cultural anthropologists to explore the cultural patterns and heritage of Japanese society so that they could occupy in the best way. But major differences exist between the Japanese and Iraqi cases, most notably uncertainty whether the United States would be willing to commit the long-term resources to the occupation of a post-Saddam Iraq.

Analysis

The panelists agreed that the September 11th terrorist attacks did not alter the structure of international relations, but they did usher in a new era of American vulnerability. America continues to occupy a unique position in the global system. On the one hand, the United States is the preeminent power without peer—a position that affords it a unique ability to act independently. On the other, it leads an international system whose governing norms and institutions bear an indelible American mark. The panel focused on whether U.S. policymakers can, and indeed even should try to, reconcile the competing pulls generated by these twin identities.

The panelists observed that the response to the 9/11 attacks, whether out of sympathy or a shared perception of threat, initially created a united front among the major powers, but also pointed to challenges that called into question the long-term durability of this international coalition against terrorism. Dr. Funabashi warned of the diverging national interests and values of the various states that constitute this "axis of good." Dr. Delpech argued that trans-Atlantic relations are being shaped by psychological and geostrategic factors that are not conducive to multilateralism. The major powers are all obsessed with their own problems, while the United States is increasingly preoccupied with security issues in the Middle East and Asia as the Europeans focus on EU enlargement to the east.

Professor Ikenberry highlighted an even more fundamental potential challenge to U.S. relations with its major European and Japanese allies. Assertive American unilateral policies related to the war on global terrorism could undermine the grand strategic bargain between the United States and its Western partners that created the most stable and prosperous international order in history. A key element of that post–World War II strategy was American strategic restraint—embedding U.S. power in multilateral security and economic institutions. That characteristic made the exercise of American power less threatening and more legitimate to other states.

In sharp contrast to the perspective on international order advanced by Professor Ikenberry, Dr. Krauthammer argued that collapse of the Cold War bipolar system had created an unprecedented "unipolar moment" that American policymakers should unabashedly seize to reshape international affairs and safeguard U.S. supreme national interests. The new American unilateralism, in fact, pre-dated the 9/11 attacks and was evidenced in the Bush administration's policies toward the Kyoto Protocol on Climate Change and multilateral arms control agreements. The September 11th attacks underscored the horrific and unacceptable consequences of a mass casualty attack perpetrated by an undeterrable terrorist group, such as al Qaeda. Meeting the diverse threats posed by rogue states and global terrorism may require the United States to undertake preemptive military action unfettered by the constraints of multilateral institutions.

Much of the panel discussion focused on this crux issue—the legitimizing political utility versus the constraining effects of multilateralism for the United States in the post–9/11 era. Dr. Delpech argued that President Bush's September 12th U.N. speech on Iraq was important because it offered a means of legitimizing U.S. actions and placed the political onus on the other permanent members of the Security Council to end Iraq's flagrant flouting of U.N. resolutions. The panel also addressed diverging perceptions of the new threats and the appropriate means to combat them. Dr. Krauthammer rejected Dr. Funabashi's suggestion that the new global terrorism should be addressed more as a law enforcement than a military problem.

Can a common approach be developed to address the transformed international security agenda? Ms. Delpech observed that the U.S. demand for complete freedom of action was unprecedented, while Dr. Funabashi warned that the U.S. doctrine of military preemption would create international chaos if other states adopted the same stance.

Professor Ikenberry advocated an international dialogue to develop new rules governing the use of force. This need was underscored not only by the September 11th attacks but also by the humanitarian interventions of the 1990s such as the NATO intervention in Kosovo that was undertaken without U.N. Security Council authorization. The forging of new rules on the use of force must take into account the increased proliferation of weapons of mass destruction to hostile states and, in particular, to nonstate actors—a trend that Dr. Delpech characterized as the "privatization of violence." According to Professor Ikenberry, this development points to the need to update key provisions of international law, such as Article 51 of the U.N. Charter, which has been traditionally interpreted as rejecting the notion of "anticipatory self-defense." While Dr. Krauthammer rejected the notion of subordinating U.S. national policy to multilateral constraints for the sake of political legitimacy, Dr. Delpech and Dr. Funabashi endorsed this proposal as a means of developing a new international consensus on the use of force.

Transcript

DR. LOREN B. THOMPSON: Thank you. Our second panel of the day deals with the contentious issue of security cooperation. In particular, it addresses the challenge of finding a suitable balance in our security efforts between self-reliance and collective action or, as some might put it, between *unilateralism* and *multilateralism*. The panel is chaired by Dr. Robert Litwak, director of International Studies at the Woodrow Wilson International Center for Scholars. The Wilson Center is a living national memorial to President Wilson, arguably the first great internationalist to leave his mark on American foreign policy. Although his efforts to forge an effective League of Nations failed, President Wilson is widely remembered today as a leader who saw that America could no longer go it alone in global affairs, retreating into hemispheric insularity when it didn't have its way.

The Wilson Center seeks to foster a continuous and contentious exchange of insights between the world of policy and the world of ideas. And Robert Litwak is a central player in that process. He comes well equipped for the task since he served on the National Security Council staff as Director of Nonproliferation and Export Controls and has authored or edited eight books on global affairs, ranging from regional security to technology controls. In addition, he teaches in the same program that I do at the School of Foreign Service at Georgetown University. He has previously held fellowships at Harvard, the Russian Academy of Science, the Graduate Institute of International Studies in Geneva, and the United States Institute of Peace. We are fortunate to have a person of his insight and breadth to anchor our second panel today. Robert Litwak.

DR. ROBERT S. LITWAK: Thank you, Loren, and good afternoon, ladies and gentlemen. The Woodrow Wilson Center is delighted to be partners with the Army and the other distinguished co-sponsors of this conference. It is particularly apt that a conference that memorializes Dwight Eisenhower's legacy is being held in a building honoring Ronald Reagan, a wing of which houses the Woodrow Wilson Center. As Loren mentioned, the Woodrow Wilson Center's mission is to improve the quality of public policy debate on the most pressing issues facing our nation through dialogue such as we're engaged in here.

The current foreign policy debate is typically framed across a broad range of issues as the choice between unilateralism and multilateralism. In short, should the United States go it alone or work in concert with others? The policy tension between unilateralism and multilateralism is not new. President Eisenhower grappled with it. It can be managed, but not resolved. That process has been made all the more challenging since the September 11 terrorist attacks, which ushered in a new age of American vulnerability and exposed the dark side of globalization.

In the war on terrorism, American policymakers must weigh the trade-offs between the utility and constraints of multilateralism. Secretary of Defense Donald Rumsfeld has baldly stated that the mission determines the coalition, not the other way around. Proponents of American unilateralism argue that the pre-9/11 constraints, such as the international legal prohibition against anticipatory self-defense, are nonsensical in an age when Osama bin Laden has said that obtaining nuclear weapons is a moral duty and when he certainly has no compunction against using them against America. President Bush argues that to protect American society, which is uniquely threatened by al Qaeda, the exigencies of the new era may require preemptive U.S. military action without the legitimizing cloak of multilateralism. Critics of this unilateralist approach respond that the pursuit of what is perceived as an American *national* agenda will erode international support for what the Bush administration has cast as a global war on terrorism. This political dynamic has been evident in the current debate over Iraq.

In the early 1990s, Madeleine Albright referred to America as the *indispensable nation*, while the book by Richard N. Haass, *The Reluctant Sheriff: The United States After the Cold War*, captured the country's ambivalent attitude

Dr. Litwak

toward international affairs. In the post–9/11 world, America remains the indispensable superpower, but global terrorism in this new era no longer permits it to be a reluctant sheriff. Extending Haass's Western metaphor: Will America be the head of an international posse or the lone ranger? To address the central issue of how the United States can cooperate with others on security problems in a globalized world, we are fortunate to have on this panel four influential thinkers, all of whom have written widely and powerfully on this theme.

John Ikenberry is the Peter Krogh Professor of Global Justice at Georgetown University's School of Foreign Service. He previously taught at the University of Pennsylvania and Princeton. He is the author of the award-winning book, *After Victory: Institutions, Strategic Restraint, and the Rebuilding of Order After Major Wars*. He has an article, "America's Imperial Ambition," in the current issue of *Foreign Affairs*, warning against the Bush administration's adoption of a geoimperial strategy.

Charles Krauthammer is a Pulitzer-Prize-winning writer whose syndicated columns appear in the *Washington Post* and *Time* Magazine. After the 1991 Gulf War, Dr. Krauthammer authored a widely discussed article on foreign affairs, "*The Unipolar Moment*," which made an unequivocal case for American unilateralism. Since September 11, he has continued to make this case. His recent columns include the following telling titles: "The New Unilateralism," " Unilateral, Yes Indeed" and "We Don't Peacekeep." Earlier in his career, Dr. Krauthammer, who received an M.D. from Harvard Medical School, was a practicing psychiatrist. In Washington's foreign policy community, he is the only person I know who goes by the title *doctor* who can actually write a prescription.

In addition to these two very different American perspectives, we will also address foreign attitudes and policies on the critical issue of security cooperation. Thérèse Delpech of France is a preeminent expert on nuclear matters, nonproliferation, and disarmament. Currently Director of Strategic Affairs at the French Atomic Energy Commission, she served in the French government as a special adviser to the prime minister for political military affairs. A recent article in the *Financial Times* cited her new book, *The Politics of Chaos, the Other Side of Globalization*.

Yoichi Funabashi is a columnist and chief diplomatic correspondent for the *Asahi Shimbun* news service and is widely recognized as Japan's leading journalist in the field of foreign policy. He is the recipient of the Japan press award known as Japan's Pulitzer Prize. Dr. Funabashi received a full Fulbright Scholarship as a Neiman Fellow at Harvard University. His publications include the award-winning study on the U.S.–Japan relationship, *Alliance Adrift*, published by the Council on Foreign Relations.

The panelists will each speak for 15 minutes in the order that I introduced them. We will give them a few minutes thereafter to interact with each other and then entertain comments and questions from the floor. Now it's my pleasure to turn the floor over to the first speaker, John Ikenberry.

DR. G. JOHN IKENBERRY: Thanks, Rob, it's great to be here. Everyone is asking the same question today, a year after 9/11: How much has the world changed? Are we entering a world where terrorism and all that comes with it is creating an environment in which the United States needs to rethink and reinvent the strategies that it's pursued over the last 50 years? Does it fundamentally need to rethink its relations with its allies and with partners around the world and with the international community embodied in international institutions and agreements? Is the old order, created perhaps in 1947—if we want to pick a date—at the beginning of the Cold War, where the Truman administration thought hard about the new environment and crafted containment and alliance partnerships—multilateral relationships—is all of that finished, requiring us to rethink all those basic organizing concepts? Well, today I want to be skeptical, optimistic, and worried.

Skeptical that the existing international system led by the United States is falling apart or is even in upheaval. In my view, we are witnessing what is really a quite mature Western order, Europe and America at the core—stumbling forward, to be sure, but forward nonetheless—mobilizing to respond to a new threat. At the end of this process, I think the United States will discover, along with its partners, that the threat of terrorism is something that we know how to handle; that the forum will be very similar to the forum we have invented and used over the decades for tackling other, perhaps less catastrophic but nonetheless global, problems: financial instability, transnational organized crime, environmental threats. That is to say, we will rely on concerted multilateral action backed by U.S. leadership. We don't need to reinvent world politics.

I'm also optimistic that the U.S. and its partners, if they play their cards right, can turn this crisis into an opportunity to renew alliance partnerships, to strengthen multilateral cooperation, and to fashion what is deeply needed, that is, new understandings about how the great powers can work together in addressing terrorist threats, weapons of mass destruction, outlaw states. And

then figure out how to use force—
what the rules are for the use of
force—which is really the next big
issue we have to tackle. Crises in the
past—great wars—have always created this moment of opportunity even
as it was a moment of peril: 1815,
1919, 1945. They are all known not
simply as wars and great moments of
risk but also of opportunity when
great powers came together in different ways, sometimes more successfully than others, in crafting a new set of
rules or rediscovering things that do,
in fact, work. Indeed, I think the
United States and the Western powers may be able to use this crisis to
further integrate Russia and China
into the existing Western-oriented
international order. In fact, perhaps
the best news we can report in the last
several years is that Russia really has

Dr. Ikenberry

articulated a new position and is integrated in important ways in the Western
security framework.

Regarding China, I think the good news is that the U.S. has discovered a
new threat and it *isn't* China. In America are many people who think this is
going to be the next crisis point. But, in fact, this is a call to action—the first
American call to action where the U.S. and its leaders have been mobilizing
American society, if you will; a call to arms, mobilizing for war—that isn't
attacking an *ism* that is embedded in another great power. Totalitarianism, fas-
cism, communism were all not just threats, but they were attached to a great
power, and that's the opportunity—that terrorism puts all the great powers
potentially on the same side. Now, America's great philosopher Yogi Berra
indicated that it's difficult to make predictions, particularly about the future.
So I'm not going to make great predictions, but I do think there is reason to
think that there are opportunities, if we play our cards right.

My third point really is that I'm worried in that I'm not sure the Bush
administration is playing its cards right. The sympathy and goodwill that we
saw swell up after 9/11 has largely ended. The United States is debating how
to deal with terrorism in rogue states, and the rest of the world is debating how
to deal with America—what looks like its high-handedness, its unilateralism,
its disrespect for multilateral rules and partnerships. My worry is that the Bush
administration is seen to be, and perhaps is, *rending* the fabric of the interna-

tional community rather than, as I said before, taking this crisis as an opportunity for strengthening that fabric.

My view is that at the end of this cycle of crisis and response, the most important thing that we need to accomplish is that U.S. power in the world is seen as legitimate and morally acceptable to Western states and the wider world; that that is the measure of whether we succeeded. It's not specific policy debates about whether we should do X or Y now or the sequence of particular approaches to Iraq. It's really this larger issue of how the U.S. protects its position and, particularly, the legitimacy of its power in the world today. And the key thesis I want to present is, to do that, the United States has to go back to the way it's done it before, particularly after World War II, which is to wrap its power in multilateral arrangements, if you will, and institutionalize its power. More on that in a moment.

I really want to make three arguments in the next 10 minutes or so, starting with thinking about the existing order that we live in today. The first argument I want to make is that, over the last 50 years, the United States has built international order by using two grand strategies. The first one is familiar. It's the realist-balancing grand strategy, forged during the Cold War, organized around deterrents, containment, balance, bipolarity, ideological rivalry, and great power alliances. The other strategy is what I call liberal grand strategy, built in the shadows of the Cold War: an earlier American strategy organized around promoting openness economically, democracy, intergovernmental multilateralism, institutions of joint management, and cooperative security. A security practice is attached to this liberal grand strategy, which both political parties have championed over the decades.

In the post–Cold War period, Bush the Elder talked about strengthening the Euro-Atlantic community, building a new political community in East Asia—taking the opportunity that now exists in the absence of the external threat that was the glue that held the Western order together to articulate a more positive view—and invoking these kind of liberal ideas. Clinton, of course, talked about engagement and enlargement in more grandiose terms. And now, the new Bush administration is talking about it less in kind of advertising ways, but nonetheless pursuing it in policies such as the new Doha trade round.

The second point I want to make is that these strategies built a remarkably successful international order, a stable, legitimate order that connects Europe, Japan, and the United States. And it's a distinctive order—an order that the world has never seen before—built around common values of capitalism and democracy as well as other values; but it's also—and this is important—an engineered political order. It's built on bargains that the United States has secured with the outside world, with Europe, in particular, and Japan, and two bargains are most important. One—a kind of realist bargain forged again during the Cold War—is that the United States will provide security to its European and Asian partners and access to American markets, technology, resources, and supplies within the context of an open-world economy. In return, these countries will provide stable partnerships, diplomacy, diplomatic support, and logistical support as the United States leads this Western order.

The other bargain is less acknowledged, less explicit, but nonetheless important. It's a liberal bargain that addresses the other feature of the world that we have been living in over the last 50 years, and that is American preeminence from the 1940s onward. In this bargain, the United States, in effect, offers to play by the rules, if you will, to be a reliable partner. In return, Asian and European countries agree to engage and connect with, rather than balance against, the United States. So there is something here that the United States is getting, but it's also something that it's giving, it's exchanging. It's what I would call institutionalized cooperation. It will play by the rules; it will make its power as benign as possible; it will make itself user-friendly. U.S. power will be made safe for the world, and other countries will agree to operate within this Western order. It's a bargain from which both parties benefit. In the background of all of this is the creation of an order that is stable and legitimate, and after five decades, these countries—these great democratic major powers—have succeeded in building a remarkably stable, multilateral, reciprocal, legitimate, and highly institutionalized political order unlike anything the world has seen before. What's remarkable, it has provided more physical security and more creation of wealth than any other international order in history. It cuts across the Atlantic and Pacific, and this order doesn't have a name. It's the trilateral world, if you will. But the key here and the secret is that the success of American policy over these decades—the secret of its brilliant career on the world stage—is that the United States has been willing to connect itself to restrain its power and connect and commit its power in loose, multilateral ways.

My third and final point is that I'm worried that the Bush administration doesn't really fully get this. That is to say, it's letting this hugely successful U.S.-centered world order slip away. Part of the problem is one that any president would have, and that is that in the 1990s we have, as Mr. Krauthammer very eloquently described, a unipolar world order; we have the U.S. so much larger than any other state that that itself is a reality that is causing an unsettling of world politics. The U.S. began the decade of the 1990s as the world's only superpower, and it had a better decade than all the other states. Its GNP grew 26 percent from 1990 to 1998 while Europe grew 16 percent and Japan 7 percent. Therefore, it's a rising power. This unipolarity makes it easier for the United States to say no and to act alone. My worry is that this is causing the kind of rethinking of this bargain, both in Washington and around the world, and you see some of this behavior in the Bush administration over the first two years. We have called it *unilateralism*—rejecting treaties and agreements—which, on balance, I think we can debate the substance of. However, I'm talking about not the content, but the form, of cooperation.

Multilateralism, I would argue, is not the enemy of primacy. There is nothing sacred about multilateralism or unilateralism. Unilateralism is a tool, as is multilateralism. Indeed, unilateralism can lead to multilateralism. We call it leadership. Britain in the early nineteenth century unilaterally attacked piracy on the open seas, and ultimately it led to a multilateral rule-based solution to that problem. The Nixon shocks of the 1970s were unilateral but led to the creation of new facilities within the IMF and the G7 process. Reagan pursued unilateral trade policy that, at the end of the cycle, led to new dispute settlement mechanisms within the GATT system. Therefore, my argument is that it's not that unilateralism is bad, but that it needs to be used as a tool toward building an international community that creates a durable institutional environment that serves American interests. Multilateralism must be a deep part of America's hegemonic strategy.

Multilateralism is not simply for wimps, nor is it, as Robert Kagan argued in a very influential piece, simply a weapon or tool of the weak. Multilateralism is also a mechanism or tool of the strong. It can deepen and expand the power and the influence of the United States. The United States would not be the superpower it is today if, during the period from 1944 to 1952, it didn't engage in this kind of hyperactive institution-building: global, regional, security, economic, political, IMF, World Bank, Bretton Woods System, the GATT system, the United Nations, NATO, the U.S.–Japan alliance. It was the most institutionally creative period in world history, and it created a foundation for American power that served this country very well. So, in effect, it makes power more profound. It also makes it, and this is important, more legitimate. It makes American power more acceptable and enormously desirable for our partners, and therefore less likely to be the subject of contestation and backlash and blowback.

Power is most profound and stable when it is restrained and institutionalized. This is a very old insight, and I don't think this insight has been fully embraced in Washington today. Therefore, the debate about multilateralism and unilateralism is not well cast today. The question is, is Kyoto [Protocol on Global Warming] good for America? Well, I think Kyoto is fundamentally flawed. I would not vote for it. But I would vote for a multilateral approach for climate warming because it's good for America's power position and its interest in the long term.

The real issue is American power. That is the nature of the dispute. The dispute is not about the specifics of particular agreements. In many ways, I think that the wheels of power today don't understand this basic insight: that institutions and restraint are not the enemy of primacy. So when I pause and worry, as intellectuals are paid to worry about issues, I echo Pericles in his funeral oration when he said, " I fear, more than the strategies of our enemies, our own mistakes." Thank you.

DR. LITWAK: Thank you. Charles Krauthammer.

DR. CHARLES KRAUTHAM-MER: Thank you. I think I'm here as the unilateralist and I intend to defend the proposition. Let me start by saying that Rob mentioned that I'm a doctor. I also used to be a psychiatrist in my youth, and I'm sometimes asked how different that is from what I do now, which is political analysis. Many years ago, and I tell people in both professions, I would spend my day studying and analyzing people who suffered from grandiosity and delusions, with the exception that in Washington, they have access to nuclear weapons. So, it makes the stakes a little higher and the work a little more interesting.

Dr. Krauthammer

I'm delighted to be here. I think this is a very important event, and I'm honored that I'm on the panel with my colleagues.

I would like to speak in defense of unilateralism, and I think it is probably the most important issue right now that we are facing in foreign policy. It underlies the debate on Iraq, it underlies the war on terrorism, and it affects just about every aspect of our defense in foreign policy. It is, I believe, the distinguishing feature of this administration's foreign policy. It's unique, it's radical, it's welcomed, and it predates September 11th. It was evident from the beginning of this administration—with its attitude toward Kyoto, the M Treaty, the Biological Weapons Convention, and others—that it would not allow itself to be drawn into and held back and restrained—in a way diminished—by multilateral arrangements the way that the previous administration had.

Now, I want to be clear; unilateralism does not necessarily mean that we want to act alone. We don't. Everyone prefers to act in concert with others, with approval and with applause. Unilateralism simply means that we do not allow ourselves to be held hostage to the opinions, policies, preferences, and interests of others, particularly when our supreme national interests are at stake. Then, we do what we have to do. It's a simple proposition. Of course, we consult, we brief, we solicit advice, and we schmooze. Why else do we have a secretary of state? There is no need to be high-handed or arrogant or to poke people in the eye by cutting them off. Unilateralism simply means that, at the end of the day, you rely on your own counsel, on your own needs, on your own assessment of the safety and necessity and morality of American action.

Why is this important? Because, I would argue, for the last 25 years establishment opinion has been obsessively, needlessly, and I would say, destructively preoccupied with the opinions of others in the conduct of American foreign policy. We have an entire literature, entire vocabulary of diplomacy-speak about the need for world opinion or international norms, or even, more powerfully, "international legality." This outward centering of American norms has infused our public policy since the early idealistic post–World War II days—the days of the founding of the United Nations. But it did not achieve dominance until Vietnam created an epidemic of American self-doubt.

It is in that quarter century of the post-Vietnam era that the dominant foreign policy school in the country—liberal internationalism—steeped in distrust of American purpose and power, sought legitimacy and validation for any significant American action from the outside. I'll give you an example of how powerful that instinct is today. You've all been watching and hearing about the debate on Iraq. You get leading Democrats like the chairman of the Senate Arms Services Committee, Senator Carl Levin, saying that he is not prepared to approve of this action until he hears from the United Nations, or essentially saying that we want to hear what the U.N. has to say if we are going to approve and legitimize this action. You've heard that from many members of Congress, from many Democrats. It's the reason that the president went to the U.N. I'm sure he didn't want to, but he understood that if he was going to get domestic support, meaning Democratic support, he had to go to the U.N., at least to make a gesture. His father understood that very well. In the Gulf War he went to the U.N., again knowing that he would need that legitimacy before he went to the Senate. As you all know, he barely got support of the Senate. The resolutions support of the Gulf War passed by 52 to 47, with the overwhelming majority of Democrats voting against, even after U.N. approval. Imagine what would have happened if he hadn't gotten it?

My question is: "Why is this such an essential requirement?" Because, it confers a legitimacy, morality, and sort of rectitude to the enterprise. I don't understand that. The Security Council is essentially a committee of the greater powers, the victors in the Second World War. They manage the world in their own interests. The Security Council is, on the rare occasion where it actually works, politics by committee. By what logic is it the repository of international morality? Why did we need the blessings of the Chinese delegation in the Gulf war—the butchers of Tiananman Square, with blood still fresh on their hands—to justify an action of liberating another people from conquest? It was beyond me then and it remains beyond me today.

Yet this thinking utterly dominates a very large school of American foreign policy thinking. I think it dominates a lot of thinking of very important, very well placed, very active political actors today. What I think one has to begin to understand is that those of us who are puzzled by this requirement are puzzled by why the approval of France or of Russia in the coming war in Iraq confers legitimacy on this enterprise? Obviously, the French and the Russians will act in their own interests. The Russians have very serious financial interest in Iraq and the French do too. They all have a price. If we meet it, we might get their approval. If we don't meet their price, we probably will not. It's true that in practice our actions might be complicated if we don't have their approval. What you have to understand: it is not the practice and the material benefits that move many people in seeking this kind of approval. It's the legitimacy, and I think that need for outside legitimacy bespeaks a very strong lack of confidence in the legitimacy of Americans acting in congress, assembled, if you like, under their own counsel. But even more important than the legitimacy that liberal internationalism seeks is the fact that it looks not just for the assent of the international community, but to act in sync with world opinion.

You often hear the argument that on myriad foreign policy issues we cannot do X because it will leave us isolated from the world. In the Clinton years, this carried the day over and over again. The Senate, for example, passed a ridiculous Chemical Weapons Convention in 1997—even though it was admittedly unenforceable—largely because of the argument that everybody else had signed it and we would be isolated if we did not. Isolation, somehow, is a diminished and even morally suspect condition, and it's a staple of critics who've assailed this administration for rejecting other unenforceable treaties or destructive treaties like the Kyoto Protocol or the amendment to the Biological Weapons Convention. My favorite example of this was the negotiations in the Land Mine Treaty in the late 1980s. Pro-treaty ads ran even recently in Washington showing the horror of land mines and noting that all of our allies signed it. We were all alone on this. Well, not quite. One of the rare dissenters who was on our side of this argument was, interestingly enough, Finland, and during these negotiations it found itself scolded by the Swedes. These negotiations were happening in Oslo in 1997, and the Swedes scolded Finland for opposing the land mine ban. The Finnish prime minister replied rather tartly that this was a very convenient pose for the other Nordic countries, because Finland was their land mine.

In many parts of the world, a thin line of American GIs is the land mine. The main reason that we opposed the Land Mine Treaty was that we need them in the DMZ against North Korea. We are the ones who man the lines. The Swedes and the French and the Canadians don't have to worry about a North Korean invasion killing thousands of their soldiers. We do. As the world superpower and the guarantor of peace in certain unstable places in the world, with very nasty enemies, we need certain weapons that others don't. The land mine example is important because it demonstrates not just that we have the right to act unilaterally, to exempt ourselves from the fashionable opinion of the day, but why we are justified in doing so.

As the Korean example illuminates, we are uniquely situated in the world. We cannot afford the comfortable truisms, the empty platitudes, the lofty sentiments of a world not quite candid enough to admit that it lives under the umbrella of American power. It's because we have these unique responsibilities that we are uniquely at risk, that we must resist the kind of easy one-worldism that countries that live in our protection can afford.

We were isolated in the Land Mine Treaty and we are on much else. So what? We are right, and we have to do what is right. There are two unique features of the international system today that highlight this uniqueness. The first, as Professor Ikenberry spoke about, I have written about extensively since that article in *Foreign Affairs* in 1990. This is a unipolar moment. This is a radical departure from the history of the world of at least the last 500 years. We have new powers rising and falling. We have always had that. However, we have never had in the last 500 years, even perhaps the last 1,500 years, a power as uniquely situated in its dominance—economic, political, military, and cultural—as the United States. That makes us uniquely vulnerable in the sense that we become a target, as we saw on September 11. It also gives us a unique opportunity.

But there is one other element of the uniqueness and the international system that makes acting unilaterally, occasionally as we must, absolutely essential. And that is the advent of weapons of mass destruction. This is something utterly new in human history, and when we apply the categories of the previous world to this world, I think we are making a grave error. Weapons of mass destruction allow small powers, sometimes even nonstate actors, the kind of power that for hundreds of years, for all of modern history, only a great power with great armies with a large economy and centrally located had. Germany had all of that in World Wars I and II and it threatened the peace of the world. In the past, you had to have been in Germany to do that. Today you can be in Iraq; you can even be an Osama, were he to acquire the weapons.

The reason that the world has changed since September 11 is not that it structurally changed; it hasn't. This has been true for a while. But September 11 has illuminated for the world, particularly for Americans, these realities. It was like a lightening strike at night; it showed that the landscape had changed during the '90s and before, when no one was watching or thinking about it. And it showed us what the future is. The future of this century is that the weapons of mass destruction will become more and more available to more and more bad actors, hostile to the United States, unless we act before they get them. To do that, we may have to act alone. This unique situation bestows on us the imperative to be able to say that while multilateralism is wonderful—that we welcome it when possible—in circumstances where our supreme national interests and beyond, the supreme interests of the world, are at stake, we must keep these weapons away from the rogue states and the terrorists of the world. We cannot be tied by these old-world concepts, which, I have tried to argue, are based on a kind of claim of legitimacy that cannot be sustained.

So I would close by saying that at this unique moment our challenge is to rekindle the sense of urgency that we felt *last* September, when we were prepared to go to Afghanistan with no one else, if necessary. Remember what happened at the time. The NATO allies passed a resolution supporting our right to self-defense, and then they basically held our coats while we fought. It was nice that we had that resolution. It may have legitimized the Afghan war for a leftist or two. But the overwhelming majority of Americans don't need a NATO resolution or even a U.N. resolution for us to act in our defense, for us to act in the name of a right.

Professor Ikenberry spoke earlier and, at the beginning of his remarks he said that we have squandered the goodwill, affection, and sympathy people had for us after September 11. In that sense, he was echoing Al Gore, who said precisely the same thing a few days ago. Well, I don't really care, because the reason that we had that outpouring last September was because the world felt sorry for us. We were the victim. It's very easy to get support and applause and sympathy when you are the victim. We don't want to *be* the victim. Therefore, when we act not as a victim but as people who refuse to be victimized, the world then stands up and says, wait a minute, hold on, you have to listen to us. We have all kinds of restraints, and we want a piece of the action or at least we want to be the ones who dictate what kind of action is taken. I think that our role in the world is not as the victim. And if that sympathy was squandered, it was going to be dissipated ultimately anyway. We were not going to play the victim forever. If the cost of acting in our self-defense and our supreme national interest is to lose the sympathy of some abroad, it is not a high price to pay. The higher price to pay is losing our security and losing our sense of purpose. Thank you very much.

DR. LITWAK: Thank you. Next, Thérèse Delpech.

DR. THÉRÈSE DELPECH: Thank you very much. You may ask why a French citizen has been selected to speak in the name of Europe on this panel, and I'll offer three different answers. The first one is that when there are turbulences over the Atlantic, the good thing about being French is that one hardly notices it; it's business as usual. And so a French speaker may therefore not dramatize the situation and, indeed, I won't do that. A second answer could be that after a particularly difficult period in Paris-Washington relationships, due notably to a diplomatic statement from our chief diplomat, there is a warming-up under way. You may have seen 15 days ago, for instance, on the front page of the *International Harold Tribune*, that our leader and Colin Powell are obviously delighted with one another. The third reason I may present is that due to some unfortunate verbal excesses during the electoral campaign of another big European country, some of the former French judgment may appear in Washington less outrageous. You're free to choose your favorite answer.

Now, let me tell you that there are, in my view, a number of superficial ways of presenting current transatlantic deficiencies. And this is very much related to the subject of our session. The first way, which I find superficial, is to rehash the release of disputes. We all know this list: the Middle East. This is at the same time boring, because it's always the same thing and sterile.

The second way I find also rather superficial is, one, revisiting the old burden-sharing debate and the old capabilities gap. When President Bush took office, his budget was about $300 billion dollars; in 2002, it's $3,050; in 2003, $3,096; and it may be $470 billion in 2007, which means about fifteen times the British defense budget. Therefore, this is no longer a gap; this is a gulf. The reason why I find this debate serious, but not essential, is because we are at the time—and this is at the core of our session, it seems to me—when America can be devastated by operations costing less than one tank. I wonder whether this is the most relevant approach for that reason.

Dr. Delpech

The third approach I find also rather superficial is the one that says that there is, I suppose, peace-loving Europe, and a part of America, probably meaning that America is no longer a reluctant sheriff. And here, if we look at the subject of unilateralism and multilateralism, you will immediately understand how superficial this is. Because concerning Europe, Europe is not always multilateral, always in favor of multilateralism. Only recently we've heard about "the German way." On the American side, certainly, America, even today, is not always unilateral, and I would certainly demur from what Charles Krauthammer said. It seems to me that the move President Bush made with his remarkable speech at the U.N., because it was a remarkable speech, and it was judged as such, at least in Europe—I don't know about the reaction in this country, but it was in Europe—the fact that this speech had been made at the U.N.

One of the reasons why I was myself strongly in favor of doing that is not because of a kind of abstract attachment to multilateralism. It's because this will force all the members of the Security Council, and I'm including my own country, to take a position and to take responsibilities. So I find that quite relevant for the world order of the twenty-first century. Therefore, these are the approaches I'm not keeping in my remarks, but I wanted to put them on the table for the debate.

What I will try to do in explaining the current situation—and let me say that I personally do worry very much about the way America has no sympathy in particular in Europe over the last year. But it seems to me that there is much more than superficial judgment about what is happening. We are facing, first, three psychological factors, which are, in my view, quite important. And secondly, three strategic factors, and these contribute to explain the current situation. The three psychological factors follow:

First, America is discovering vulnerability at the time when Europe no longer wants to hear about it. You may find that strange unless you take into account the fact that Europe has known, since the seventeenth century, one major war by generation, and the twentieth century as such in Europe can be defined as the *tragedy of war*. Perhaps you may understand a bit more about that.

Secondly, America is insisting on sovereignty and freedom of action as never before, and at a time when Europe's daily life and, indeed, Europe's very existence are about abandoning sovereignty. It's about accepting voluntary interdependence and, again, it may be difficult for America to understand this process. But this is our life. And this is what we are trying to do, as well, with enlargement. And I'll speak about that afterwards. This is *the* great achievement we have before us in the coming decades: the unity of Europe again. And this is done as a multilateral task, because there is no other way to do it.

The third psychological factor is about time. And here it seems important to say that America is very much a present tense and future oriented, and I admire that. This is part of America's dynamism. But we have to recognize that on our side we are having exactly the opposite psyche. I mean, we are loaded with the past and the past is quite often unpleasant, to use an understatement. I give you my own experience. When I was at the prime minister's office, one of the most unpleasant parts of what I was doing was that we were discovering, still now, tons of chemical weapons from World War I. And this was something I didn't know before I entered this work. There are some more unpleasant discoveries still. We are still discovering mass graves around Europe. What I mean by that is that the past is present for us. It is something distinctly different from what you have on your side. Of course, we also had some impatient figures in European history. One of the best known was Napoleon. You know what he said before leaving for Moscow? He said, "Let's go forward, and then we'll see." You know the result of this story, I suppose. So, I personally would prefer more patience.

There are also three strategic factors we face on both sides of the Atlantic. First is the fact of the centrality of European security. The fact that in some sense Europe's security was the strategic issue has vanished. I believe that the

Balkans may have maintained the illusion for 10 years that Europe's security still mattered and, in particular, still mattered here in Washington. But it seems to me that the war in Afghanistan has definitely evaporated this illusion.

The second geostrategic factor is, of course, to answer the question, "What is at the center stage now, if not Europe?" Here, in my view, we have two realities. One is Asia security, and this is probably the reason why we have Dr. Funabashi with us here, and the second is something that has no center precisely, which is *global terrorism*. And I would say that on both counts, Europe and the relations with Europe are somehow problematic. I'll come back quickly to that.

The third geostrategic factor is the fact that the center of gravity is moving in the opposite direction. The center of gravity for America is moving west, because of Asia in particular, and the center of gravity in Europe is moving east, because of the enlargement. So we also have these facts we can do nothing about. It's a reality.

Now, I come back quickly to the reason why the two questions at the center stage, Asia and terrorism, are part of the problem. Concerning Asia, Europe is neither a problem nor a solution. Asia simply is not, and I regret it, on the European radar. I believe it's a mistake because there is a great potential for conventions in Asia, whether we speak about West Asia, where there are almost indefinite occasions for conventions, or South Asia, with India and Pakistan. Each year when the snow melts, we can hear a nuclear war. Southeast Asia and the very difficult situation of the sea lanes, and East Asia, which my neighbor will speak to much better than I would.

Terrorism is, no doubt, a common threat. Even if I agree that the U.S. may be uniquely at risk, which is perhaps, by the way, why it needs the rest of the world, Europe is also under terrorist threat. There is absolutely no problem about that. The networks are in Europe, and we have found in Afghanistan some explanations for that; the reason why they like to be in Europe. Secondly, a large number of attacks have already been foiled, including at least three in my own country. And thirdly, all the experts on terrorism in Europe say the worst is to come. The worst is before us, not behind. So, the threat is common. But the problem is—and here I would be a critic of my own part of the world—there has been no public debate on the subject. There is no serious investment. Yes, there has been military cooperation and, even more, non-military cooperation with the United States. The nonmilitary cooperation is much less because part of these networks were known in Europe because they have their roots, in particular, in Nigeria. But Europe is not at war, and this is a big difference.

I will conclude by saying the following: First, a general conclusion. It seems to me that we are facing, together, I mean all of us, two major problems in this century. One is the way technology and violence are meeting, the way the privatization of violence could be today the privatization of extreme violence. This is a common major problem. Secondly, all the major powers are self-obsessed for different reasons. America is obsessed by the protection of its homeland, something I can fully understand. The Europeans are self-obsessed with enlargement, which is *their* problem. Russia is self-obsessed with a long list of internal problems. And China is still not an international actor. China is interested in the rest of the world only if it is affected. It's not good for multi-lateralism, certainly not.

The second conclusion concerns America and Europe. Concerning America, it seems to me that it would be nice to keep what Jefferson called "a decent respect for the opinion of mankind." Secondly, it would also be good to recognize that power, particularly military power, is more relative than ever. I regret that this is a reality at the time of global terrorism. On the European side, we have to enlarge our vision while we enlarge our territory. And we have to make peace with the use of force, provided that rules for the use of force are defined. And here I completely agree with John.

I will now, as the third conclusion, say that instead of exploiting our differences to fuel anti-Europeanism in America and anti-Americanism in Europe, we should take advantage of these differences to jointly contribute to the challenges of this century. Who said, "The magnitude of our shared responsibilities makes our disagreement look so small"? I believe it was the President of the United States, in Germany, in May 2002. Thank you.

DR. LITWAK: Thank you, Dr. Funabashi.

DR. YOICHI FUNABASHI: Thank you very much. I'm very glad to be here. I would like to share some of my thoughts and reflections on 9/11 and its aftermath. Particularly, I'd like to say that many of America's allies—Japan, Germany, and the others—share this sense of a critical juncture, urgency, in fighting terrorism. At the same time, I think that the allies have increasingly come to be concerned about some aspects of the antiterror war and politics. Therese mentioned Germany's very cynical campaign, and I think I share her view. It has really undermined the alliance, and I think you have to pay a high price for that. It may take some time to mend fences, but at the same time, I think we have to ask the question: "Why have German people actually responded to that very blatant anti-American rhetoric and the opposition to the war on Iraq so much that it seems to have made a critical difference in the result of the election?" If, say, we would have that election in Japan, for instance, perhaps this issue also could be made, a sort of national referendum on its commitment to war on Iraq and its rationale, and yes or no to the war on Iraq. Perhaps in some European Union countries we might conceivably, perhaps, see a similar result. I think, in the case of Japan, more than 70 percent of the Japanese public is opposed to war on Iraq. It's not only peaceniks who have expressed that position to the war on Iraq. I think America's allies

are very much wary of another war at
this moment. Actually, it's a remarkable turnabout in little more than one
year, when America's allies expressed
their sincere solidarity and sympathy
with the victims of the attack.

Dr. Krauthammer said that he
doesn't care that much. But I think
the American people should care for
good reason. Because this has something to do with their moral fabric
value system, which we should
defend, we must defend, and which
the terrorists attacked. Therefore, this
is the common thread of America's
relationship with the world that is the
underpinning of that whole world
vision and order. So they should care.

It is perhaps more troubling to
say why and how this swelling sympathy and solidarity seem to have
evaporated, at least on the surface.

Mr. Funabashi

Perhaps there are many reasons for that. But as far as America's allies and
friends are concerned, I think that they have not been able to digest the Bush
doctrine, which has evolved in a surprising way during a single year. First, I
think the Bush doctrine has three tenets. The first one is, the mission determines the coalition doctrine—no "axis of evil"—and then, being followed by
this preemptive action and war doctrine. I think this has raised a serious question among America's friends, where this administration is really heading and
how the United States will pursue its long-term strategy. They are not convinced, and the explanation of the rationale of those doctrines has not been
sufficient to match this very quick pace of the policy formulation.

Take the example of "axis of evil." Certainly, Saddam Hussein has
remained a major threat, and we have to do something about it, but as for
North Korea, President Bush just has announced his decision to dispatch that
delegation to Asia. Therefore, it's obvious that this engagement policy still continues. In the most recent national security strategy document, there is not
even a mention of Iran in the whole document. Therefore, this axis of evil has
not been able to hold too long, clearly.

With regard to the initial terms of the coalition, this makes the allies very
much nervous. They perceive that America's new partners—Russia, India,
China—haven't elevated to the status of making dinner, while they have been
relegated to doing dishes, and some likened them to garbage collectors. I do

not think this is a fair characterization, and I also think that America's other allies don't object to America's better relationship with Russia, India, and China. John mentioned that the U.S. could even seize the opportunity of getting that relationship, with particularly China and Russia, in a much better way by taking advantage of this mutual common front to fight the terrorist war. And it's a welcome one. But again, I think we should have a more sobering view here that the national interests of great powers like China and Russia will not change so easily, and I do not think that America and China share the values, the international order vision, so easily. They cannot accommodate so easily on Taiwan, for instance, and human rights, and also maritime security, as Therese mentioned. So I do not think this axis of good, this partnership with Russia, India, China, will hold too long, either.

What about this preemptive action? This is perhaps the most important new doctrine in the Bush administration. It's very radical and fundamental, but at the same time, it could really ensue in chaos, and it could put the world into a medieval crusade era. Certainly, their allies agree that there is a serious threat we confront coming from this terrorist attack and terrorism. This is going to be the primary enemy in the coming years, not only to the United States but also to the world. It is an elusive enemy and, certainly, the allies would find nothing amiss with a reservation that terrorists do not seek to attack us using conventional means. The greater risk is the risk of inaction, and I think the Bush administration is not wrong in pointing this out. So this is the new threat, the new challenge we confront. But the introduction of this preemptive action could really dismantle, undercut, in one fell swoop, the whole international system and institutions—the United Nations, U.S.-centered alliance system—the U.S. fathered and in which the U.S. has put so much investment in the past half century. Is it worthwhile? I think we really should ask hard this question.

Another issue is the allies' uneasiness with too much doctrinization of policy, a generalization of ad-hoc policies. We are not living in the Truman era. The nature of the threat is very much different. And I think that the allies perhaps feel that we should attack the specific problems with specific policies, not allow one huge and encompassing doctrine to solve. And I think that doctrinization also could very much blur the real objectives, means, and costs, and that is where we still have yet to articulate those factors—those variables—sufficiently.

I want to caution that it is a mistake to try to invent a new doctrine, particularly a war doctrine, for a new threat. Perhaps our energies would be better spent trying to find another way to address these new problems. We could instead perhaps regard terrorism as a crime, applying the methods of law enforcement. It is certainly very hard to come to terms with this. But we must not expect ever to terminate terrorism once and for all. Like all crime, it will never be totally defeated. We have to learn how to contain it. And we may even be able to preempt it, as we do with a crime.

This morning I was hearing Professor Douglass North's comments on consciousness, and I found it very interesting, thought provoking. He suggested that this innate violence cannot be eradicated. All we should expect is to contain and to deal with this fanatical mass murder. And I think that perhaps may be a case that we should also ponder.

In the morning session, we also were hearing about the de-Baathification of Iraq as a day-after question, and we have heard a lot of talk applying the MacArthur formula to Iraq recently. Well, the United States occupation forces stayed in Japan for 6 years and 8 months, with more than 100,000 troops, including 450,000 stationed in 1946. They also counted on the Japanese emperor as a symbol of integrity and stability to bring [the country] back to the political center to achieve that democratic transition. I doubt there are comparable means available in Iraq. With regard to the occupational strategy of Japan, the State Department actually started to develop this plan within less than a year of the Pearl Harbor attack, and it took three years to complete it. They did really good homework, and they mobilized the best anthropologists to really explore the cultural pattern and heritage of Japanese society, so that they should occupy in the best way.

I want to mention, briefly, one more thing—a question of deterrence. It may be true that traditional concepts of deterrence would not work against a terrorist enemy whose tactics of wanton destruction include targeting of innocent people as the National Security Strategy Report says. However, does Saddam Hussein fit this characterization? He is clearly more passionate for homicide than suicide. He's a status-quo, risk-averse adversary, deterrable as he has been for the past decade.

Lastly, a few words on U.S. leadership. John eloquently mentioned that critical nature of U.S. leadership, and I'd just like to echo what he said. American leadership has, of course, helped immeasurably in securing peace and security for the entire world and America's allies in the past half century. But America's allies are worried that this might change as the U.S. pursues new doctrine. If America fails in Afghanistan, for instance, or in nation building, or in Saddam Hussein's post-Ottoman empire, and democratizing Iraq or the Middle East more widely, it could swing toward becoming an inward-looking and isolationist nation. The allies are worried whether the United States will remain a staying power. The United States will continue to be extremely critical for world peace, but this can only derive from legitimate and stable leadership. Above all, allies expect the U.S. to provide leadership, not naked power. But there now seems to be a danger of the U.S. role being destabilized. And if this center is destabilized, how can you expect the world to be stable? Thank you.

DR. LITWAK: Thank you very much, Dr. Funabashi. Before turning to the floor for comments and questions, I'd like to give our panelists an opportunity to respond to the others' presentations if they wish. If not, we can go to the floor. But if there was a point that was raised that you would like to preemptively respond to before we turn to the floor, you may do so. Therese?

DR. DELPECH: It's not about preemption, certainly not, but I want to ask one or two questions, and to make a comment. First, I would love to have from John, if he wishes, some development about what he said concerning the definition of new rules to use power, because it seems to me this is a very important question. Secondly, to Yuichi, I'd like his view on the following point. It seems to me that China is still a unilateral actor in a much more radical way than the United States. So, I'd like to have your view on the way this can evolve. And, to Dr. Krauthammer, I have one question and one comment. The question is the following. You said, and it seems to me rightly so, that unilateralism predates September 11. My question is: Does not September 11 bring back the need precisely of the rest of the world? Because it seems to me again that this is quite a serious question. The fact that unilateralism was here before is something which is not necessarily explaining the situation after September 11.

And my comment is related to Iraq only to say two things. First, I'm not in a fighting mood here because I'm just arriving. I stay here for one day, and I'm very happy to be in Washington. But I want to say that concerning France and Russia, I'm really upset by the way that we are always put together on this subject, because the situation is quite different now for some years. Let me give you only *one* example. When Colin Powell came back from the Middle East with this idea of smart sanctions—which had the liberation part, all the economic parts with no military potential, but also parts to control the legal trafficking in the Middle East—he got immediate support from Robin Cook. They were coming back. He had a meeting in London, immediate support. This was never reflected in the American press.

Now, currently, let me tell you first for Russia, the problem number one is not contrast. The problem number one is Georgia, in my view. Concerning France, the problem with Iraq—and you have to take into account the interview my president gave some time ago in the *New York Times*, which was much more open than you could have expected some time ago. But the position of France has not much to do with commercial interests right now in Iraq. The main problem, from what I've heard—and I hear a lot on the subject because I'm the U.N. commissioner—is concern about the release; it's concern about a number of things which could go bad. These are legitimate concerns—the way WMD could be used—because now Saddam would have this idea of regime change and then the possibility of urban warfare. This is what I heard. I haven't heard about contrasts.

To close the subject, it seems to me that one of the reasons why the U.N. is so important concerning Iraq—and here I want your reaction as well—it's because we are in the unique situation where the legitimacy of what we are going to do is related to a cease-fire conditional to the implementation of a number of resolutions that have been violated by Iraq. So, the U.N. Security Council is at the very center of the stage. And, again, not to ask the Security Council to implement its own policy, in my view, would have been a mistake. Thank you.

DR. KRAUTHAMMER: In the spirit of not ceding the chairmanship of the meeting to the delegate from France, I'll not take debate on the questions. I'll only make one remark regarding France's role on Iraq. I find it somewhat odd to make the case for Iraq's ardency on this issue, its immediate support of a policy proposed that would have weakened sanctions on Iraq. Let me respond to what Dr. Funabashi said just earlier, which I think is the heart of the unilateral case. He made two points I wanted to respond to as quickly as I can.

First, he suggested that we should respond to terrorism as crime, rather than war. I find that absolutely astonishing. What we realized on September 11 is that our previous treatment of terrorism precisely as a matter of crime, rather than a war, is what brought us to September 11. The policy of the Clinton administration and the other administrations before was to go after terrorists as individuals, put them on trial, lock them up, and it was utterly ineffectual, because it's entire conception was wrong. This is a war on America. Arresting individuals is an absurd way to go about it. We displayed in Afghanistan precisely why that is. Had we arrested a few culprits, it would have made no difference. What we showed the world in what was essentially a demonstrating war was the price of harboring a terrorist in your territory. And that lesson was learned around the world. That's how you respond to terrorism, and that, in part, explains why what everybody expected after September 11—the second shoe to drop—did not happen, because the enemy was attacked, dispersed, and scattered, and the lesson of the price of harboring a terrorist as a sovereign state was learned by the destruction of the Taliban.

On one other issue, the issue of multilateralism—which is at the center of our discussion—I think the key is to understand that the structures of multilateralism, of which all of my fellow panelists are rather nostalgic, were developed, many of them, *ex nihilo*, after the Second World War, to face two new realities: a bipolar world which had not existed before and the advent of nuclear weapons. Moreover, it worked by creating a new structure—a remarkable idea—the balance of terror, which maintained the peace. Unless we have the courage to re-create our structures, rather than nostalgically looking at structures that are no longer relevant—the world is not bipolar and the threats are almost ubiquitous—that's number one.

Secondly, what we have are not stable relations with an adversary like Russia, but unstable relations with state actors, substate actors, and rogue states. Unless we face the new structure in the world and the new threat of disseminated nuclear, biological, and chemical weapons by relying on old structures, we will endanger our security and the security of the world. Unless we are willing to create new realities like the doctrine of preemption, which is entirely suited and required in a world in which you cannot see an enemy mobilizing by moving his trains, mobilizing his army, and preparing himself—who can strike by stealth, like on September 11—unless we do that, we are endangering not just our security but the security of the world.

DR. IKENBERRY: Multilateralism as an American grand strategy is not simply an artifact of war. It pre-dated the war by using its momentary advantage to create a structure that would return dividends over many decades. It was a positive vision reinforced by the Cold War, but it pre-dated and postdated the Cold War. We have seen a lot of it in the 1990s because we realize it's a good investment of our resources; it creates an environment that we want to live in. And I think that the problem with the so-called new unilateralism is that it doesn't have a vision of what the international order should be like, other than a kind of coercive American bully getting its way, and in the process, in my view, creating a more divided and conflict-ridden world where the United States can't secure its interests as successfully as it can in a world where it's created a structure.

The new unilateralism is intellectually and historically bankrupt. The oddest statement I think I've heard so far today is the view that a great power trying to secure its interests and build a framework for its power through the search for a kind of a legitimate settlement among other powers is somehow a sign of lack of confidence. I've never heard that argument made in public before and, as I'm off to Europe tonight, I'll scratch my head over the Atlantic thinking about that. I think it's absolutely the opposite that, in fact, it's an insecurity about your power that leads you to not realize that there are opportunities to concert it, to combine it, to leverage it through cooperation. I think that's why Bush went to the United Nations and that's why I think he wonderfully transformed the debate about Iraq by doing so. There was a palpable difference after that little talk by that one individual in front of that one podium at that one building. It changed things overnight because it sent a message that this is not the U.S. against a particular threat, it's the world community. And that is remarkable.

Legitimacy is not something that academics puzzle about. It's something that is real. It's an aspect of power. It's also a fundamental misreading of American history to argue that it's not something that the United States has cared about or used with great success. One of the great differences between the United States and the Soviet Union after World War II was that the Soviet Union, in effect, was a unilateralist. It pursued its own narrow interests of gaining territory and possessional strategy in Eastern Europe. The United

States pursued what you might call a milieu strategy, where it combined its power with its colleagues and the other democratic countries, helping to create democracy and to build institutions. And that institutional project, that infrastructure, if you will, was designed not simply to wage the Cold War, but to create a structure economically, politically, in security that would bring old adversaries together and create a framework where American power was seen as something that other countries wanted to work with rather than against.

The greatest danger for America is not to seize this moment of unipolarity to create that framework, which entails doing something new, not simply resting on something old. It means that the form of cooperation and leadership is like, in the past, enlightened and built on a strategy of creating structures that last and including structures about the use of force, determining threats. What won't work is a world order that a new unilateralist might envisage where God speaks to the American president about what is evil and what isn't and the American government goes out and attacks evil and says, "You are either with us or against us," and the rest of the world is faced with some kind of decision. The more successful strategy for the U.S. is if the United States uses a leadership of a different sort, working with the other great powers, which it uniquely can today because the other great powers are uniquely eager to cooperate multilaterally with the United States to create rules of the game— rules of the game that don't require the United States to cede any right to protect its own interests, including in the final instance, the unilateral use of force. But multilateralism is not something sacred. It's something that, when used strategically, is the epitome of what it means to be clever.

DR. KRAUTHAMMER: I think this is the crux of the argument, and I think this is where the debate between unilateralism and multilateralism hinges. I'm happy to have international legitimacy and everybody on the board and the U.N. applauding and clapping as you are. That's lovely. The question is, "What do you do when you go to the U.N. and they say no?" The Germans have said no. What if the French and Russians say no? That is the issue. I say we act anyway. And unless you are a fair-weather multilateralist, if you believe what you're saying about the importance of this great structure, you have to say no. And is that what you say? That's my question.

DR. LITWAK: I want to give Dr. Funabashi an opportunity to jump in if he wishes to comment on the exchange here.

DR. FUNABASHI: Thank you. Two points. I think that fits in better with crime. On the political level, it has been all war and, understandably, I think we are committed to be part of this antiterror war as allies. But how can you end this war? Even the first chapter? How can you close? We all know that this will be never-ending war, a long, long process, a lasting war. But politically, you have to at least close the first chapter. And I think that rebuilding Afghanistan, after terminating al Qaeda and the others, should be the first chapter. And we should not just seek one war after another; I think we have to finish the war. And then perhaps we should explore morphing antiterror war into enforcement, so that the composition of the crime, law enforcement, should increase. That is perhaps a much better balanced way of attacking terrorism.

Quickly, with regard to Therese's inquiry about China, about the policy streak, I would rather frame it a different way. I think China has entered into a more multilateralist process and framework. And they entered, particularly, into the WTO, and they had no choice but to play a multilateral role in the economic and investment trade field. But at the same time, I think China would also perhaps explore its tribute system figuring the East Asia region. The China Free-Trade Agreement could perhaps evolve into that. People are already very much fearful of China's retaliation and closing their market to them, so I think they would perhaps play both games.

On the question of the policy of the United Nations, they certainly have played a nuisance-value role. They tried to put their veto cards on the highest bid price, and they have rarely taken a new initiative as a builder, a constructor of that world. So I do not think that China will change very much fundamentally here. China has not participated in peacekeeping operations since the conversion peace settlement. Somehow they have not participated since 1993. But I think we should perhaps give the benefit of doubt to China, because China is more interested in building multilateralism, but particularly in the antiterror campaign. They have been very enthusiastic, and I think the United States also should participate as a legitimate and most important player and a stabilizer in Central Asia. China has been conspicuously absent from that cabal, the Korean Energy Development Organization. They have wanted to play an independent role here by forging a special relationship with North Korea. I think that after the talks, perhaps it would be conducive to China to be more interested in participating in a multilateral framework. Thank you.

DR. LITWAK: Thank you very much. Let's turn now to the audience and the participants in the conference and invite comments and questions. There are microphones available. If the questioners would please stand, identify themselves, and provide their affiliation.

AUDIENCE MEMBER: Thank you. I'm from the Embassy of France. I apologize to John Ikenberry because what I will say might hurt his standing in Washington, but I fully agree with what you've said regarding the issue of preemption and unilateralism. It's difficult for people close to the American allies to understand how a doctrine that in theory stems from the feeling of vulnerability and isolation and the need to respond to it, as Dr. Krauthammer indicated, seems to many of us to have such strong potential to make the U.S. both less secure and more alone.

I had a question for Dr. Krauthammer. Regarding the issue of the role of the United Nations in the authorization of force. We can disagree about the legitimacy, but it seems very difficult to disagree about the legality, not only from the point of view of international law, but even as far as U.S. law is concerned. The day that the U.S. Senate ratified the treaty and the United States became a state party of the United Nations, the United Nations Charter became, in effect, the law of the land, including the provisions on the use of force and the very specific circumstances in which they can be authorized. It seems to me that radicalism without the willingness to take the logic to its end is nothing but posture. And my question is, therefore, would you be ready or do you feel it would be necessary for the United States Senate to repudiate the San Francisco Treaty and the U.N. Charter? Thank you.

DR. KRAUTHAMMER: If I could respond, I take it you were unaware of the fact that the war on Serbia was conducted without U.N. Security Council approval. I guess in that case, since it was a European interest, that might have put it in a slightly different perspective and, therefore, you didn't raise it in your question. So, it seems to me, speaking about parochialism, the hypocrisy, let's look at both sides of the coin. I think this entire notion of determining how to act in the national interest of the United States, particularly in our case today, of the supreme security interest of the United States in terms of treaty language, is absurd. That would require an hour of discussion, but I think it is the least important of the elements of any discussion. I think if you have enough smart lawyers at the State Department, that they ought to be able to find a loophole if you are searching for one, and that's why we hire them.

If we had not had U.N. approval for the war in Afghanistan would we not have acted? It's a question that answers itself. The idea of putting this war response to those who've attacked us in terms of legalism or, as we have just heard, looking at it as a form of law enforcement, is similarly absurd. When the USS *Cole* was attacked, how did the U.S. respond? Dispatched a few FBI agents to Yemen to get the culprits. We all know what happened. It was a farce and a sham. They got no cooperation; nothing happened. Osama, himself, has said, derisively, looking at the response of the United States in the '90s to the attack on the first World Trade Center attack, the attack on the *Cole*, the attack on our embassies in Africa, how risible and absurd those reactions were, all within the context of law enforcement, and how it emboldened him, imagining that America was weak and spineless and would hide behind legalism in trying to minimize its response. So, I would say that if, when you are attacked, you don't look to international law or to the FBI. It's not how you respond.

DR. LITWAK: Thank you, Charles. John?

DR. IKENBERRY: I think the more important issue is how we move after Iraq into a world where there is some agreement on the rules for the use of force, for addressing these new threats, which are dangerous and play havoc with traditional Article 51 United Nations Understandings of Self-Defense. Things have to be done because of the presence of weapons of mass destruction or technologies of violence that are available and can be put into the hands of smaller and smaller groups with agendas and motivations that are not—either because they are willing to die for their cause or do not have a home address—deterrable.

So there is a class of threat that is very dangerous. I would also stipulate that the United States, at the moment, is probably correct in determining that it is more likely the target of that kind of violence than other major states. But it is not a class of threats that necessarily, in principle, pits the major states against each other. This is really an area where we can extend rules and thereby concert power, as well as legitimate it, in ways that leverage a power to address this issue. Because there is just no way that the United States is going to be on the other side of this threat without the cooperative behavior of the other major states and a lot of other states as well. It's just a question of practical reality. How do we marshal our resources? For me, it's really not simply putting your fist in the air and saying, when push comes to shove we will use force against threats that we face. That may be true, but words matter, process matters. Not that those should in any fundamental sense, if you are legitimately threatened, constrain your options, but that it makes good practical sense. So I think that is the issue and that's where we will be as an international community, on the other side of Iraq.

DR. LITWAK: You had a two-finger comment on this question.

DR. DELPECH: Yes, it seems to me extraordinary to say at the same time that the strike is ubiquitous and the U.S. is at risk, and not to conclude that only cooperation will work and that the world will be punished collectively or not at all. And here I have to say I'm not speaking as a delegate of France, but as a sensible mind.

I want to come back to the question of the U.N. approval concerning Afghanistan because there is something so important I cannot let it slide. The point is not that you would not have acted if the U.N. would not have approved, because of course I would have found it absolutely legitimate that the U.S. would have acted even without any kind of U.N. approval there, because it seems that self-defense was clear. The point is what did the U.N. approval bring with it? It brought, in my view, two things, which are absolutely essential. And in the first one, it brought the recognition that for the first time in history a terrorist act was not justifying only police, law enforcement, intelligence, but military operation. And this was not recognized only by the victim, the United States, but the entire world. So this was an historic moment for that very reason. Secondly, and this is important as well, it gave the United States international support which is embodied in the resolution, I believe 1373, obliging all the countries of the world to fight terrorism. Is that irrelevant? It seems to me it's very relevant, so I wanted to make those two points.

DR. LITWAK: We are down to a few minutes left. Is there is a question that maybe stands as a comment because we have to adjourn on time?

AUDIENCE MEMBER: Let me back up from this discussion and link it to a couple of incidents. I appreciate the honesty of our foreign guests in terms of what they said about the views of others. But it causes me to make the following observations. This is not a discussion of U.S. unilateralism. It's a discussion of European unilateralism and Japanese unilateralism as well. Dr. Delpech was correct in saying that Europe doesn't want another war. Europe is busy with its own affairs, moving eastward, quite appropriately one might argue. Japan is concerned about the consequences of the way we are pursuing the war and about other issues, because Japan's security situation right now is very good. It's a very self-serving view, and I don't mean that in a positive sense. It seems to me, to go over to Dr. Ikenberry, the problem with the institutional argument is there has to be a common view about the problem or parallel interests or parallel tracks, in a strategic sense. I don't see it. We can say that the U.S. has its own unilateral view but, quite clearly, so does Europe; quite clearly, so does Japan. The real security issue is not how we handle Iraq or how we handle the war on terrorism. It is, as we go in different directions in terms of our basic definition of security interests, how do we collectively keep those institutions from just blowing apart or creating new ones?

DR. LITWAK: We are down to two minutes. Dr. Funabashi and Therese Delpech, any final brief words?

DR. FUNABASHI: I think that the question is what kind of world we really would like to envision. I think that is perhaps the ultimate question that we confront now. And I think that the U.S. will particularly be the most critical. And as I said, it seems to be that role being very much shaken, if not destabilized. And it would be extremely difficult for the world to envision the post–9/11 new vision, based on this destabilizing at the center of the order.

DR. DELPECH: In my conclusion, you've noticed that I said one of the major problems we have in the world is the self-obsession of all the major powers. I'll conclude with what John Ikenberry said in his own conclusion, when he was quoting: "We have to look first at our own mistakes, because this is where the danger lies." And the first thing to do is to go out of this self-obsession, not only in the United States, I totally agree, also in Europe.

DR. LITWAK: Charles, I'll give you the last word. Other than my own last word.

DR. KRAUTHAMMER: Well, there are obsessions and there are obsessions. Europe is obsessed with integration. It's a fine and noble goal. What is now obsessing the United States is the prospect of nuclear weapons exploding in New York, in Washington, in San Francisco, in London, in Paris—all around the world. That, I would argue, is an obsession of a different order. It's not an obsession, it's an emergency. And to make the parallel between European unilateralism and American is simply incorrect. The point I want to leave you with is this. We can have all our arguments about multilateral and unilateral American action. As I indicated before, there is nothing intrinsic in the position that is hostile to any of these institutions or arrangements. But the question of the day is this: If you go to these institutions as we have to the U.N.—and I pose that question to all the multilateralists—and we need to act in the supreme security interest of our country, not an obvious act of self-defense as Afghanistan was, but a more subtle one as in Iraq, do we rely on our judgment or the judgment of the world? Of course, we would love to have everybody's support. The question is: If the French and Russians and Chinese and Germans and others say no, is that decisive? My answer to that is absolutely not. Thank you very much.

DR. LITWAK: Thank you very much, thank you to the panel. I think that this discussion has brought out the cleavages in the debate and has tried to move that debate beyond caricature. So thank you for your attendance, and this session is adjourned.

KEYNOTE ADDRESS

HOMELAND SECURITY—THE CHALLENGE OF SECURING AMERICA'S TRANSPORTATION

The Honorable Norman Y. Mineta, Secretary of Transportation

Introduction by: The Honorable Lee H. Hamilton, Director, Woodrow Wilson International Center for Scholars

Summary

• Today we confront a more dangerous world than any of us could have imagined a year ago.

1. The Department of Transportation has worked to ensure that terrorists can never again use our transportation technologies as a weapon against us.

2. All of us understand that in this war on terrorism, the home front is the primary front. Ultimately, our ability to respond to these dynamic challenges rests upon the very virtues that we seek to defend: liberty, democracy, and free and open markets.

3. The strongest, most vibrant economy in the world depends on the safest, most efficient transportation system in the world. We have a solemn obligation to ensure that we retain those distinctions.

4. Our transportation systems are more secure today than at any time in our history, and tomorrow they will be more secure still.

• President Bush's *National Security Strategy* is based upon a doctrine of preempting the new threats to our national security, rather than relying exclusively on the Cold War era doctrines of containment and deterrence.

1. The fight against terrorists will not conclude in a matter of months or even a few years. We must not expect the quick and decisive victory of the 1991 Gulf War nor a high-tech, air-only campaign like Kosovo. Rather, the war on terrorism is a global enterprise of uncertain duration.

2. Where we cannot pre-empt threats to our nation, we must detect and prevent terrorist attacks within the United States, reduce America's vulnerability to terrorism, and minimize the damage and recover from any attacks that do occur.

• President Bush previously announced a major restructuring of the federal government leading to the creation of a new Department of Homeland Security. The President's plan recognizes that we are fighting a new kind of enemy, one that plots to turn our twenty-first century technology, transportation, and economy against us.

1. Currently, homeland security responsibilities are scattered across more than 100 different federal agencies, resulting in a lack of accountability and responsiveness. The President's plan envisions an efficient, coordinated, and agile federal defense against terrorism.

2. We have an opportunity to create an agency that takes full advantage of twenty-first century technology and management techniques, ready to fight tomorrow's battles and not yesterday's.

3. Under the President's plan, more than half of the new agency's personnel and budget would come from two organizations that are currently part of the Department of Transportation: the United States Coast Guard and the Transportation Security Administration.

• In the aftermath of the horrific and devastating attacks of September 2001, President Bush asked the Department of Transportation (DOT) to design an aviation security system that will allow travelers to arrive safely at their destinations, free from the threat of terrorism, but also free from unnecessary burdens or intrusions, and we have done our best to respond.

1. The DOT is focused on developing a new system of systems that combines world-class security with world-class customer service.

2. The Transportation Security Administration has already placed federal screeners at more than 122 of America's 429 airports, including many of our busiest.

• DOT is also developing heightened security procedures and awareness across every mode of transportation, including rail, highways, transit, maritime, and pipelines.

• Another key piece of our ongoing transportation security effort entails securing our nation's ports and maritime transportation system.

1. The numbers give you an idea of the complexity of the challenge: in addition to roughly 360 seaports, our maritime border consists of nearly 95,000 miles of open shoreline, 25,000 miles of navigable waterways and more than 3.4 million square miles of exclusive economic zoning.

2. DOT is implementing a layered defense of the maritime domain with a full range of concentric maritime security measures and is working to effectively push our borders out as far as possible so that we can intercept potential threats long before they arrive on our docks.

3. DOT will maintain an increased level of maritime security operations directed against terrorism.

4. DOT must create a more comprehensive awareness of threats and activities in the maritime domain.

5. DOT must expand and transform the core competence of the United States Coast Guard and modernize its most vital assets, especially our deep-water force. We will continue to deploy maritime safety and security teams and to expand our sea marshal program.

6. DOT must strengthen the physical security of our seaports and reduce their vulnerability.

Analysis

In his remarks, Secretary Mineta appropriately highlighted the essential role of the United States' transportation assets and infrastructure and the continued challenge of protecting those resources. Secretary Mineta built upon Mr. Grasso's earlier remarks by emphasizing that transportation is an indispensable underpinning to both our economy and to our national security. The challenge to secure these assets is compounded by the shear magnitude of the nation's transportation assets and tests both policy and organizational solutions.

Secretary Mineta highlighted the key role DOT has had in implementing the new *National Security Strategy*. Through both its aggressive aviation security system and through the creation of the TSA, the DOT has worked to both reduce vulnerabilities and detect and prevent attacks against all modes of transportation. The department continues to work to minimize the damage caused by any attack and to be ready to recover after an attack.

As Secretary Mineta states, President Bush's proposal to create a Department of Homeland Security includes transferring the Coast Guard and the TSA away from the Department of Transportation. This move would separate responsibilities for the economic aspects of our transportation infrastructure and the responsibilities for transportation security between the two departments. Secretary Mineta views this move as an essential step to protecting our homeland and providing defense against global terrorism. The largest challenge, in his view, remains maritime security because of the amount of coastline in the United States and the enormous amount of goods that are transferred through our ports. He believes the new department will be better postured to deter, prevent, and respond to these attacks.

While Secretary Mineta fully supported the administration's positions and the new National Security Strategy, he was quite candid in his assessment of the challenge posed by securing our transportation infrastructure. And, while the DOT has been the most criticized federal organization since last year's terrorist attacks, he clearly emphasized many of the department's successes and the initiatives that have been taken to prevent future attacks and to better secure the nation's resources. His remarks provided an adept turning point in the conference from the previous discussions about the security environment and security strategies to a substantive discussion about the organizations and capabilities needed to execute those strategies in the security environment of today and tomorrow.

Transcript

DR. LOREN B. THOMPSON: Hello again. Hey, I feel like I just lost on *American Idol*. Our keynote address this evening will be delivered by Secretary of Transportation Norman Mineta, whose exceedingly complex job became even more demanding and important in the wake of 9/11. We've found a person of suitable stature to introduce Secretary Mineta—a person whose legislative and academic life exemplifies the spirit of the Eisenhower Series. He's the Honorable Lee H. Hamilton, Director of the Woodrow Wilson International Center for Scholars. That position is uniquely well suited to Lee Hamilton because, for more than 30 years, he was a vital and highly visible voice of moderation in Congress, working tirelessly to forge a bipartisan foreign policy.

Congressman Hamilton represented Indiana's Ninth District from the early days of America's involvement in Vietnam until the last year of the American century, and during that time he came to be regarded as one of the most influential shapers of foreign policy in the lower chamber. Among other things, he was the Chairman of the Committee on International Relations, Chairman of the Joint Economic Committee, Chairman of the Permanent Select Committee on Intelligence, and Chairman of the Iran Contra Committee. By the 1990s, Congressman Hamilton had become such a key member of the House leadership that candidate Bill Clinton seriously considered him for the vice president's job in 1991. One reason was his considerable stature in foreign affairs.

Congressman Hamilton was one of the first legislators to grasp how the proliferation of weapons of mass destruction was transforming the landscape of global security. He saw the need to open China to global trade and the need to take an even hand in our policies toward the Middle East. But most importantly, Lee Hamilton saw that partisanship had to end at the shoreline, and that America's effectiveness in global affairs depended on a foreign policy that transcended party lines. For all those reasons, and for all of his contributions, we are pleased that Lee Hamilton is with us tonight to introduce our keynote speaker, Lee Hamilton.

CONGRESSMAN LEE H. HAMILTON: Good evening. It is my pleasure to introduce this evening's keynote speaker, the Secretary of Transportation and a very good friend of mine, Norman Mineta. The Wilson Center is honored to co-sponsor the Eisenhower National Security Conference, along with the Drucker Foundation, the Lexington Institute, the Office of the Secretary of

Defense for Net Assessment, the Conference Board, and, of course, the United States Army.

I want to acknowledge the Chief of Staff of the United States Army, Eric Shinseki, whose leadership and vision have enabled the Eisenhower National Security Series to become a valuable dialogue for the national security community. It has been a high personal pleasure for me to work with him and his staff. I welcome, of course, all of you this evening and am especially pleased to welcome Secretary Mineta.

By any measure, Norman Mineta is one of the nation's outstanding public servants of my generation. One of these days, I'm going to establish a hall of fame for public servants, and Norm Mineta will go into it on the first ballot. Only a few Cabinet officials in the history of this country have served Democratic *and* Republican presidents. Norm has, and he has done so with distinction. He told me a moment ago that the last time that was done was in 1871. So he really is genuinely an historic figure.

His career includes ten terms in the United States House of Representatives from California, a year as Secretary of Commerce under President Clinton, and now nearly two years as head of the Department of Transportation under President George W. Bush. He also served his country in the United States Army and has had a notable record of success in the private sector. He served in the Congress from 1975 to 1995, and he represented California's Silicon Valley. As a congressman, he worked diligently on behalf of his district and state and became a leader on many issues, particularly in transportation and infrastructure. He was Chairman of the House Public Works and Transportation Committee, also Chairman of the Aviation Subcommittee and its Surface Transportation Subcommittee. After leaving Congress, he continued his involvement with national transportation issues, chairing the National Civil Aviation Review Commission in 1997.

Secretary Mineta heads a department with 100,000 employees, a $58 billion budget, a transportation system that includes 3.9 million miles of public roads, 120,000 miles of railroads, and 5,000 public-use airports. He does so at a time when our nation's infrastructure faces unprecedented threats of terrorism. Ports, pipelines, waterways, highways, and airports are all possible targets. Secretary Mineta has worked to secure our nation without losing sight of the key role that our transportation system plays in generating and enabling economic growth.

Norm is a man of the highest integrity, with a keen intelligence and a deep commitment to his country. He is a consensus builder, a man who enjoys working with people of all persuasions, and a man who is genuinely liked by his constituents and his peers.

His extraordinary life story is an American saga. He and his family were among the 120,000 Americans of Japanese ancestry who were forced into internment camps during World War II. Instead of turning his back on his

Congressman Hamilton

country, he served it with a profound sense of purpose and gratitude. In 1988, as a member of Congress, his work led to the passage of the Civil Liberties Act of 1988, which officially apologized for the injustices endured by Japanese-Americans during World War II. Suffering injustice as a young boy, he lived to prompt his government to account for the actions that caused him, his family, and thousands of others pain, humiliation, and hardship.

I've asked myself how I would have reacted if my country had placed me in an internment camp at an early age because of my ethnicity. I cannot, of course, answer this question or any of the other what-ifs of my life, but having talked to Norm about his experience several times on the floor of the House, I'm reasonably sure that I would not have emerged from that experience with the same positive and constructive attitude that marks his life and his leadership.

I am very pleased that Secretary Mineta is our Secretary of Transportation at this important time in the country's history. I am pleased that he speaks to us tonight about homeland security—the challenge of securing America's transportation. Mr. Secretary, thank you for joining us. We look forward to your remarks.

SECRETARY NORMAN Y. MINETA: Lee, thank you very, very much for that warm and kind and generous introduction. When you hear something like that, you wonder where are your kids when you want them to hear something good about you?

As all of you know, I had the great privilege of serving with Lee in the United States House of Representatives for more than two decades, and I can attest that in challenging times such as these, America is truly fortunate to have patriots such as Lee Hamilton in the forefront of these policy discussions. I cherish the counsel and advice that I have gotten over the years from Lee. And my wife, Denny, and I also cherish the friendship that has been extended to us by Nancy, his wife, and Lee, and we thank you very, very much.

Today we confront a more dangerous world than any of us could have imagined just a short year ago, and this conference provides an important forum to discuss and develop the strategic responses appropriate to this new threat environment. Last week, President Bush enunciated a new national strategy—one based upon a doctrine of preempting the new threats to our national security rather than relying exclusively on the Cold War era doctrines of containment and deterrence.

The fight against terrorists will not conclude in a matter of months or even a few years. We ought not to expect the quick and decisive victory of the 1991 Gulf War or a high-tech, air-only campaign like Kosovo. Rather, as the national security strategy spells out, the war on terrorism is a global enterprise of uncertain duration. And where we cannot preempt threats to our nation, we must detect and prevent terrorist attacks within

Secretary Mineta

the United States, reduce America's vulnerability to terrorism, and minimize the damage and recover from any attacks that do occur.

Now, earlier this summer the president announced a major restructuring of the federal government leading to the creation of a new Department of Homeland Security. The president's plan recognizes that we are fighting a new kind of enemy—one that plots to turn our twenty-first century technology, transportation, and economy against us. Currently, as all of you are very well aware, homeland security responsibilities are scattered across more than 100 different federal agencies, resulting in a lack of accountability and responsiveness. And the president's plan envisions an efficient, coordinated, and agile federal defense against terrorism. And so I urge the Congress, and in particular, the United States Senate, to match the president's bold vision with equally bold execution. We have an opportunity to create an agency that takes full advantage of twenty-first century technology and twenty-first century management techniques, ready to fight tomorrow's battles and not yesterday's.

Under the president's plan, more than half of the new agency's personnel and budget would come from two organizations that are currently part of the Department of Transportation—namely, the United States Coast Guard and the Transportation Security Administration. Now, while I am very, very proud to serve as the Secretary of the United States Coast Guard and to serve as the Secretary of Transportation over the Transportation Security Administration, I am also fully committed to working with the Congress to make this new agency a reality.

Tonight, I want to address some of the challenges of securing America's transportation system. We have learned a lot since September 11th, and so, I suspect, has Osama bin Laden. He knows now that he cannot attack America with impunity. He now knows that he cannot hijack our spirit or our resolve. And if he doesn't know it by now, I would tell him this: Our transportation systems are more secure today than at any time in our history, and tomorrow they will be even more secure still.

In the aftermath of the horrific, devastating attacks of last September, President Bush asked the Department of Transportation to design an aviation security system that will allow travelers to arrive safely at their destinations, free from the threat of terrorism, but also free from unnecessary burdens or intrusions. And we have done our best to respond. We are well on our way to a new system of systems that combines world-class security with world-class customer service.

The Transportation Security Administration—otherwise known as TSA— has already placed federal screeners at more than 122 of America's 429 commercial airports, including many of our busiest. Today, on this single day, more than a million and a quarter passengers will pass through airports with federalized checkpoints, and that represents about 63 percent of total daily emplanements. Now, contrary to some published reports, we have hired nearly all of the federal passenger screeners that we will need in order to meet our November 19 deadline for replacing the current contract private screeners. And by the end of the year, we plan to have a full complement of new, highly trained federal security personnel on duty at all of our airports.

As you are aware, the Aviation and Transportation Security Act, signed into law by President Bush on November 19, 2001, sets more than two dozen deadlines for the TSA. And thus far, the TSA has met every one of them, and we will continue to meet all of the remaining deadlines that are in the legislation. I am pleased to say that our success at strengthening aviation security has not gone unnoticed. The editor of *Aviation Security International* magazine—someone who visits airports around the globe—applauds the job that we are doing. He says that on a recent trip, "Every x-ray operator seemed on the job. Training was in progress, and the quality of the searches carried out were some of the best I have ever seen anywhere in the world." Heightened security has not created an impediment to travel. In fact, data from the Bureau of Transportation Statistics show that only one of every eight passengers had to wait more than 30 minutes in order to complete passenger screening, and fewer than one in ten expressed dissatisfaction with their experience at the security checkpoint. And most importantly, a recent American Automobile Association poll found that a full three-fourths of all travelers surveyed think flying is safe—up from just a third of those surveyed two months after the September 11 attack.

Although much of the media attention has focused on our aviation efforts, we are also developing heightened security procedures and awareness across every mode of transportation, including rail, highways, transit, maritime, and pipelines. Of course, transportation and national defense have long-established links. In 1919, a young Army colonel traversed the country from Washington, D.C., to San Francisco, California, as part of a program to encourage the national government to invest in a new highway system. Traveling on muddy roads and rickety bridges, his trip required two months. And based on his experience, that soldier advocated—nearly two decades later—for the transcontinental highway system that would come to bear his name: the Dwight D. Eisenhower System of Interstate and Defense Highways.

The president's national homeland security strategy also recognizes this linkage when it says, "Virtually every community in America is connected to the global transportation network by the seaports, airports, highways, pipelines, railroads, and waterways that move people and goods into, within, and out of the nation. We must therefore promote the efficient and reliable flow of people, goods, and services across borders, while preventing terrorists from using transportation conveyances or systems to deliver implements of destruction."

As I indicated in my remarks to the Fletcher Conference last March, another key piece of our ongoing transportation security effort entails securing our nation's ports and maritime transportation system. The numbers give you an idea of the complexity of the challenge, and that is, in addition to roughly 360 seaports, our maritime border consists of nearly 95,000 miles of open shoreline, 25,000 miles of navigable waterways, and more than 3.4 million square miles of exclusive economic zoning.

Our strategy has matured somewhat over the months since we first announced it, with several key components. First, we are implementing a layered defense of the maritime domain—just as we have with aviation security—with a full range of concentric maritime security measures. And we want to effectively push our borders out as far as possible so that we can intercept potential threats long before they arrive on our docks.

Secondly, we will maintain an increased level of maritime security operations directed against terrorism. The care with which we treated the *Palmero Senator*—the Liberian-flagged container ship recently held at sea for several days—until we determined that the trace radiation detected in the cargo did not arise from a security threat typifies this new normalcy.

Thirdly, we must create a more comprehensive awareness of threats and activities in the maritime domain. Prior to September 11, we focused mainly on first-response capability and consequence management. Obviously, in the face of the new threat environment, we must look forward—cognizant not only of last year's threat but preparing for next year's as well.

Fourth, we plan to expand and transform the core competence of the United States Coast Guard and to modernize its most vital assets, especially our deep-water force. We will continue to deploy maritime safety and security teams and to expand our Sea Marshal Program. These improvements will take several years to fully achieve, but the president remains committed to obtaining the resources to do the job.

And finally, we must strengthen the physical security of our seaports and reduce their vulnerability. The Department of Transportation, in an effort coordinated by the Maritime Administration, the Coast Guard, and the Transportation Security Administration, recently awarded $92.3 million in port security grants, most of which was earmarked for security measures such as fences and cameras. I was very proud of the agency's ability to cut through red tape to get those grants out to the ports in record time. And we intend to provide an additional $125 million for port security grants sometime in the near future.

These grants are only the beginning in our quest to make our ports safe from terrorism. All of the department transportation modes have actively engaged within the agency, with our colleagues in other federal and state agencies, and with our partners in the private sector to reduce vulnerabilities to transportation-critical infrastructure, to develop secure and intelligent supply chains, to test credentialing of workers in the transportation industry, to cultivate smart and efficient borders, and to create new ways of sharing security information with an engaged and concerned transportation industry. Throughout the agency, men and women of the Department of Transportation have worked literally day and night to ensure that terrorists can never again use our transportation technologies as a weapon against us. All of us understand that in this war on terrorism, the home front is the primary front. Ultimately, our ability to respond to these dynamic challenges rests upon the very virtues that we seek to defend: liberty, democracy, and free and open markets. The strongest, most vibrant economy in the world depends on the safest, most efficient transportation system in the world. We have a solemn obligation to ensure that we retain those distinctions.

God bless all of you. Travel safely. And God bless America.

DR. THOMPSON: Thank you, Secretary Mineta. You know when President Johnson got together a dozen or so other organizations to form a new Cabinet agency called the Department of Transportation, the only thing that all the parts had in common was that they were all moving. This was a very complicated job, even before 9/11, and I guess that complication has now been squared. I certainly don't envy you the burden that you have. Thank you for finding the time to come tonight.

We're done for the day. We will resume tomorrow morning at 8 o'clock, when we hear an address from Frances Hesselbein of the Drucker Foundation.

The Honorable Tom White, Secretary of the Army, will introduce her, and if you want to come earlier, we will have an informal reception starting at 7 o'clock. I guess as most of you know, General Myers, the Chairman of the Joint Chiefs of Staff, will give a concluding address tomorrow in the early afternoon.

Thank you all very much for coming today. We hope you enjoyed it. Don't forget to fill out those questionnaires and tell us how we can improve this. And I'll see you tomorrow.

MORNING ADDRESS

THE CHALLENGE OF MANAGING CHANGE

Mrs. Frances Hesselbein, Chairman of the Board of Governors, Peter F. Drucker Foundation for Nonprofit Management

Introduction by: Dr. Daniel Goure, Vice President, The Lexington Institute

The Honorable Thomas E. White, Secretary of the Army

Summary

Dr. Daniel Goure, Vice President, The Lexington Institute

• The U.S. military today is conducting defense planning in an era of uncertainty and working to engender the transformation of the U.S. military. So it is not only the environment that is changing, but so is the U.S. military.

• Transformation is loosely defined as a set of significant changes in equipment, organization, doctrine, training, and personnel that together result in order-of-magnitude improvement in overall military capability or effectiveness. This is a more complex phenomenon.

• The U.S. military is well into this process of transformation.

• It is quite something to argue that you are going to separate yourself from the traditional notions of how land forces are supposed to operate, how they're supposed to relate to one another—well beyond the idea of just using modern technology. So the Army, along with the other services, has much to be proud of in its transformation efforts.

Mrs. Frances Hesselbein, Chairman, Board of Governors, Peter F. Drucker Foundation for Nonprofit Management

• The challenge for leaders today in any type of organization is successfully managing change, leading change, creating change.

    1. For the future, the challenges will be exceeded only by the opportunities to lead, to innovate, to change lives, to shape the future. Leading change is the great leadership imperative.

    2. The great challenge is leading change with innovation and daily discipline to create a new dimension of performance.

3. The most effective way to manage change successfully is to create it. But experience has shown that grafting innovation onto a traditional enterprise does not work.

4. To create change, the organization itself must be seen as an agent for change.

5. To make the military and all other national security organizations change agents, we exercise tough discipline in moving innovation across the total enterprise, getting our house in order as we hurtle into a future, a tenuous future.

• And in this crucible of massive change, there is no time to negotiate with nostalgia for outmoded, irrelevant policies, practices, procedures, and assumptions.

1. We have to have the managerial courage to say, "In this organization, there are no sacred cows," so we practice planned abandonment that forces us to challenge the status quo.

2. We challenge the gospel of the status quo, the direction, the assumptions of the past, and we deliver only those plans and projects and policies and procedures that will be relevant in the future, viable and relevant for those we serve.

3. Planned abandonment means keeping mission and values and vision the soul of the organization, centered and aligned as the organization moves beyond the vestiges of the past that spell irrelevance in the future.

• Today, leaders in all sectors are finding that the old answers do not fit the new questions. Across all sectors, it is common questions, common challenges, and a call for principled leadership.

• The future calls our country and countries around the world for effective, ethical leaders in every sector at every level of every enterprise, not *a* leader or *the* leader, but many leaders dispersing the responsibilities of leadership right across the organization. It calls for leaders with a moral compass that works full time, leaders who are healers and unifiers who embody the mission, who live the values, who keep the faith.

• We define leadership in our own terms. This is my definition of leadership: Leadership is a matter of *how to be*, not *how to do it*. You and I spend most of our lives learning how to do it and teaching other people how to do it, yet in the end, it is the quality and the character of the leader that determine the performance and results.

Analysis

Mrs. Hesselbein's remarks reinforced those made by David Gergen and Dick Grasso about the importance of leadership in any organization and the importance of leadership during times of change. Her remarks have great applicability to any organization facing the dual challenges of the dawning of the Information Age and increasing economic globalization, but are especially relevant to the military services during this period of transformation and other public security organizations reorienting after last year's terrorist attacks on the United States.

Mrs. Hesselbein's definition of leadership is familiar to those in the military services and becoming more familiar to leaders in the corporate and nonprofit sectors. She emphasizes the importance of principled leadership based on strongly held morals, ethics, and values. Principled leaders understand their organizations and are able to set a positive example. They can also clearly articulate a vision, objectives, and standards for their organizations. In today's security and economic environment, organizations need these capabilities.

Mrs. Hesselbein appropriately highlights the challenge of leading in a time of change and of managing that change. Organizations in all sectors have been forced to change and to continue adapting to avoid irrelevance. Successful leaders must balance the need for creative thinking and innovation against the need to maintain routines and discipline within the organization. However, while maintaining this balance, leaders must continue to pursue and drive actual change in the organization. To be successful, this change must be measured and evaluated against well-defined performance goals and objectives. Both defining these standards and measuring progress can inhibit or retard change.

For change to be successful, Mrs. Hesselbein articulated the need to break with the past and to discard standards, procedures, and policies that continue out of habit and not relevance to the organization. Many organizations' cultures are closely linked to their past experience and successes. Leaders must carefully break from the past while sustaining both the organization's core competencies and the constructive aspects of its culture.

Mrs. Hesselbein's address focused the conference discussion on the broad challenge of leadership, not only in the national security arena but also in all organizations' sectors. Her comments helped highlight commonalities and shared challenges faced by public, private, and nonprofit institutions providing effective leadership for today and in the future.

Transcript

BACKSTAGE ANNOUNCER: Ladies and gentlemen, please welcome today's master of ceremonies, Dr. Daniel Goure.

DR. DANIEL GOURE: Good morning and welcome to the second day of the Eisenhower Series Conference on National Security in the Twenty-First Century. Yesterday, we learned that we are facing a complex and extremely difficult security environment. We also learned that there is really no consensus regarding who we will fight, how we will fight them, with whom we will be allied, and how we will conduct either the current conflict or future ones. Indeed, if we listened carefully to Professor North, we aren't even sure if we know why we're fighting or why the other side is fighting. Altogether, I think it was a very satisfying first day.

To compound this difficulty, we are now looking at trying to do defense planning in an era of uncertainty and to promote, create, or engender the transformation of the U.S. military. Therefore, it's not only the environment that must change, but so must we, so must the United States military. In some sense, therefore, it's a matter of not knowing where we are going necessarily, or how far we want to go, as well as where the environment is.

Dr. Goure

Transformation is loosely defined, and I stress that, as a set of significant changes in equipment, organization, doctrine, training, and personnel that together, in some fashion, result in an order-of-magnitude or orders-of-magnitude improvement in overall military capability or effectiveness. It's not as simple as getting more bang for the buck or more power per unit of weight. This is a more complex phenomenon. We know from history that often times new ways of using existing capabilities are transformational. Often, experts in this field point to the German blitzkrieg, with particular mention of the inferiority of German armor to that of many of its foes in Europe, at least early in the war. Therefore, it's not just technology or primarily technology, although technology does have a lot to do with it.

Over the last several years, we have come to learn that transformation, like beauty, is in the eye of the beholder. I was tempted to use the expression once applied by former Justice of the Supreme Court Byron White to another topic, not knowing what it is but knowing it when he sees it. But I thought that was a little much for this particularly august body. The fact that we really don't know entirely, or perhaps shouldn't know yet what we mean by transformation—what it is, what all the steps are to achieve it—is a source of enormous frustration. I'm certain, for some of the people in this room, for people who have to observe the process, for those on Capitol Hill who are being asked to pay for it. Yet we ought to recognize that whether we know it, whether we have done it deliberately, the U.S. military is well into its process of transformation, which is the subject of today's panel sessions. That process is now well under way.

In some sense, like Dorothy in Kansas, in *The Wizard of Oz*, our heart's desire is right here in our front yard, and we've really had it all the time. Afghanistan, just to use that example, demonstrates the degree of transformation in small, significant ways—the relationship between the tactical air controller on the ground using a laser pointer and a GPS (Global Positioning System) to command B52 strategic bombers. Never have so few, or, perhaps in some sense, so low, done so much in such quick time. Each of the services are acquiring new capabilities and creating new doctrines and concepts of operation that are transformational by almost anybody's view of the subject. Whatever one thinks of the mix, it's certainly a quantum leap in technology:

- The Air Force airborne laser.
- The F–22/JSF combination.
- GPS-guided weapons, particularly air-delivered, but there are others.
- Persistent ISR (Intelligence, Surveillance, Reconnaissance), the bringing to the table of UAVs (Unmanned Aerial Vehicles), not only in the Air Force but also in other services; however, the Air Force may be a little bit ahead.
- Effects-based operations. This is not just an Air Force concept. They've done a lot to kick-start the process of thinking about how to be more precise, not simply in the targeting of weapons or the direction of forces but also in the kind of military and political effects we want to achieve. The Navy and Marine Corps are similarly heavily engaged, heavily invested in this kind of process. I would point to the CVNX, the new carrier, which, with the full system that includes the command and control and the electric drive, could be a platform not only for air operations but also for advanced lasers and other technologies.
- The conversion of the SSBNs to SSGNs—a completely new concept—and the way we are going to try to use those.
- The expeditionary maneuver warfare the Marine Corps has invested in, which relies on AAAV, V22, and a number of technologies, but it's the concept that's important.
- The Army Stryker, which is now being produced at a very successful rate, and was used in Millennium Challenge '02—the first time we've actually had a unit out there.
- The Comanche, which will come on line, we hope, in 2009, and beyond that, the future combat system and the objective force, with the land warrior.

More importantly for the Army are new concepts for land warfare. In some ways, I would argue the Army effort at transformation has been the boldest of all. It's quite something to argue that you are going to separate yourself from the traditional notions of how land forces are supposed to operate, how they're supposed to relate to one another, which is well beyond the idea of just using modern technology. The Army, along with the other services, has much to be proud of in its transformation efforts.

I ended talking about the Army as a very clever way to segue into my introduction of the next gentleman to come up, who is the Secretary of the Army, the Honorable Thomas White. The Secretary took over the Army at a very interesting time, and he has been very bold in his efforts to move the Army forward, not just with respect to transformation but also with respect to readiness and personnel. These are all issues that have to be treated together. One can't simply talk transformation and ignore the realities of today. Secretary White is extraordinarily experienced in Army issues, and in the broader issues of transformation, bringing business to the fore, and applying different tactics, different strategies for moving the Army along. He's a graduate of West Point, and in his career as a brigadier general, he has attended a number of military-related schools, including the Naval Postgraduate School and the Army War College. He is here to introduce our keynote speaker. Mr. Secretary.

SECRETARY THOMAS E. WHITE: Transformation—what a great topic for us as we try not to become collateral damage of the IMF protesters. I love the smell of tires burning in the morning. General Shinseki, it's great to see you, Chief. Three years ago next month, at the AUSA Conference, which will run next month, the chief of staff laid down the marker for the direction and the vision of Army transformation. With his leadership, we have stuck to it religiously for those three years, and that's why we are in such a wonderful position today as we field Striker, as we solidify the vision of the future combat system, the objective force, Comanche, and the other things such as personnel transformation. Therefore, I'd just like to publicly salute the chief for being the Army's change agent.

General Vuono, it's wonderful to see you here this morning, bright and early, as is your custom. General Meigs, my old friend, great to see you here. It's a pleasure to introduce our keynote speaker this morning, the former National Executive Director of the Girl Scouts of America, Frances Hesselbein. She is now the Chairman of the Board of Directors, Board of Governors of the Peter F. Drucker Foundation for Nonprofit Management, which is one of the co-sponsors of our Eisenhower National Security Conference. She is the Chairman of the Board of Governors of the Josephson Institute for the Advancement of Ethics. Her management ideas are studied at distinguished institutions like the Harvard Business School, which has turned her Girl Scouts work into a substantial case study.

In August, Mrs. Hesselbein released her new book *Hesselbein on Leadership*. Recognized worldwide, Frances was featured on the covers of

Secretary White

both *Business Week* and *Savvy* for her managerial excellence. In 1989, President George Bush appointed Mrs. Hesselbein to his advisory committee on the Points Of Light Foundation, and in 1991, he appointed her to the Board of Directors of the Commission on National and Community Service. She is the only woman and the only member of the human services sector to serve on that commission. In January 1998, President Clinton presented her with the Presidential Medal of Freedom, the nation's highest civilian honor. We are privileged to have her with us today to speak on a tremendously relevant topic—the subject of managing change. Ladies and gentlemen, please extend a warm welcome to Mrs. Frances Hesselbein.

MRS. FRANCES HESSELBEIN: Thank you, Mr. Secretary, and Secretary White, we are deeply grateful for your leadership in the transformation of the Army. You inspire us. General Shinseki, distinguished members of this conference, I would like to extend my deepest gratitude for all of the partners of this conference because it is the great example of collaboration so essential in our society. The partners sponsoring the Eisenhower Conference have been aware of the great responsibility and the great honor that we share, and we are grateful to Susan and the Eisenhower family for the gift of General Eisenhower's name and his inspiration for this conference.

This is a high honor to be with you this morning as we look at the great leadership imperative of our times: managing change. In 2002, it is the challenge of leading change, creating change, and I bring you warm greetings from the people of the Drucker Foundation.

Peter Drucker celebrated his 92nd birthday in November by teaching a class, full schedule, at Claremont; working on a new book; and on November 7, in the *Economist* magazine, with a seminal article, "The Next Society, Survey of the Near Future." Peter's wisdom is spread across twenty incredible pages, and one observation is most relevant to our discussion: seeing the organization as a change agent. Now, you and I are used to hearing that we must be change agents, but as Peter writes, "To survive and succeed, every organization will

have to turn itself into a change
agent. The most effective way to manage change successfully is to create it.
But experience has shown that grafting innovation onto a traditional
enterprise does not work; the enterprise has to become a change agent."
And he continues, "It requires the
exploitation of successes, especially
those unexpected and unplanned-for
ones, and it requires systematic innovation. The point of becoming a
change agent is that it changes the
mindset of the entire organization.
And then, instead of seeing change as
a threat, its people will come to consider it an opportunity."

Peter delivers a powerful leadership imperative: Making the organization, the military, a change agent,
and all of the partners in our national security, change agents. This

Mrs. Hesselbein

means that we exercise tough discipline in moving innovation across the total
enterprise, getting our house in order as we hurtle into a tenuous future. In
this crucible of massive change, there is no time to negotiate with nostalgia
for outmoded, irrelevant policies, practices, procedures, and assumptions.
Our turbulent times do not accommodate that "we have always done it this
way" strategy. We have to have the managerial courage to say, "In this organization, there are no sacred cows, so we practice planned abandonment that
forces us to challenge the status quo."

We challenge the gospel of the status quo, the direction, the assumptions
of the past, and we deliver only those plans, projects, policies, and procedures
that will be relevant in the future, viable and relevant to those with whom we
serve, for those we serve. And in this new world that we will build, planned
abandonment means keeping mission and values and vision the soul of the
organization, centered and aligned as we slough off the vestiges of the past that
spell irrelevance in the future. It is time to put our house in order, whether we
are the United States Army, the Salvation Army, or Chevron/Texaco.

On Wednesday here in Washington, I spoke to the U.S. Department of
Commerce Minority Business Leaders Conference on the entrepreneurial leader
of the future, and I shared with them—there were 500 minority business leaders present—that I cheered when I read an article in the November 8 New York
Times about the United States Army rethinking its priorities. The article closes

quoting the Army Chief of Staff: "Many foot draggers are in the Army itself, but General Shinseki has a warning for them: 'If you don't like change,' he likes to say to his commanders, 'you'll like irrelevance even less.'" The conference loved it because it's all about leadership. It's all about change, no matter which conference, no matter what the subject—for all of us, for our fellow travelers on a long journey toward an uncertain future, where the challenges will be exceeded only by the opportunities to lead, to innovate, to change lives, to shape the future, where leading change is the great leadership imperative.

Today, leaders in all three sectors are finding that the old answers do not fit the new questions. Across the three sectors, it is common questions, common challenges, a call for principled leadership. For the future calls our country and countries around the world for effective, ethical leaders in every sector at every level of every enterprise, not a leader or the leader, but many leaders dispersing the responsibilities of leadership right across the organization. It calls for leaders with a moral compass that works full time, leaders who are healers and unifiers who embody the mission, who live the values, who keep the faith. Today, for leaders in all three sectors, the great challenge is leading change with innovation, the daily discipline. We use this definition for innovation: *change that creates a new dimension of performance, always the focus on performance and results.*

Let me share some personal background on leading change that may be relevant. On July 4, 1976, as the tall ships sailed into New York harbor on that auspicious day, I arrived in New York to become the Chief Executive Officer of Girl Scouts of the U.S.A. I left a small town in the mountains of western Pennsylvania to lead the largest organization for girls and women in the world. It was an organization of enormous complexity. Over 3 million members and 650,000 men and women serving 2 1/2 million girls, and there were 335 local chartered councils and cookie sales, grossing one-third of a billion dollars every year. It was an organization of long history and proud tradition. It was a great American institution. But, in 1976, most organizations were reeling from the seismic changes of the 1960s and the early 1970s.

Gatherings of corporate and organizational chief executives had few female faces, but some CEOs—and I was one of them—developed our own philosophy, our own style, and our own leadership language. Instinctively banning the old hierarchy, we took our people out of those old rigid boxes into the concentric circles of a flat and fluid flexible structure and system that I call *circular management.* And circular management released the energies of our people, released the human spirit. Now, in 1976, I did not know that our society was entering a period of the most massive change in more than 200 years, since the American Revolution. I just knew that the practices of the past were not relevant to the present I was living and the future I envisioned, and I knew with that equal access, building a richly diverse organization, was an indispensable part of a demographics-driven, customer-driven future.

I understood the power of example and the power of mission and values and vision and the power of language. Therefore, I worked hard on the language, until the answer came clearly, and it would be my definition for the next 20 years. We managed for the mission. Later I added the indispensable companions for the journey. We managed for the mission, we managed for innovation, and we managed for diversity. And this permeated the total organization. It became a leadership benchmark, a very simple and powerful way to describe the management and the focus of a great institution.

Then and now, I did what each of us must do—define leadership in our own terms. Therefore, after much introspection, this is my definition of leadership: *Leadership is a matter of how to be, not how to do it.* You and I spend most of our lives learning how to do it and teaching other people how to do it, yet in the end, it is the quality and the character of the leader that determines the performance and results. Leadership is a matter of how to be, not how to do it. It was my thesis in those early days. It is my thesis today. And the power of language is indispensable on our journey to transformation. And we learn to mobilize our people, and we are talking about more than three-quarters of a million adults. We learn to mobilize our people around mission, why we do what we do, our purpose, and our reason for being. And with a passionate goal of equal access, we built a richly diverse organization, tripling racial/ethnic representation right across the organization at every level highly visible.

Now, you don't achieve this by sitting at a desk in New York and waving your hand and saying, "Let there be diversity." As the Army knows, it happens on the ground. It happens in the neighborhoods where the people are. And when we look at this wonderfully diverse country and we look at the wonderfully diverse people that we wanted to bring in, we asked ourselves a powerful question: All these people we want to bring in, when they look at us—at our boards of directors, the management team, the workforce, the visual materials—can they find themselves? The answer was a resounding yes, and the results are documented, as Secretary White said, in a Harvard Business School case that is used by business schools around the world, and it's always interesting if I'm in Manila speaking to graduate MBA students of the Asia Institute for Management to have two of them come up and say, "We used your case last week. We have a few questions about the Girl Scout cookie sale."

The organization became mission-focused, values-based, demographics-driven, and the power of language was the indispensable companion on the journey to transformation. In addition, from our own people, I learned the power of persuasion, for by then I was leading a workforce of 788,000 men and women and, of those, fewer than 1 percent employed staff. The rest could leave if they weren't happy. And from them, I learned that change and innovation and diversity are the power that drives and transforms an organization—as true in 2002 as in 1976. When I left the Girl Scouts of the U.S.A on February 1, 1990, we had achieved the greatest diversity in 78 years—the highest membership with the greatest cohesion in our history. We were one great movement, and we were passionately mobilized around the mission. We had changed the program for girls, with a heavy focus on math, science, and technology. We changed the way we developed leaders, the way we delivered services by market segment, not geography. We even dared to change the pin, the logo, but never the values, never the beliefs, the principles, the soul of the organization, and the promise that begins, "On my honor, I will serve God and my country."

As I led the largest organization of girls and women in the world, and I did this for 13 1/2 years—that's 5,000 days—I never had a bad day. I had tough ones, but never a bad one. Moreover, that last year—a carefully planned 12 months of leadership transition—was the most exuberant year of my whole career. Leaving well is the last great gift that a leader can make to the organization. I am happy to tell you that since then, the organization has grown and thrived, and it now has one million adults and three million girls. Leading change was the great leadership imperative for that great movement. A slow and genteel decline was the alternative.

On my desk in New York is the 1999 United States Army leadership manual. I keep it there. It has a very simple cover. There are only three words: "Be, Know, Do." That says it all. It's Army shorthand for leadership. I mentioned this in a roundtable I was part of for the December *Harvard Business Review*. We had the chairman of Merck and the chairman of FedEx as part of this little group of six. In the dialogue, I mentioned, "be, know, do," the Army's leadership manual, and then in our leadership journal and on the web site was an article "A Time for Leaders" where I mentioned the Army leadership manual. Immediately, we were getting flooded with e-mails and calls from people who had read the December *Harvard Business Review* or downloaded the article, and all of them asking, "Where can I get a copy of the Army leadership manual? Where can I get 'Be, Know, Do?' How do I order it?" And I thought, "Oh, what have I done?" I called Suzanne Carlton in fear and trembling, and I said, "Oh, I do hope it's declassified." She said, "Oh, yes indeed, here is the 800 number." We put the 800 number up on our web site and could answer all the calls in a very positive way.

Now, think about this. We are helping civilians order the Army leadership manual. I don't believe that would have happened ten years ago. Today, people are hungry for leadership. They are hungry for meaning. Leaders are hungry for significance. And somehow, the Army leadership manual and those three words touched and connected. Indeed, leadership is a matter of how to be, not how to do it.

I'm traveling two or three times a week. I have a sense of great urgency right now. Therefore, I spend a third of my time with corporate leaders, a third on the campuses of colleges and universities, and somewhere in there is always the military. This spring, I spent some time with the faculty at West Point and a couple of weeks later with the faculty at the Naval Academy. At both, I had the privilege of working with cadets or midshipmen, and last year, before September 11, I worked with Admiral Loy at his command conference, and the subject he gave me, and this was a year ago, had one word—*transformation*. In the past few months I've spoken to the leaders of the California Highway Patrol and to corrections and parole officers of California. Wednesday, I spoke to that remarkable conference for minority business leaders, and last Thursday, I worked with Chevron in this marvelous example of a great American corporation bringing together nonprofit leaders.

The Drucker Foundation and Chevron have worked together for seven years. Where it was Texaco, now it is Chevron/Texaco. And this time, they designed the three-day management institute for the presidents of local urban leagues and the officers of the National Urban League. This is another example of collaboration right across the sectors, and next week I'm doing something quite unusual. Microsoft has invited me to come to their campus in Seattle to talk to their people about my new book, *Hesselbein on Leadership*. For the first time, I received five questions, and Microsoft said, "Please answer these questions, and we will print this in our corporate newsletter that goes out to all of our people." Two of the questions, I'll share with you; not the answers. How would you answer these two? "Who is your favorite historical figure?" And the second tough one: "If you could give to only one organization, which would it be?"

The highlight of the year was this. On June 25, in collaboration, the Conference Board, the U.S. Army, and the Drucker Foundation brought ten Army leaders, ten corporate leaders, and ten nonprofit leaders to West Point for an off-the-record conference on Leadership in an Age of Discontinuity. They arrived at West Point, ten, ten, ten—three very different groups. Moreover, I could tell that some of them weren't sure how they were going to relate to these other groups. Three days later, they left—one powerful, cohesive group, very articulate and determined to continue the dialogue, for we spoke a common language, the language of today's leadership in management. With this common language, we found common ground. And those three days changed lives. And on August 29, a foundation chairman, who has his own foundation and who participated in this conference, met with representatives of the Conference Board and our foundation and the U.S. Army to brainstorm the follow-up of an incredible experience, and we'll meet again in October.

Whenever the officers of our military can work with civilian leaders, it is an incredible gift. They change minds and they change lives, and the quality and the character of our military people embody the qualities of leadership and character so needed in all three sectors. They inspire us all as they have for over 200 years.

Now, in these two days together, we have been developing some powerful messages of leading change, of redefining the future. It is not an intellectual exercise. Everything this remarkable Eisenhower Conference will develop converges into a new leadership imperative. Every word, every act, every initiative tested against the imperative of leading change in a world that has changed forever. That's the message. Long ago, early in another century, George Bernard Shaw left this message for you and me: "I am of the opinion that my life belongs to the community, and as long as I live, it is my privilege to do for it whatever I can. I want to be thoroughly used up when I die, for the harder I work, the more I live. Life is no brief candle for me. It is a sort of splendid torch which I have got hold of for a short moment, and I want to make it burn as brightly as possible before handing it on to future generations." Now, when the roll is called in 2010, you and I do not know what that world is going to be like, but the leaders in this room will help define that future, and whether in the United States or abroad, all of us are struggling with this seismic transformation of the global society and its institutions in a world at war. Ten years from now, when the history of the United States military and its partners is written, may they write of you: "For a little while, they held a splendid torch. The future called, and they responded. They kept the faith." Thank you very much. We have time for a few questions.

AUDIENCE MEMBER: Hi, ma'am. I'm Major Todd Key and I'm the proud father of an 8-year-old daughter who is a Girl Scout, and I tell you, those cookie sales are tough. However, they emphasize a question I have, which is about decentralized execution. You know, tremendous organization where cookies are stacked up in your house, you're getting them out, your daughters are out there selling, you want to keep your log, your tooth-to-tail ratio down because you got to live in the house. The question is about how decentralized execution seems to me to be a picture of the future in enabling your people to do more, trusting them to do more, with the focus of leadership that you discussed. Could you please elaborate just a little more on the decentralized aspect of that?

MRS. HESSELBEIN: Yes. If you look at the giant and complex organization and you're part of that Army of 788,000 men and women, bigness does not inspire anyone. How then do we mobilize the people? We do it through mission, and we had this wonderful 1912 statement of purpose. It was beautiful, and it was very long. We knew what it meant, but we couldn't always remember all of it. Therefore, we distilled that statement into a mission statement that had only nine words: *To help each girl reach her own highest potential.* We put that into place right up front. It wasn't bigness; it wasn't power. It was, "We exist for one little 8-year-old girl, to help her reach her own highest potential." That mobilized the country, and like most national organizations/movements, over here is the national organization and somewhere on another island is the field, and until they become one powerful movement, you can never become what you should be. With that mission and the total focus on girls growing up—with that as a passionate focus—and every speech, the stationery, the visuals, they all beamed not twenty messages, but about five, and that was one of them.

While it is far-flung, I think the secret to building this powerful, cohesive organization is to have standards and policies that everyone must adhere to—standards that guide us—but not a thousand, a manageable handful, all focused on why we do what we do. That's when you don't even think of decentralization. When I looked at the 6,000 staff members out there, I knew I couldn't go anywhere in leading unless they knew they were the indispensable members of my team. Therefore, every year, for the local executive directors and 100 national staff members, 500 people, we had a leadership development conference we called *An Adventure in Excellence*, where Warren Bennis, or Peter Drucker, or the great thought leaders of the day would speak. That sent a message that only the best is good enough for those who serve girls.

When we talk about values, and values permeate the organization and the leaders in everything they do—they embody the values that we preach—you build the kind of palpable culture, the kind of palpable cohesion that you usually only dream about. This is a long answer to a very important question, and I hope that next year your garage has a thousand more boxes of cookies. If your daughter will call me or send me a card, I would like to buy one box of each flavor. Thank you.

AUDIENCE MEMBER: Ma'am, my name is Larry Wood. I'm a retired Army colonel. I now work for Computer Sciences Corporation. I apologize for asking a second question, but the issue of leadership is one that has certainly challenged me throughout the course of my military and now civilian career. I spent four wonderful years as a brigade commander in the United States Army Cadet Command, where their business was leadership. Yesterday, we listened to a variety of economic experts and strategists and intellectuals and so forth discuss similar topics with a range of disparate views. The dilemma for leaders—General Shinseki, Secretary White, yourself—when all is said and done, if you have a collaborative approach to leadership and you listen to all the opposing views, you alone as the leader must make a decision. What is the one leadership characteristic, or tenet, or value that is most critical in making those very difficult, alone decisions that leaders must make.

MRS. HESSELBEIN: In my experience, you take the question, you take the challenge, and the first questions we ask ourselves is, "Will it further the organization? Will it further the mission?" Mission is the big question—will it further the mission of the United States Army, whatever the organization is in all three sectors? Is it consistent with the values? We have lots of offers, ideas, opinions, but we test them first against the mission. If it does not further the mission, if it would diminish the mission, if it would alter the values, we say, "Thank you very much," and we don't do it, because that's what holds us together in this powerful way. When we look at our young people in the military and where we send them, they know why they're there. As leaders, we have to be very tough. If it doesn't further the mission, we say, "Thank you very much." We are mission-focused, values-based, and we never forget it. Please?

AUDIENCE MEMBER: I have a small question for you. Of the challenges that the organized militaries face for the future, the most important one, in my mind, is the environment that exists now, which is a very dehumanizing kind of an environment, where the contenders don't follow the normal route they've followed in the past—where uniformed people fought uniformed people. These dehumanizing experiences I allude to are people walking into churches shooting people, flying planes into buildings, walking into temples—all areas that were forbidden in the past. What recipe would you have for preparing the military to challenge and overcome people who have such dehumanized psychologies?

MRS. HESSELBEIN: Sir, if I had that recipe, I would now be not only the Chief of Staff of the United States Army, I would be the Secretary of the Army as well. You're asking a question that not just the military agonizes over but all of us, because the United States Army, the United States military, belongs to us, the civilians. When we have enemies that do not play by the rules—and I'm not so sure that in every war, people have played by the rules—all we can do is give the young men and women we send out, wherever we send them, a powerful sense of support that we care for each one of them as an individual. There is a personal caring. This is what I hear as I work with the Army. The Army cares about its people. People come first. Now, how do you prepare for the unimaginable, the unthinkable? We send our young people into that abyss and all we can do is help them understand why and give them the best training and the best equipment. Nothing is spared, and when we ask the American public, "In which institution do you have your greatest confidence?" the military is number one.

You've asked a grievous question because we don't even know some of the places we will send our people, but we have to believe that if we do the best possible job of preparing them, somehow that indomitable American spirit that has been with us since the day the country was born will travel with them. We have to think of new ways to support and we all have to work. We are all in it together. Sometimes, when I talk to the military, I try to explain, because I don't think they understand how the American public really feels. Because, if you look at me, I am the daughter of a soldier, and I am the mother of a soldier, and I am the great-granddaughter of soldiers marching back through history to the American Revolution. The United States Army, its culture, and its history are part of my family's culture and history, and there are millions and millions of Americans just like me. Therefore, you have this vast, vast army of civilian support. It is passionate and it is total, and that's my best answer to a very difficult question that has no answer. Thank you, sir. We have three minutes before we say good-bye.

AUDIENCE MEMBER: Thank you very much. I have a follow-up of the question just asked because it seems to me this is one of the most important questions we may ask for the security of this country. I'm personally convinced that the unknown soldiers of this century will be the civilians. In the last century, what we have seen is that in World War I, only 10 percent of the victims were civilians. In World War II, they were 60 percent. In the wars of the '90s, they were up to 90 percent, with the extermination of the civilian population as the target of the wars in certain parts of the world. Now, it seems to me that what we have discovered with this concept, adequate or not, of asymmetric warfare is that even in developed countries, we might have the civilians targeted as such because the military are themselves so well protected. I find the question of the Indian gentleman so important that I ask it again. What, in your view, should be the part of the civil defense now in the budget of our ministries of defense?

MRS. HESSELBEIN: If I were writing the check, it would be unlimited, because all of us are in it together, and what you said is very true. But in the end, the military and the passion of the citizens are what sustain the democracy, and so we have faith in one another and we move forward into a very uncertain future. With this focus, and with the total support of the military, we will sustain the democracy. Thank you very much for your question. Thank you.

DR. GOURE: Before we break for coffee, I have a couple of announcements. One is that as part of the Eisenhower Series over the last year, there was a seminar or forum conducted on Investing in America, much the same topic that we listened to Mrs. Hesselbein discuss just a few minutes ago—bringing together leaders of the military, corporate America, and nonprofit organizations and looking at how to manage change in large organizations. The report of that is available to all of you. In addition, the proceedings of yesterday's session are now on the web at www.eisenhowerseries.com. If you want to actually get the visuals, as well as text forms of the various presentations, you can download that. With that, we will end the first session and move to coffee. Thank you very much.

PANEL III

BUILDING CAPABILITIES—REALIZING MILITARY TRANSFORMATION

Co-sponsor: The Lexington Institute

Chair: Dr. Loren B. Thompson, Chief Operations Officer, The Lexington Institute

Historical Perspectives on Military Change: Dr. Michael E. O'Hanlon, Senior Fellow, Brookings Institution

Perspectives on Defense Transformation: Dr. David Johnson, Senior Policy Analyst, RAND

Transforming America's Military: Dr. Hans Binnendijk, National Defense University

Joint Implementation of the Transformation Vision: Major General James M. Dubik, Director for Joint Experimentation (J9), Joint Forces Command

---

Panel Charter

Transforming the U.S. military into a twenty-first century force is the Bush administration's Number 1 national security objective. As discussed in the Quadrennial Defense Review, the changing international security environment that seems poised to spawn a generation of new and unpredictable threats necessitates such a transformation. This situation is made worse by the proliferation of advanced technology giving rise to the concern that even small state adversaries and terrorist groups might be able to obtain and employ weapons of mass destruction against our forces abroad, our friends and allies, and even the U.S. homeland.

There is no single agreed-on definition of what constitutes transformation. Generally, it can be defined as an order-of-magnitude change in the ability of military forces to fight. Many definitions exist, both within and outside DoD. Some focus on new technology, others on organizational change, and still others on new doctrine and strategy. An often-used example of such a transformation is the German Blitzkrieg, which was a mix of technological, organiza-

Left to right: *Dr. Loren B. Thompson, Dr. Michael E. O'Hanlon, Major General James M. Dubik, Mrs. Francis Hesselbein, General Eric K. Shinseki, Dr. Daniel Goure, Dr. David Johnson, Dr. Hans Bennendijk*

tional, and doctrinal change. The Department of Defense has identified six transformational goals:

- Protect the U.S. homeland and bases overseas.
- Project and sustain power in distant theaters.
- Deny enemies sanctuary.
- Protect information networks from attack.
- Use information technology to link up different kinds of U.S. forces so that they can fight jointly.
- Maintain unhindered access to space and protect space capabilities from enemy attack.

The challenge confronting DoD and the services alike is how to translate these goals into concrete programs, new organizational schema, and/or novel concepts of operation. Further complicating the situation is the fact that DoD must simultaneously fight a global war on terrorism as well as ensure the essential modernization of existing forces. As a result, budgetary competition between the transformation accounts and those for people, operations and maintenance, and modernization are likely to intensify over the next 5 to 10 years.

The objective of the transformation panel is to bring some clarity to this rather murky subject. The panelists will be asked to address three questions as part of their presentations. First, are DoD's goals and those of the services realistic? Second, what progress has been made or will be made in the near term? Third, why will the final outcome of the process, assuming all goes well, result in a transformation? Panelists will also be asked to identify programs and activities that they believe are the best examples of transformation.

Summary

Dr. Loren B. Thompson, Chief Operations Officer, The Lexington Institute

• Every new administration tries to find some word or some phrase that captures the essence of its security posture. Presidents know that if they don't come up with their own phrase, they'll get tagged with one by the media that will probably be a good deal less congenial.

1. When President Eisenhower first entered office, he developed a national security posture that relied more on air power and on atomic weapons. He wanted to call it the New Look, but critics called it massive retaliation and that's the phrase that stuck.

2. The Bush administration's preferred term for its efforts is transformation, which is understood to mean a wholesale reorganization of policy and priorities in response to emerging threats.

3. The national security community must discuss what transformation has meant in the past and what it may mean for our current preparations as we enter a new millennium.

Dr. Hans Binnendijk, National Defense University

• Transformation is the process of creating and harnessing a revolution in military affairs.

• It is useful to go back and look at previous revolutions in military affairs.

1. They take place on the average of once every 50 to 60 years.

2. They all have three elements in common: fundamental change in the underlying technology, new operational concepts that are designed to take that technology and use it on the battlefield, and organizational changes that are introduced in order to implement those new concepts.

3. Generally, a new theory of war accompanies these changes and, often, combined arms is emphasized. The technology that fuels these revolutions often comes from the commercial sector.

4. These revolutions often allow small forces to win over large forces. And we also find that even with battlefield successes, they are not a panacea.

• The current revolution in military affairs can be traced back to the end of the Vietnam War, when our military began to figure out what went wrong, to reorganize itself, and to make use of the new technologies.

1. DESERT STORM clearly had elements of the revolution in military affairs already present: stealth technology, precision strike, enhanced com-

mand and control, night vision, a new tank with a stabilized gun, speed, laser range finders, and cruise missiles.

2. What we did not have at that time were new operational concepts. We still fought DESERT STORM in a fairly traditional fashion. But, we already see elements of effects-based operations, in Kosovo and even more so in Afghanistan.

3. A key document in the transformation process was *Joint Vision 2010*, which focused on massing fire rather than massing forces.

• What happened in the last 7 or 8 years to begin to change this?

1. The shift in operational focus since the Cold War toward agility, which has become a key element of thinking in the transformation process.

2. New emphasis on anti-access and area denial problems, where a potential enemy has access to a lot of this new technology.

3. An emphasis on reducing casualties and on getting to the battlefield rapidly.

4. More emphasis on robotics, more thinking about swarming techniques.

5. An improvement in computers and computer networks and in the ability of almost everyone to use this technology, which has led to network-centric warfare.

6. Some improvements in precision strike, allowing us to rely more on inorganic firepower.

7. Despite implementation of this process having been very much service-driven, the joint element is now coming into play.

• The Army has recognized the nature of its problem: a gap exists, which is clearly stated in the Army road map, and it has to do with becoming more expeditionary and getting to the battlefield more quickly.

1. The Army has taken a fairly radical approach to transformation, much more so than the other services. Its very comprehensive approach sets out clear priorities and includes budgets for each priority.

2. The Army's process is tremendously under resourced, thereby creating risk. First, very little is being spent today on research and development to improve the legacy force. Second, the interim force does not have sufficient combat power for demanding offensive missions. Finally, the risk for the objective force is technology.

3. There is a concern that essentially two transformations are under way: the Army's transformation to the Objective Force and Secretary Rumsfeld's view of Army transformation. If you combine these two transformations, does the Army transformation replace the Abrams and the Bradley and the Rumsfeld transformation replace Crusader and maybe Comanche? What's left?

• The Navy and the Air Force are working very well together, and that is clear in their road map. They have come up with a number of new concepts.

1. The Navy's key problem is determining how to budget for everything it wants to do.

2. The Air Force, similarly, has a very strong road map with six transformational goals tied to seven operational concepts and specific technological needs and capabilities.

3. The Air Force now has two problems. One, it is not focusing enough on the seams between what it delivers for ground forces, which includes lift, mobility, space assets, and close air support. The Air Force is basically talking about what it does on its own. It needs to think much more about what it does for other services. The Air Force plan is basically unaffordable at this point.

• The next step in this process is to make it joint. We need to develop better joint operating concepts. And the key to this is joint experimentation.

• Transformation has to be broadly based. We cannot just think about air/ground operations but about issues like focused logistics, the acquisition process, and spiral development. We have to think about transformation in the interagency context and even with NGOs. And we have to include the allies.

• We have to fight the notion that if something is not transformational, it's no good. We have to pay more attention to the vulnerability of information technology. We have to be careful not to overemphasize the strength that transformation gives us. We have to keep in mind the limitations to this process. Finally, we do not want war to become the chosen instrument of American diplomacy.

Major General James M. Dubik, Director for Joint Experimentation (J9), Joint Forces Command:

• The military must perform a relatively complex range of operations, and that range extends from one end, which is to be solved in a high-tech way to the other end, which is very low tech, where physical mass and physical presence still count. Even in one operation, some aspects may admit to very technical solutions, where others absolutely do not.

• We've seen the impact of the Information Age trend, the globalization trend, and the emergence of the new political order strategic environment after the Cold War. We see the impact of these on our social systems and organizations, our political systems and organizations, our fiscal systems, our economic systems, our corporate systems. This should be no surprise, for they have had a major impact on our military systems, organizations, and procedures.

• One of the difficulties in transformation from a practitioner's standpoint is that the past is not always a guide to our future. Our reasoning process is not how it worked in the past and how can we project it into the future, but how do we change to adapt to a new future. It's an entirely different reasoning process, and that's a big challenge.

• *Full Spectrum Dominance*: we are going to be asked to fight and win war in all its various forms; not war defined as conventional combat, but war in all its varieties. We've been asked to use force to compel adversaries to do our will.

1. Not every conflict will submit to a rapid, decisive conclusion. We may have a rapid, decisive conclusion to the initial operation, but have to follow up with other operations. We've also been asked to provide more options to military leaders.

2. We'll have to build our joint, combined, interagency teams quickly without being ad hoc. The way we formed joint task forces in the past has been very successful, but we want to diminish the ad hoc aspect and increase the stable side of the kind of quick operations that we may have to execute in the future.

• Some guiding principles in transformation that are important:

1. First, as much as we would like to get it right, we should understand that the real operating principle is not to get it too wrong. Our challenge is not to get it too far off and to produce leaders who can adapt what we've given them to the new set of circumstances—leaders who can adapt to something that none of us can predict.

2. Second, while materiel solutions are very important, they are not as important as the training, organizational development, leader development, and doctrine portions of transformation. Having technology doesn't win wars; using technology better than your opponent wins wars.

3. Third, our transformation must be much more inclusive of each of our regional combatant commanders, all the services, our allies or potential allies or coalition partners, interagency operations, and the nongovernmental and private organizations that are included in operations all over the world.

• Joint Forces Command is on a dual-path strategy in this regard for the next several years.

1. One is to subject the joint capstone concepts, as well as the functional concepts and the integrating concepts that result from them, to significant experimentation for the next couple of years.

2. The second is to expand effects-based operations beyond the initial offering, expand a concept called operational net assessment that takes intelligence preparation in the battlefield to the next level, field a collaborative information environment, and refine the joint interagency work.

Dr. David Johnson, Senior Policy Analyst, RAND

• The U.S. Army never developed an equivalent of the transformation of the German blitzkrieg in the years between the two world wars. *Blitzkrieg* is defined as the joint capability derived from combining ground mechanizing maneuver and air power.

• World War I was a seminal experience for the U.S. Army. It was the first major war off our shores. The most important lesson the Army's leaders took from that war was that manpower and industrial mobilization were the keys to success in modern warfare.

• Two new technologies confronted the U.S. Army in the aftermath of the war: the tank and the airplane. But, given the environment in which the tank and the airplane were developed in the interwar Army, it would have been very surprising if an American version of the blitzkrieg had been developed.

• The interwar Army experience offers insights about innovation and transformation.

1. During periods of relatively low threats to national survival, the services and their branches tend to focus on internal imperatives. They try to highlight their particular contributions to the national defense in their quest for greater budget and mission share. Thus, innovation happens on the margins, and the leadership is generally more prone to enforce orthodoxy.

2. The Army's interwar experience also reinforces how we are all, in many ways, captives of the institutions within which we serve. To be accepted practitioners and to get ahead, we embrace the norms of our services and how they fight. We also tend to espouse the unique value of our service and the belief that its contributions to national defense are more important than those of the other services. This is clearly an impediment to realizing true jointness within the defense establishment.

Dr. Michael E. O'Hanlon, Senior Fellow, Brookings Institution

• Transformation is a paradox. You have to try to do it to try to speed up innovation. But you have to also expect that most of what you try may not work, may be a bad idea, and may interfere with pressing requirements and other national security priorities that simply must remain as high as they've been.

• At this time in history, we have to try to innovate even more than we have in previous periods for a number of reasons:

1. We now find ourselves as the only superpower. Historically, that tends to mean that there's only one place to go, and that's down. People tend to aim at you, they want to compete with you. You tend to get a little bit complacent, and if you're not careful, pretty soon you're no longer the superpower.

2. In a more immediate and security-oriented way, we, of course, see new threats. We do not have the same kind of concerns of head-on, force-on-force warfare that we saw during the Cold War. We have new threats in two different forms: the state-centered form and the terrorist-centered form.

3. People aren't going to try to compete with us in the air or on the open terrain of battlefield: they're going to try to prevent us from getting into

theater, they're going to try to raise the risk of casualties, they're going to talk about urban combat strategy.

• The terrorist threat is a different kind of asymmetric capability. DoD cannot expect to have first "dibs" on national security resources anymore. For a number of reasons, we have to look at changing the way the military deals with new kinds of threats and do so as economically as possible, even though transformations are usually not cheap.

• Another reason to keep pushing for change and innovation is the computer revolution. We should see how far we can push electronics and computing because they are at a historic point in terms of how fast they're changing and the opportunities they provide.

• Those are the reasons to try to innovate, even more than we have in the past. But there are also reasons to be wary and reasons to be careful, which is the paradox of transformation.

1. We cannot afford to lose sight of all the things we're doing well today. We have an extremely well trained and extremely capable force. We must continue to emphasize, as our top priority, the need for readiness and for people to be continually reinforced.

2. Our geostrategic place in the world is remarkable. We are the superpower that no one is trying to balance against, except possibly one or two countries. So we cannot afford to lose this particular strategic situation. It is unprecedented and even more impressive than the military capabilities of the United States in technology terms.

• Our Number 1 national security asset is the men and women of the armed forces; the Number 2 asset is the global alliance system; and the Number 3 asset is our technology and the concepts that we are trying to improve by way of transformation. Transformation is actually the third priority relative to maintaining the excellence and the readiness of our armed forces and maintaining this global alliance system.

Analysis

Dr. Loren Thompson, Chief Operating Officer, The Lexington Institute

The military transformation panel heard on the second day of the 2002 Eisenhower Conference was arguably its most controversial. Four respected scholars offered distinctly different interpretations of transformation, and each expressed concerns about how the present process of accelerated change might go wrong.

Transformation is the Bush administration's preferred term for its efforts to foster fundamental change in military doctrine, organization, and culture. The concept traces its origins to efforts among military leaders and intellectuals following the collapse of communism. With the defining threat of the Cold War

gone, future military requirements were less clear than at any time since the
mid-twentieth century. Not surprisingly, there was disagreement as to the
goals the military should pursue in the early years of the new millennium and
the level of resources needed to realize those goals.

During the Clinton years, transformation came to mean two things: coping with more diverse threats and assimilating the technological benefits of the
information revolution. The new threats were said to include proliferating
weapons of mass destruction, rogue states, transnational terrorists, and countries unable to enforce internal order ("failing states"). The new technologies
most frequently cited as having military salience were digital networks, precision-guided munitions, multispectral sensors, and machine intelligence. The
military services produced a series of vision statements during the 1990s that
sought to explain how emerging technologies could enable warfighting concepts suited to dealing with new dangers.

Critics complained that these efforts were too timid, in part because military bureaucracies were reluctant to part with tradition. In 1997, a group of
outside experts called the National Defense Panel offered a counterpoint to the
Quadrennial Defense Review and called for major changes in the nation's military posture and popularized the notion of transformation.

Even before he was elected president, George W. Bush signaled his support for the proponents of military change. In a campaign speech at the Citadel
in 1999, Bush argued, "our military is still organized more for Cold War
threats than for the challenges of a new century—for Industrial Age operations
rather than Information Age battles." Bush said that, if elected, he would give
his defense secretary a broad mandate to "challenge the status quo and envision a new architecture of American defense."

Secretary Rumsfeld has done precisely that, soliciting ideas from outsiders
and repeatedly pressing the military to justify its priorities. After a year of
reflection and frequent detours, the administration released a transformation
framework focusing on six overarching goals:

• Protecting bases of operation and defeating weapons of mass destruction.

• Assuring information systems and conducting information operations.

• Projecting and sustaining U.S. forces against antiaccess threats.

• Denying enemies sanctuary through persistent surveillance, tracking,
and engagement.

• Preserving and exploiting superiority in space.

• Developing joint information architecture for warfighting, including a
common operating picture.

The administration's plans for implementing transformation borrow heavily from the thinking of pioneers such as Andrew Krepinevich and the
National Defense Panel, emphasizing joint operations, interoperability, and
rigorous experimentation to test new warfighting concepts. However, military
transformation is still in its infancy and could take many different paths,

depending on security developments, political priorities, and budgetary resources. The purpose of the transformation panel at the 2002 Eisenhower Conference was to explore which paths are likely to be most fruitful.

The Bush administration has made military transformation a central pillar of its defense posture. What began as a modest collection of ideas and initiatives in the Clinton years has now grown to embrace every facet of military endeavor. Transformational thinking pervades the strategic pronouncements of senior policymakers and the spending plans of the military services.

But like every new idea that captures the imagination of political leaders, transformation carries with it dangers and difficulties. Revolutions often descend into excess or provoke countervailing forces that generate unforeseen consequences. The potential pitfalls of new ideas are roughly proportional to the amount of change they demand, and military transformation seems to demand huge change.

There is little doubt that the military needs to change. The threats to national security today are different from those that drove defense preparations during the Cold War. New technologies really do enable new concepts of warfighting, and even if America chooses to ignore those concepts, its enemies may not. Nonetheless, it is important to recognize the many ways in which transformation might go wrong and to be prepared for a quick shift in direction.

First of all, transformation is about the future, and the future is not knowable, as most of the participants on the conference panel pointed out. There may have been a time during the Middle Ages when social and economic stagnation made the next generation of warfare easy to anticipate, but today all the forces shaping future conflict are highly dynamic. The risk associated with any particular course of action—the risk of getting it wrong, as General Dubik put it—is fairly high. Arguing for a "capabilities-based" rather than a "threat-based" approach to military preparations doesn't help much with this problem because capabilities are the fastest-changing feature of the geopolitical landscape.

Second, the revolutionary warfighting potential of information technologies is substantially devalued by the likelihood that future adversaries will possess many of the same tools. Even those enemies who do not possess them may understand emerging technologies well enough to defeat or circumvent them. When Pakistani authorities apprehended a key member of the al Qaeda terrorist organization in October 2002, they found him surrounded in his apartment by three satellite telephones and five laptop computers linked to the Internet. U.S. warfighters must understand the full potential of such tools, but it would be a profound error to assume that only Americans will have cutting-edge technology in the future.

Third, the emerging technologies that drive military transformation are not simply tools for enhanced warfighting; they are also potential sources of vulnerability. Anytime a military force becomes heavily dependent upon a particular technology—be it digital networks or satellite guidance or machine intelligence—it is critical for that force to understand all the potential consequences of such dependency. A senior admiral recently conceded that once the Navy adapts its doctrine and organization to network-centric warfare, loss of access to the network could actually make the Navy more vulnerable than it is today. That is a danger the military services have barely begun to think through.

Finally is the matter of opportunity costs. Much of the funding for transformation will be generated by cutting existing programs, including those intended to modernize the military's Cold War arsenal. However, that arsenal is now growing decrepit with age and overuse, raising doubts about whether capabilities can be maintained during the transition to next-generation warfare. When proponents of transformation first raised the possibility of taking near-term risks to leap ahead in capability, the world looked a good deal less threatening than it now does. Policymakers will need to be mindful of the opportunity costs that transformation imposes on current-generation warfighters, particularly if they involve further deferral of long-delayed modernization plans.

Despite the potential problems with transformation, it is hard to escape the conclusion that some such process was required to shake the military services out of their post–Cold War lethargy. While the armed forces have not descended into the bureaucratic insularity David Johnson described in his discussion of the interwar Army, there is plenty of evidence that external pressure was required to encourage greater imagination. If the material and doctrinal benefits of military transformation ultimately prove to be modest, that will not change the fact that it was a concept worth exploring fully at a time of unprecedented global ferment.

Transcript

BACKSTAGE ANNOUCNCER: Ladies and gentlemen, Dr. Daniel Goure.

DR. DANIEL GOURE: Ladies and gentlemen, I have the distinct honor, privilege, and, for myself, a unique experience so far in the year and a half of working with Dr. Loren Thompson, my colleague at Lexington Institute, to introduce him to this forum as the Chair of this panel. One of the reasons that he was selected is that Dr. Thompson has been at the leading edge of the current debate on transformation. He comes to us with a wealth of experience from all perspectives—years in academia, in defense consulting, and in the think-tank world. One of the reasons he has been so successful in energizing the debate on transformation is that he looks at it not simply from the point of view of a single service, not simply from a particular kind of conflict, and not simply from the level of the military forces themselves. His vision spans the range of sectors in which transformation is occurring or must occur—all the way from the defense industrial sector, which is really civil-industrial based, that will support transformation, through the military forces that will be both the beneficiaries and the embodiment of transformation. His vision continues into the policy community, which must understand the nature of that force that is transformed or transforming, how to use it, and perhaps, in some cases at least, how not to use it. He is a friend, a colleague, a distinguished scholar. Ladies and gentlemen, Dr. Loren Thompson.

DR. LOREN B. THOMPSON: Thank you, Dr. Goure. We call Dan Dr. Gourmet around the office because he only imbibes the finest wines from the vineyards of ideas. I'd like to believe that someday I will understand these things as well as he does, but I know I'm never going to understand this as well as he does. He just has too good a mind, and he's been reading for too long.

Every new administration tries to find some word or phrase that captures the essence of its security posture. Presidents know that if they don't come up with their own phrase, they'll get tagged with one by the media that will probably be a good deal less congenial. When President Eisenhower first entered office 50 years ago, he developed a national security posture that relied more on air power and on atomic weapons. He wanted to call it the New Look, but critics called it massive retaliation, and that's the phrase that stuck.

The Bush administration's preferred term for its efforts is transformation, which is understood to mean a wholesale reorganization of policy and priorities in response to emerging threats. Mr. Bush first used that concept, the term transformation, in a speech almost exactly three years ago at the Citadel in which he set forth his priorities if he were elected president in terms of preparing the nation for future security challenges. Since that time, the word transformation has been woven into almost every one of his major security pronouncements. In the new national security strategy released last week, for example, the term transformation was used in a number of different ways to describe federal government reorganization and response to the terrorist threat and to describe military modernization in response to the information revolution. It was even used to describe changes in our policies toward India. Therein lies the problem. Many people use this term in many different ways. It's similar to the use of the word paradigm, which academics once discovered was being used 22 different ways in a single article.

Pentagon transformation guru Admiral Arthur Cebrowski says that, simply, transformation is the application of information technologies to the conduct of warfare. But if you've paid any attention to this debate, you know that for some people, it means a good deal more. It means changes in doctrine, in organization, in business practice, and in culture. The purpose of this morning's panel is to discuss what transformation has meant in the past and what it may mean for our current preparations as we enter a new millennium. We have four respected experts with us to explore and debate the meaning of transformation.

First is Hans Binnendijk, Theodore Roosevelt Chair and Director of the Center for Technology and National Security Policy at the National Defense University. He previously served on the National Security Council as Special Assistant to the President and Senior Director for Defense Policy and Arms Control. Over the course of a distinguished career, Hans has served as principal deputy director of the State Department's principal planning staff, Deputy Director of the International Institute for Strategic Studies, and Director of the Institute for the Study of Diplomacy at Georgetown University.

Major General James M. Dubik is director of Joint Experimentation at the U.S. Joint Forces Command, a key position in which many of the concepts we hear regarding transformation are actually put to practical test. General Dubik has served in command roles in overseas operations ranging from Bosnia to Haiti, has occupied senior positions on the Army Staff, and has commanded a number of operational units, including the 25th Infantry Division. He also has a list of academic credentials that would put most professors to shame, having successfully completed programs at Johns Hopkins University, Harvard University's Kennedy School of Government, Syracuse University's Maxwell School of Public Affairs, and MIT.

Dr. David Johnson is a senior policy analyst with the RAND Corporation in Washington, focusing primarily on military transformation, technology, training, and doctrine. He is the author of numerous well-received books and studies, including most notably Fat Tanks and Heavy Bombers, Innovation in the U.S. Army, 1917 to 1945, which is published by Cornell University Press. Dr. Johnson holds a doctorate from Duke University and is considered to be one of the leading academic experts on the revolution in military affairs.

Finally, Michael O'Hanlon is a senior fellow at the Brookings Institution, where he specializes in defense strategy and budgeting, military technology, and regional security. Dr. O'Hanlon has published many authoritative studies on security issues, including most recently, Technological Change and the Future of Warfare, which assesses a thesis that a revolution in military affairs is currently unfolding. He holds a doctorate from Princeton University and other degrees in the physical sciences from Princeton—it's kind of a novel idea for a public commentator in transformation to have some grounding in the physical sciences—and he is a member on both the Council on Foreign Relations and the International Institute for Strategic Studies. Please welcome our panel.

DR. THOMPSON: Why don't we begin? Why don't we just do it in alphabetical order and begin with Dr. Binnendijk.

DR. HANS BINNENDIJK: Well, it is a real pleasure for me to be with you here today. What I thought I would try to contribute to the proceedings is first a couple of quick lessons from history, then a notion of how transformation has evolved over the last quarter of a century. I actually believe that transformation is a process that has been under way for some time. I will then take a look at the current process—where the services are. I have some particular comments about the Army and its transformation process and then a couple of cautionary notes. However, let me begin by adding to the voluminous list of definitions of transformation. We did a search the other day and found at least a dozen official definitions. So I tend to look at transformation as the process of creating and harnessing a revolution in military affairs. With that in mind, it's useful to look at previous revolutions in military affairs.

Dr. Binnendijk

If you look back at, say, the last 700 years, you can find at least a dozen of them. We don't have time to go through all of them, but it is useful to note that they take place on the average of once every 50 to 60 years. They all have three elements in common. There is a fundamental change in the underlying technology, there are new operational concepts that are designed to take that technology and use it on the battlefield, and then there are organizational changes that are introduced in order to implement those new concepts. There is generally a new theory of war that accompanies these changes, and there is often an emphasis on combined arms. The technology that comes from these—that fuels these revolutions in military affairs—often comes from the commercial sector, but not always. Recent examples are nuclear weapons and stealth. For example, look at the artillery revolution of about 500 years ago; the basic technology there came from new designs of casting bells. The Napoleonic revolution really was fueled by the Industrial Revolution. The same thing is true for the revolution that took place between World Wars I and II. Again, the technology came primarily from the commercial sector, and that's what we find in this current process.

Much of the technology is coming from the information technology arena. That means that these revolutions in military affairs are available to others, as well, and the leads that we develop may not be long lasting, so we need to keep that in mind. Historically, these revolutions in military affairs have had a powerful impact not just on the battlefield, and we can list a whole series of different battles from Crecy and Agincourt to Blitzkrieg, but what I find perhaps even more interesting is the effect that they have had on society as a result of the impact they've had on the battlefield.

One can look to the stirrup. Some historians will trace feudalism to the development of the stirrup. The artillery revolution leads, some argue, to the end of feudalism. The development of large ships in the 1500s with cannon aboard leads to colonialism. The Napoleonic revolution and the mass conscription leads to modern nationalism. The revolution in the mid-1800s that we experienced during the Civil War really led to defensive warfare. By the end of the Civil War, we were in trenches, and we stayed there through World War I.

The interwar revolution between World Wars I and II got us out of the defense and back into the offense. So this phenomenon is powerful not just on the battlefield but more broadly in society. These revolutions often allow small forces to win over large forces. That's certainly true in the case of the Swedes around 1700. It's true of the Israelis, but by and large if you look back, the results of these revolutions in military affairs are not cost savings. You end up with more expensive and larger militaries. Mistakes have been made. In many ways, the nuclear revolution—look back to about 1950–55 as we put tactical battlefield nuclear weapons throughout the inventory. That was clearly, in retrospect, a mistake, once it was concluded that we couldn't use these things in most cases and we had to go back. That's part of the military that fought the Vietnam War. So mistakes can be made. We also find that even with battlefield successes. Look at Napoleon and Hitler; they had revolutions in military affairs that led to success on the battlefield, but they overextended themselves. Therefore, it is not a panacea.

Now, let's look at the current revolution in military affairs. In my view, we can trace this back to the end of the Vietnam War when our military began to figure out what went wrong in that war and to reorganize itself and to make use of the new technologies. DESERT STORM clearly had elements of the revolution in military affairs already present. Stealth technology, precision strike, enhanced command and control, night vision, a new tank with a stabilized gun, speed, laser range finders, cruise missiles were available. So, a lot of the technology was already available about 1990–91. What we didn't have at that time was some new operational concepts. We still fought DESERT STORM in a fairly traditional fashion. But if you look forward to the 1990s and Kosovo, you already see elements of effects-based operations in Kosovo and even more so in Afghanistan.

In the mid-1990s, a key document in the transformation process was *Joint Vision 2010*—General Shalikashvili. This was really a product of Bill Owens and Wes Clark and sort of a compromise that emerged in *Joint Vision 2010*, but in that vision you have the heart of transformational thinking, which is to mass

fire, rather than to mass mass. You don't use tanks in the same way in the battlefield. You have much more reliance on inorganic firepower. Therefore,
already you can look back to Joint Vision 2010 and see the very basics of it
there.

Now, what happened in the last seven or eight years to begin to change
this? First, we have had a number of shifts in the nature of the mission from
two major theater wars to a conflict in Bosnia and more of an emphasis on
smaller-scale contingencies. A couple of years ago we had a new focus on
China as the potential enemy. Very quickly we moved to a war on terrorism.
Now we've almost come full circle when we're talking about Iraq. We're back
to the major theater war notion. That requires agility, and agility has become
a key element of thinking in the transformation process. We've also had, in the
last six or seven years, a new emphasis on anti-access and area denial problems, where a potential enemy, in fact, has access to a lot of this new technology. We've also had an emphasis on reducing casualties and on getting to the
battlefield rapidly. So all of that translates into the need for small network plat-
forms, more emphasis on robotics, more thinking about swarming techniques.

Third, we have seen an improvement in computers and computer networks. We have seen an improvement in the ability of almost everyone now to
use this technology. That has led to network-centric warfare. We have had
some improvements in precision strike, not necessarily the accuracy, but with
JDAMs we now have much cheaper versions of these systems that can give us
precision strike, and they are plentiful with the advent of the small-diameter
bomb. We can begin to rely more on inorganic firepower. So, these are some
of the changes that have taken place over the last four or five years to begin to
shape the transformation process.

Now, as was indicated earlier, this became an element in the last presidential election at the Citadel when candidate Bush came in. We had the
strategic review, which was quite disruptive back in the spring of last year. The
QDR tended to settle things down, but now we have a transformation czar, a
transformation budget, and things are on track. So, let me talk a little bit about
how the process is now being implemented and let me say, first, that this is
very much, at this point, a service-driven process. The joint element is just
now coming into play. I'll spend most of my time on the Army.

The Army, in my view, has recognized the nature of its problem. There is
a gap. It's clearly stated in the Army road map. It has to do with becoming
more expeditionary—getting to the battlefield more quickly. To deal with that,
the Army has taken a fairly radical approach to transformation, much more so
than the other services. The approach has been very comprehensive, if you
look at the road map. It sets out clear priorities. Budgets are attached to each
of those priorities. In that sense, the Army is on a reasonable trajectory; however, some real risks have to be addressed. They relate, in part, to resources.
In my view, the Army's process is tremendously under resourced. The Army

comes up quite short when you compare what is going to be spent on procurement and R&D in the Army to the other services. That, in turn, creates risks.

First, the legacy force, which is what we have to fight with today and it's also the hedge. Very little is being spent today on research and development to improve the legacy force. If you go around and talk to the Army research labs, as I have done in the last six months, 95 percent of the spending is on the objective force, and very little is going into improving the legacy force. In my view, that's a problem, and it creates risks.

Secondly, the interim force—the Striker brigades—the risk there in my view is that these brigades do not have sufficient combat power for demanding offensive missions. They were not intended for that purpose, but the problem is that this is now the element of the Army force that is able to be forward-deployed quickly because it fits in a C-130 with an inch or two to spare. Therefore, this is the force most likely to be inserted quickly, and it may well be put in a position where it is faced with high-intensity conflict, even though it is not designed for that purpose. Therefore, I see a risk here.

Finally, the objective force—the risk here is technology. I'll touch on three or four elements of technology. This is all being worked on by the Army research labs and others, but if you talk to them, they will tell you that these are very hard propositions to deal with. You need a new network architecture to take the network and put it on the move. That's hard to do. With no land lines, you need to develop better armor for this 18- to 20-ton future combat system. You need to put a lethal gun on it that doesn't affect this light vehicle, and you need to maintain the lethality, and that is a very difficult proposition. You have a much greater reliance on sensors, anti-mine sensors, for example. That is a difficult proposition. So there is real technological risk in the future combat system, and we need to hedge very heavily, it seems to me, against the proposition that it may not be there.

In addition, if you look at organizational change in the Army, there are some proposed organizational changes and more are being considered, but the Army needs to think more boldly about organizational change. I also have a concern that there are essentially two transformations under way. There is the Army's transformation to the instrument objective force, and then Secretary Rumsfeld has his own view of Army transformation. So, if you combine these two transformations, you have the Army transformation replacing the Abrams and the Bradley, and you have the Rumsfeld transformation replacing Crusader and maybe Comanche. What's left?

What's left is a future combat system, and I've just gone through some of the technical problems that need to be solved in order to deliver that. The Army needs to think about the risks that it's taking. Again, I salute the Army for its bold thinking, but it needs a Plan B, in case the technology doesn't prove out.

I'll touch very briefly on the Navy and Air Force. The Navy and Air Force are working very well together, and that is clear in their road map. They have come up with a number of new concepts: force net, expeditionary strike groups, C shield, C strike, C trial, C basing—there's a common theme here you can see. The key Navy problem is that it has to figure out how to budget for everything it wants to do. The Air Force, similarly, has a very strong road map that it's put forward, with six transformational goals tied to seven operational concepts, specific technological needs, and capabilities.

So all three of the services really have done a pretty good job in developing their road maps and have moved the process forward. However, I think the Air Force has two problems. One, it's not focusing enough on the seams between what it delivers for ground forces, which includes lift, mobility, space assets, and close air support. If you look at the Air Force, it is basically talking about what it does on its own. It needs to think much more about what it does for other services. The Air Force plan is basically unaffordable at this point, even though we're going to be spending more on the Air Force than any of the other services. So, it has to pull back a little bit.

The next step in this process is to make it joint, and this is what you're going to be focusing on. We have to close the gaps and work at the seams of what the services are doing. We need to focus on the C^4ISR problem. Everybody agrees that this is the key to transformation, but there is not enough top-down direction being given, in my view, to how we do this so that we have true interoperability in this area. We need to develop better joint operating concepts. Each of the services has its own now. The Army has rapid and decisive operations, much as the Navy has network-centric warfare. The Air Force has effects-based operations. What we need to do now is to combine these and come up with a unifying theory. The Joint Staff is working on that as we speak. The key to this also, in my view—and this is a segue, perhaps, to the general's presentation—is joint experimentation. I believe in the first rule of wing walking. You don't let go with one hand until you have a firm grasp with the other hand, and the way you do that in the transformation business is joint experimentation, so this is key to the process. I'll just note that this is under way.

Lastly, let me make two quick points. First, as we think about transformation, it has to be broadly based. We can't think only about what is at the heart of it—in my view, air-ground operations—but we have to think about things like focused logistics. We also have to think about the acquisition process and spiral development and how to improve these processes to deliver to the core. We have to think about transformation in the interagency context, even with NGOs. We can perhaps win the war militarily, but we can't win the peace militarily; therefore, we have to bring these agencies in. I would also commend to you the PDT 56 process, which was developed in another context, but it provides a way of thinking about transformation here. However, we have to broaden it to include the allies. We have seen some real progress in this area in the last day or two, with the NATO response force and with the NATO defense ministers having accepted that. Therefore, if we don't transform NATO as we transform ourselves, we will destroy NATO by developing gaps that will destroy its basic underpinning.

There are some dangers here that we have to be aware of. I've talked about some of the risks already in the service process. We have to fight the notion that if something is not transformational, it's no good. The notion now is that everything is transformational because if it's not, it isn't funded, and that's a dangerous notion. We have to pay more attention to information technology vulnerability, which is at the heart of the transformation process. Yet we have some real vulnerabilities to EMP, to jamming, to hacking. We have to spend a lot of time on information assurance. We have to be careful not to overemphasize the strength that transformation gives us. I would ask you to think about the Vietnam War. If we had to fight the Vietnam War with a transformed force—the one we are envisioning—but we had to fight it under the same ground rules and the same terrain, with the same political and diplomatic constraints, would we win? It's not at all clear to me that we would. So we have to keep in mind the limitations to this process.

Finally, the obverse to that point is that as we begin to be able to win fairly easily with few casualties in places like Afghanistan and Kosovo, we don't want war to become the chosen instrument of American diplomacy. It should be an important arrow in the quiver, but it's not the first one you want to reach for. As transformation becomes successful, and it will, we have to make sure that we don't reach for that military arrow too quickly. Thank you.

DR. THOMPSON: General Dubik.

MAJOR GENERAL JAMES M. DUBIK: Thanks. Well, that's a good segue, and actually, the panel is well-placed in terms of the two-day program in that military transformation is well understood as part of a larger context of transformation that's going on. Yesterday several speakers pointed this out. We are, to say it mildly, in a new strategic environment. We in uniform have been asked to do a range of military operations, and that range is relatively complex: from one end to be solved in a high-tech way, to the other end in very low-tech way, where physical mass and physical presence still count. In one operation there might be some aspects that admit to very technical solutions and others that absolutely do not admit to technical solutions.

So the new strategic environment we find ourselves in is an important thing to keep in mind as we talk about how we transform ourselves and also the globalization and hypercompetition, which is another part of the context in which we have to operate, and last, the Information Age and the tools that the Information Age makes available to us as practitioners.

We've seen the impact of these three major trends, the Information Age trend, the globalization trend, and the emergence of whatever will be the new political order strategic environment after the Cold War. We see the impact of these on our social systems and organizations, our political systems and organizations, our fiscal systems, our economic systems, our corporate systems. There should be no surprise that these are going to have, and have had, major impact on our military systems and organizations and procedures. As Hans said, the services have all tried to come to grips with this over the last X number of years. Now it's the joint services' turn to come to grips with this because there's an important aspect on joint warfighting as well.

General Dubik

One of the difficulties in transformation from a practitioner's standpoint is that the past is not always a guide to our future. As practitioners, all of us in uniform are very adept at linear projection of our past into the future. That's not a very good guide in many cases right now. Now, our reasoning process is not, "How did it work in the past and how can we project it into the future?" but "How do we change to adapt to a new future?" It's an entirely different reasoning process, and that's a big challenge for us. How we structured our problems, how we decided upon solutions, how we acted in the past are not always reliable. I'm not saying they're never reliable—I'm choosing my words carefully here—they're just not always a reliable guide for our future.

When you visit—whether it's services or any component underneath a service—you'll see a chart or two saying, "We're moving from" and a list of places "to" and a list of things. At a time like this, when there's so much shifting from/to, it's how much you can learn and adapt that comes to the fore, rather than how much you know and used before. These are, for practitioners, major shifts in how we have to solve our problems. Now, where is the environment and where are the new tools taking us as a set of professionals? I'll use what I hope to be one of few buzzwords—full spectrum dominance. We're going to be asked to fight, we have been asked to fight and win war in all its varieties; not war as defined as conventional combat, but war in all its varieties. We've been asked to use force to compel adversaries to do our will. That's the definition of war. Our aim in every case here is to try to end this as quickly as possible on terms friendly to the U.S. and its allies. Or, if we can't end the conflict quickly, we strive to end the initial operations in such a way to as to set up for success in a longer campaign—an aspect of fighting that we can't lose track of.

Not every conflict will admit to a rapid, decisive conclusion. We may have a rapid, decisive conclusion of the initial operation, but we will have to follow up with other operations. We're also going to try to provide more options, or have been asked to provide more options to military leaders—something all of our predecessors have had to do. Now we're asked to do the same thing. We'll have to build our teams quickly—our joint, combined, interagency teams—without being ad hoc. The way we formed joint task forces in the past worked very well, but the kind of quick operations that we may have to execute now, we want to diminish the ad hoc aspect of it and increase the stable side.

As I implied, they're not just joint but also combined interagency operations where, right from the start, at the operational level, each of us can plan and prepare our operations together in a collaborative way, and then execute them in a relatively seamless way—where each service uses the forces and combat power of the other services at the point of battle—at the tactical level where we close with and destroy the enemy, at the operational level where we try to decide how to use tactical operations to attain strategic means, and at the strategic level, where we want to make sure that our use of the military element of power is in concert with the other elements of national power and the other elements of a coalition.

What we're talking about here from the joint level, and in many aspects in the services, is new professional, technical knowledge. Our profession has to come to grips with new aspects. Many professions in the past, not just military, have had to do this as technology or other items have forced them to change. We're now in that position. We have new technical military professional knowledge. We have to turn around, understand, operationalize, and educate ourselves about that.

Now, some important guiding principles on transformation. The first—as much as we would like to get it right—we should understand that the real operating principle is, "Don't get it too wrong." The future is still the future. None of us can predict it. What we produce now, in 25 years another set of leaders is going to have to use; and in 50 years, another set of leaders. Our challenge is to not get it too far off and to produce a set of leaders who are adaptive enough to use what we've given them in a new set of circumstances. It's through the leadership and their way of thinking that transformation will provide its greatest benefit to our nation and to the world; it's through leaders who can adapt to something that none of us can predict.

The second guiding principle is that while material solutions are very important, they are not as important as the training portions of transformation, the organization portions, the leader development portions, and the doctrine portions. It's not having technology that wins wars. It's using technology better than your opponent that wins wars. Using technology means you train correctly, you develop your leaders correctly, you're organized correctly, and your doctrine is better than your opponents'.

Third, especially in the joint area, but true of all the services and especially in light of Hans's comments, our transformation must be much more inclusive—inclusive of each of our regional combatant commanders; inclusive of all the services; inclusive of our allies, or potential allies, or coalition partners; and inclusive of interagency operations, as well as nongovernment organizations and private organizations in operations all over the world. This will be a very difficult challenge, but as we build to our future, it's the inclusive process, as difficult as that may be, that will be very important to us.

Last, in terms of a guiding principle, concepts and ideas should drive materiel, not the other way around. It's a tension, I understand that. It's not either-or. You want to glean good ideas that come from materiel solutions, but you also want the materiel solutions to respond to how we want to fight the concept side. Joint Forces Command—I'm not going to pretend that I have a whole lot of experience there since I've been in the job just one month, but we're on a two-path strategy here for the next several years. One path is to take the joint capstone concepts that the Joint Staff is working on right now—as well as the functional concepts and integrating concepts that will result from them—on a pathway for significant experimentation for the next couple of years. That will include our multinational partners and interagency partners, as well as the services. The second path is to take some of the concepts worked in Millennium Challenge—that finished a few months ago—and refine those: expand effects-based operations beyond their initial offering; expand a concept called Operational Net Assessment that takes intelligence preparation of the battlefield to the next level; field a collaborative information environment so that we can plan, prepare, and execute in a collaborative way throughout the joint force; and refine the joint interagency work so that we can use the military aspect of power with the other elements of national power. These two pathways will be worked collaboratively, and these two pathways will work in a continuous experimentation environment.

In conclusion, I'll just say that, in my opinion, we're all making history—those in uniform and not in uniform—people associated with the transformation. Unlike writing about history, making history is messy, it's hard, it's risk-laden, and none of it is free. When you make history, it's like going west; you have two aspects with you in your pocket all the time—high excitement and high anxiety—and you can't get rid of either of them when you're transforming. When the wagons went west, everyone was excited and anxious. For my part, I say, "Westward ho." Let's get it on.

DR. THOMPSON: Dr. Johnson.

Dr. Johnson

DR. DAVID JOHNSON: Thank you. As an historian, I'm going to make sure we're going west. That's my challenge. The topic of my talk this morning is "Whither the American Blitzkrieg: Transformation Insights from the Interwar U.S. Army," and the title reflects my belief that the American Army never developed an equivalent of the transformation of the German blitzkrieg in the years between the two world wars. By blitzkrieg, I mean the joint capability derived from combining ground-mechanizing maneuver and air power. I'll also try to draw some insights from that era that are relevant for today's military, particularly in its transformation efforts, because I believe the effects of the interwar era and World War II still resonate in our service cultures and that they reward our ability to create a truly joint force. I must note that this talk reflects my personal views, not necessarily those of RAND or any of its sponsors. I'll begin with a discussion of the U.S. Army's experience during World War I and then move to an assessment of the interwar development of tanks and airplanes and the concept for their use and how they fared in World War II. I'll conclude with my thoughts about what I think it all means.

World War I was a seminal experience for the American Army. It was the first major war off our shores. The most important lesson the Army's leaders took from the war was that manpower and industrial mobilization were the keys to success in modern warfare. In the words of then-Army Chief of Staff Peyton March, the Great War "was not won by some new and terrible development of modern science. It was won as every other war in history, by men, munitions, and morale." Thus, the Army believed it needed a much larger peacetime establishment and adjustments to its structure. Also, two new technologies confronted the American Army in the aftermath of the war—the tank and the airplane. They, like everybody else that moved from the Western Front back to their capitals would have to contend with both of these over the next 20 years.

The Army's wartime experiences would frame the early decision about these weapons. In the case of tanks, the American experience in the Great War was quite limited. In the closing days of the war, Colonel George Patton led the only American tank brigade during the battle of St. Mihiel and the Meuse-Argonne Offensive. His slow, mechanically unreliable French Renault tanks fought in an infantry support role. Thus, at the end of the war, the widely held view in the American Army was that tanks were infantry support weapons. As with tanks, the vast majority of aircraft were supplied to the Americans by the British and the French.

Radically different from the tank experience, however, was the astonishing and very visible progress aviation technology made during the war. From flimsy scout planes to sophisticated fighters and long-range bombers, aviation also made a significant contribution to operations, adding a third dimension to warfare. Consequently, the interwar discussion about the future of military aviation was much broader and more informed by combat experience than was the debate about the tank. Indeed, advocates envisioned air power as the decisive weapon of the future—one not wedded to the ground battle. Others, principally ground officers, had a more conservative view and saw aviation as simply long-range artillery. I would submit that these differing views soon ignited a controversy that is still not fully resolved to this day.

The context for the interwar is also important. The Army brought its postwar plans to a Congress that was in a mood to economize, and the absence of any threat after "the war to end all wars" didn't believe the Army needed to be expanded greatly. The Army wanted 500,000 men. Congress authorized 250,000 and appropriated funds for less than 150,000 till just before World War II. The tank corps was abolished—with very little controversy, I might add—and tanks were moved into the infantry, although the cavalry eventually got a chance to play with the new technology in the 1930s. Additionally, Congress established the air service after scotching an attempt by air power advocates to establish an independent, international Department Of Aeronautics.

The Army also created combat arms chiefs with major generals at their heads to strengthen the voice of the line in the War Department. What soon evolved was a very decentralized program with powerful and parochial branch chiefs jealously guarding their authority over doctrine, personnel, and materiel. In the aftermath of the act, the Army largely focused its appropriation on maintaining its manpower and filling out its skeletal structure, often at the expense of R&D. The exception was the Army's air component, which fixated on development of technology and a concept that could realize claims that air power could be decisive and thus justify an independent Air Force. Consequently, there was a much greater affinity in the air arm for R&D, indeed, which was supported by Congress and private industry, largely because of its obvious dual-use potential.

Turning now to tanks, it's not surprising that the infantry, once in charge of technology, focused on making the tank the ultimate infantry support weapon. Indeed, the 1922 War Department directive concerning tank development specified, "the priority mission of the tank is to facilitate the uninterrupted advance of riflemen in the attack" and that any future tanks "must operate efficiently at the pace of walking infantrymen." The War Department, however, complicated R&D efforts when they placed a crucial constraint on any future tanks—they could not weigh more than 15 tons. This limit was dictated because 15 tons was the weight capacity of the divisional pontoon bridge, and the chief of engineers who was in charge of this technology refused to change the bridge requirement. Consequently, when the infantry specified the characteristics it wanted in tank mobility, lethality, and survivability, the ordnance department could not meet them within the 15-ton limit.

In the area of operational concepts, successive chiefs of infantry were ruthless in enforcing the branch orthodoxy that tanks existed only to support infantry. They repressed or chased away officers with different views about tanks—officers like Dwight Eisenhower and George Patton, who were both experienced tank officers—were foolish enough to advocate independent tank operations. After a chastening by the chief of infantry, Eisenhower quit tanks, never to return. Patton soon followed suit and returned to the cavalry where he spent the next 20 years extolling the virtues of horse cavalry and designing the last cavalry saber.

In the 1930s, the cavalry also began to develop tanks, calling them combat cars because the infantry owned all the tanks. The growing group of cavalrymen embraced mechanization in this cultural impediment, where they wanted them to be light, fast, iron horses that were going to support traditional cavalry missions. Unfortunately for cavalry mechanization efforts, the chief of cavalry determined where his budget went and in a zero-sum resource environment, most refused to give up horse cavalry structure to further mechanization. As a consequence, the Army had only one mechanized cavalry brigade in 1940. No cavalryman was more convinced of the utility of horses in war than the last chief, Major General John Herr, who I sometimes think was born so I could write about him. He proposed to transform his branch by giving horses strategic mobility. The concept was to load them on tractor-trailers, drive them to battlefields, unload them, and their tactical prowess could finally be realized. Herr's favorite saying was, "When better roller skates are made, cavalry horses will wear them."

What's alarming is his inability to grasp the realities of modern warfare, which became blatantly apparent during the meeting he had with George C. Marshall in 1942—a meeting that took place after the fall of Poland, France, and much of the rest of Europe to the Nazi blitzkrieg. Herr pleaded with Marshall, "In the interest of national defense in this crisis, I urge upon you the necessity of an immediate increase in horse cavalry." As you'll recall, this was Herr's last meeting with Marshall.

In 1940, the Army belatedly formed an armored force over the objections of the chiefs of infantry and cavalry, who argued that by law, tanks belonged to them. The armored force, dominated by cavalrymen, became a captive of mechanized cavalry doctrine. Consequently, it focused on exploitation and penetration missions and paid little attention to combined arms or air support. There wasn't much concern the Army and American tanks would eventually confront other tanks because lightly armored fast tank destroyers with heavy guns championed by probably the most powerful man in the Army, General Leslie J. McNair, would take care of any tank threats. Finally, Army Regulation 850-15 limited tanks to 30 tons in weight, an increase from 15, with the understandable goal of facilitating their deployment to theaters of war. This restriction was in effect until late 1944. Unfortunately, as one Army ordinance specialist pointed out, "Hitler's tanks violated this American rule."

The story of the airplane in the Army was much different than that of the tank. Billy Mitchell widely publicized the idea of air power when he sank a number of ships in the 1920s with bombers. Mitchell proclaimed that the days of armies and navies were over. He was eventually taken to task and, I might add, trial by the War Department. As a result, he became a martyr to the cause of air power. More importantly, however, Mitchell empowered a generation of air officers to transfer their loyalty from the Army to the idea of an independent air arm and to conduct an insurgency to that end within the Army.

By the 1930s, the Air Corps developed a strategic bombing concept designed to prove the proposition that air power could be decisive by itself. That doctrine, based on untested assumptions, became a dogma: to maintain that daylight, high-altitude, unescorted bomber formations would always get to the target with acceptable losses; to conduct precision bombing against the vital nodes of an enemy's industrial web; thus, air power could destroy an enemy's ability to wage war. In short, air power could win a war independently. Not surprisingly, in the opinion of air power advocates, such an Air Force had to be under the control of air officers to be effective. This focus on strategic bombing became the Air Corps' orthodoxy, and those with other ideas, like Claire Chenault, were marginalized.

Before moving on, I feel obligated to note in passing that the Navy also had its transformation issues. They're epitomized in my mind by the caption accompanying the picture of the battleship U.S.S. Arizona from the November 29, 1941, Army-Navy football game program. The text accompanying the picture reads, "A bow on view the USS *Arizona* as she plows into a huge swell. It is significant that despite the claims of air enthusiasts, no battleship has yet been sunk by bombs." A little over a week later, after this Army-Navy game, Japanese air enthusiasts sank the Arizona at Pearl Harbor.

I turn now to wartime consequences of the decisions made by the interwar Army and its officers about tanks and airplanes. Before doing so, however, I want to spend a moment on what the Army had to do to get itself in a position where it could prosecute a war. In 1942, General George Marshall used an executive order to reorganize the war development in the ground, air, and service forces. Gone were the branch chiefs, and many senior officers were forced to retire. Quite simply, the structure of many of the leaders that had nurtured the Army between the wars were not up to the task of taking it to war. Additionally, George Marshall sanctioned a strategy that called for the Army to conduct two wars: one in the air, and one on the ground. I now turn to how American tankers and airmen fared in the unforgiving crucible of World War II.

American tankers paid a heavy price for the Army's decisions about tank weight and doctrine. American armored vehicles were clearly outclassed by the much more lethal and survivable German Panthers. American Shermans had to maneuver for flank and close-in rear shots to take out German Panthers and Tigers, while the Nazi tanks could take out Shermans and American tank destroyers head on at 2,000 meters. American tanks, contrary to Army doctrine, had to fight German tanks, and they did so at great disadvantage and heavy cost. Omar Bradley's 12th Army Group alone lost over 4,000 tanks between D–Day and the end of the war in May of the next year. But evolving in Europe was a war of attrition with overwhelming air and artillery support making up for the shortcomings of American armor. Close air support techniques, however, had to be worked out in theaters of war by those fighting and dying because they had not been developed by the War Department. The Air Force doctrine of unescorted daylight strategic bombing came to an end in October 1943. The Luftwaffe realized that this was a mechanical problem. They used airplanes that could fly as fast as B–17s and B–24s, but they carried standoff weapons like cannons, rockets, or bombs to attack the bomber formations with impunity from outside the range of their .50-caliber machine guns. These slow-flying German aircraft could do this because there were no American escort fighters to contend with. Bomber losses became too heavy to endure. In 10 days in October, the 8th Air Force lost 164 bombers. Losses among bomber crews trying to finish 25 missions were nearly 70 percent at this time in the war. Missions into Germany were suspended until drop tanks could be fielded for the P–47 and P–51 fighter planes, allowing an escort bomber formation for the duration of all their missions.

Finally, and this is a statistic that alarmed me more any when I read it: The Army Air Forces lost over 54,000 airmen in the war, as compared with 19,600 Marines. This gets us to the question of why there was no American blitzkrieg in 1944, even after the Army had several years to observe an obviously successful German model. My view is that the tank was the captive of conservative branches that tried to adapt it to their parochial interests, or worse, as in the case of the last chief of cavalry, who actually thwarted its development to protect horses. Furthermore, American tank forces were retarded by arbitrary weight limitations, first 15 tons, then 30, until 1944—this, despite the fact that it was known that the Germans were designing more survivable and lethal and, thus heavier tanks by 1942. The airplane on the other hand became a tool in the quest for independence by air power insurgents bent on freeing themselves from the conservative ground Army and unwilling to cede control of the air weapon in any form to ground officers. Thus, an interwar institutional approach to ground combined arms and air support that joined us at the heart of the blitzkrieg was never demanded or developed.

Finally, and perhaps most disturbingly, both ground and air components of the Army demanded loyalty from their officers, and silences within the other viewers. There was no debate about alternative concepts or futures. This leads me to conclude that, given the environment in which the tank and the airplane were developed in the interwar Army, it would have been very surprising if an American version of the blitzkrieg had been developed.

I want to turn briefly to the question of "so what?" I do believe that the interwar Army experience offers insights about innovation and transformation. First, during periods of relatively low threats to national survival, the services and their branches tend to focus on internal imperatives. They try to highlight their particular contribution to the national defense and in their quest for greater budget and mission share. Thus, innovation happens on the margins, and the leadership is generally more prone to enforce orthodoxy—practical technologies of those that don't collide with the institution's views about warfare. Clearly, artifacts of past successful conflicts have amazing staying power, and alternative systems have a hard time competing with accepted systems or concepts. Quite frankly, many never see the light of day. In short, military institutions grounded in the past and very preoccupied with the present are not particularly adept at dealing with the future.

The Army's interwar experience also reinforces in my mind how we are all, in many ways, captives of the institutions within which we serve. To be accepted practitioners and to get ahead, we embrace the norms of our services and how they fight. We also tend to espouse the unique value of our service, and its contributions to national defense is more important than that of the other services. This is clearly an impediment to realizing true jointness within our defense establishment. Initially most officers buy into what questions are okay to ask, as well as many of the answers. In closing, I would note my sense that the heart of the Army's interwar transformation difficulties was the unwillingness of most officers to question the ruling orthodoxy, which is quite understandable given the environment the Army's leadership had created. Consequently, there was little debate to inform critical thinking. I'll close by saying that given the obvious stakes for our nation's future, today's leaders must do a better job than their predecessors. Thank you.

DR. THOMPSON: Dr. O'Hanlon.

DR. MICHAEL E. O'HANLON: Thank you, Loren. It's a great honor to be here on this excellent panel. A lot has been covered already, and in the interest of saving time, I'll make a couple of broad points fairly quickly. They build,

Dr. O'Hanlon

to a large extent, on what we've already heard. I would sum them up by describing my thesis as, "There's a paradox about transformation." You have to try to do it. You have to try to speed up innovation, but you have to also expect that most of what you try may not work, may be a bad idea, and may interfere with pressing requirements and other national security priorities that simply must remain as high as they've been. In this sense, if there's a single strawman I would go after and set myself up in a debate against, it would be some of the tone of the 1997 National Defense Panel Report, which suggested that transformation should become, in many ways, the pressing priority of the United States military.

I do not agree with that thesis, and my apologies if anyone thinks I'm misportraying the thesis of that NDP Report, but just to have something to aim at, I'd like to hold that up even though it was a very good report in other ways. So, what's the paradox? Well, the paradox is that where we are in history—and Hans gave some sense of this with his review of the last few centuries of combat—we have to try to innovate, perhaps even more than we have in previous periods. There are a number of reasons for this. One, we now find ourselves as the only superpower. Historically, that tends to mean that there's only one place to go, and that's down. People tend to aim at you, they want to compete with you. You tend to get a little bit complacent, and if you're not careful, pretty soon you're no longer the superpower. This is Paul Kennedy's famous thesis from the late 1980s. It tends to be the historical norm.

So what do you do if you're in that position? You have to try to change. You have to try to be the country that continues to be hungry and continues to look for new opportunities. That's the natural tendency of the underdog or the weaker power. You have to try to make that your own tendency, even as the superpower. Therefore, it's sort of a broad historical imperative for change. In a more immediate and security-oriented way we see new threats. We don't have the same kind of concerns of head-on, force-on-force warfare that we saw during the Cold War—at least not to the same extent. We have new threats in two different forms. One is the state-centered form; the other is the terrorist-centered form.

The state-centered kind of threat is often described as being oriented toward an anti-access strategy. People aren't going to try to compete with us in the air or on the open terrain of battlefield—they're going to try to prevent us from getting into theater; they're going to try to raise the risk of casualties; they're going to talk about urban combat strategy. That's actually more of a symmetric tactic, in many ways, that Saddam is talking about now, but it still, in a way, plays to our selective potential weaknesses. Also, the fact that we have to move large amounts of materiel across the world to fight people we'd generally be fighting in their neighborhoods requires us to move things that are vulnerable. So anti-access becomes a natural concern and a natural temptation for exploitation for many adversaries. This is a broad, historical trend that is in many ways produced by our success in classic force-on-force terms and also by our position in the world needing to project power overseas.

With the terrorist threat, we now have seen a whole different kind of asymmetric capability, which suggests a few things to me; one of which is the DoD can't expect to always have first dibs on national security resources anymore. If I had to choose, if we were not in a political environment that allowed increased resources on a substantial level for both DoD and homeland security, I would choose the latter. I would prioritize that as being the area of more pressing concern at the moment. In the military, we need to keep that concept clear, because there's a political reality here, or a potential political reality—I shouldn't describe it as a reality just yet, but a potential political dynamic that could actually put a little bit of a lid on national security resources in the military sphere, to the extent that others share my view and the politics change—the politics of the post 9/11 world, where everybody basically gets what they want, because so far there's no major objection to that. So, there are a number of reasons why we have to be looking to change the military dealing with new kinds of threats and doing so as economically as possible, even though as Hans pointed out, transformations are usually not cheap.

Finally, in historical terms, there's one more reason we need to keep pushing for change and innovation and that's because the computer revolution offers this opportunity. This is a more optimistic and a more positive way to think about where we stand in history. It's not just a question of new threats, it's not just a question of the potential complacency of being the superpower; it's a question of new opportunity. Therefore, we should see how far we can push electronics and computing because they're at an historic point in terms of how fast they're changing and the opportunities they may provide. Those are all the reasons to try to innovate even more than we have in the past.

There are also reasons to be wary and reasons to be careful. This is the paradox of transformation, or of the transformer. Let me give two broad categories of rationale and try to be quick. One of them is strategic. We cannot afford to lose sight of all the things we're doing well today. We have, obviously, an extremely well trained and extremely capable force, and I give credit to all the services for always highlighting that people are their top asset. Sometimes in the RMA and transformation debates, it sounds more like technology is the top asset, but when you talk to the services and people in uniform, they don't tend to make that mistake. They don't tend to blur that line. They emphasize the need for readiness and for people to be continually reinforced as our top priority. That's one thing we have to always keep our eye on.

A second thing is our place in the world—our broad, geostrategic place in the world. It is nothing short of remarkable. We are the superpower that no one is trying to balance against, except possibly one or two countries. But we're still pretty fortunate that it's not very many. Look at the fact that the global alliance system led by the United States now accounts for 75 to 80 percent of global economic output and about that same percentage of global military spending. This is unprecedented. The entire history of the nation today is the history of when somebody gets on top, people below start looking for ways to ally against the top power. They start looking for ways to compete with the top power, even if it's a relatively benign top power like Britain in the nineteenth century, by which I don't mean to say that Britain's motives in that time period were entirely benign or broad in terms of their interests for their nation. They obviously had imperialistic and colonial ambitions, and Hans talked about that too, but even when it's a relatively benign power, people tend to go after them.

That's not happening. We're about to admit seven new countries into NATO. People are trying to get into this global alliance, as big as it already is. Even countries that we potentially have to worry about as rivals or as competitors, most explicitly China, seem not to have quite decided just how much they want to fight this alliance system and how much they simply want to develop some kind of a quasi-cooperative, quasi-competitive relationship. It's not strictly competitive. Therefore, we cannot afford to lose this particular strategic situation. It is unprecedented and, to my mind, even more impressive than the military capabilities of the United States in technology terms.

So if I was going to rate our national security assets, I would say the number-one asset is the men and women of the armed forces, the number-two asset is the global alliance system, and the number-three asset is our technology and the concepts that we are trying now to improve by way of transformation. So to me, transformation is actually the third priority relative to maintaining the excellence of our armed forces, maintaining the readiness of our armed forces, and maintaining this global alliance system. That has big implications for resource allocation when budgets get tight. Transformers may not get as much money as the NDP suggested if tough choices have to be made. Those are the strategic arguments.

We have tremendous potential today from computers and electronics. We should try to push that, but is it really so unprecedented, the pace at which we are changing technology today? I'm not so sure. Here I will again use my national defense panel. It's a little bit unfair to take a group that I admire so much and a report that I admire as my strawman, but for the sake of argument, I'm going to do so and point out that if you read the NDP Report, it says that we are in a period where technology is turning over every 18 to 24 months. We have essentially a new generation of technology every 18 to 24 months. That's the way they put it. In other words, they imply this is a broad characteristic of our era for many technologies. That's simply not true. It's only true for computers and electronics. That is the only area of technology in which we're getting that rapid pace of turnover.

I would argue, and this is a little bit of a sweeping comment and certainly one that could incite some discussion or disagreement, but I would argue that the only other area where we are seeing remarkable progress that's of historically unprecedented pace is largely in the area of biological understanding—many of the medical sciences, many of our understandings of DNA, and so forth. That area is also moving quickly, with some implications, obviously, for the military but not perhaps yet as much as for computers and electronics.

If you look at the major vehicles and the major technologies underlying American military vehicles today, I am struck by the fact that, if anything, the technology is changing less quickly than it has in the last half century, and certainly not more quickly. Whether it's the speed of airplanes, I think you can look from one generation to another and see more sophisticated materials, higher engine temperatures, somewhat greater fuel efficiency. The F-22 is obviously ahead of the F-15 in terms of the performance of the best systems. However, if you look at the basic way in which we move about the world and about the battlefield, we still rely on the internal combustion engine in many of our ground vehicles. We still rely on armor that is better than it used to be, which has more composite features, but in my mind is evolving in a very gradual way over a period of many decades.

We still rely on ships that typically go 20 to 30 knots, and there's the hope that we can do some catamaran shapes and some other above-water kinds of ships for tactical operations or for very specific purposes. However, these things tend to be quite expensive, and for the most part, we're going to be stuck moving things with airplanes that fly at 500 miles per hour and ships that go 30 knots as far out as I can see in terms of our major capability to move things around the world and the major way in which we deploy forces. Therefore, I am struck when I look at technology by how much we still have to do. When you're talking about a new, fast, globally deployable American military that's also lethal and survivable, we got a lot of work to do before we can attain that kind of capability, and I, frankly, am dubious that we can attain it anytime soon.

Therefore, I'm more comfortable thinking of transformation in terms of a slightly accelerated rapid evolution, and I'm a big skeptic on whether we really have to claim we are in a period of revolution. Because that implies discontinuity. That implies that you have to put a lot more resources into changing technology and all the associated concepts of operations and organization that go with it, and I'm not sure that we want to potentially risk sacrificing the quality of our people, of our training, or of our global alliance commitments to do that.

To summarize and conclude, there's a paradox of transformation. There are enough reasons today to try to push innovation, that we should try to push it, but there are a lot of reasons to think it's not going to be smooth and it's not going to be easy, and maybe it should not even be our top priority as we go out there in the future national security environment. Thank you.

DR. THOMPSON: Well, thank you very much. We'll take some questions now. I'd like to begin by asking a question of Dr. O'Hanlon. In addition to your doctorate, you have degrees in physics and in engineering from Princeton. It seems as though many of the most strident proponents of transformation are a little thin in the tactical credentials department. Is this a problem?

DR. O'HANLON: Well, it's a good question. I guess I'm tempted to think about the debate between a lot of people who haven't been in the military, just as I haven't been, who are promoting war against Iraq, versus a lot of people who are in the military who are a little more skeptical. I would tend to actually defend both camps in regard to both questions. In other words, it's important to have people who look in broad historical terms and push that first argument and say, "Listen, we cannot afford to be complacent. We have to push more than we want to; we have to push in a way that makes us a little uncomfortable." Sometimes, being unencumbered by too much knowledge helps us do that—as long as those people don't ultimately make the decisions by themselves.

I like the fact that the services are a bit pragmatic and conservative. Dave Johnson has made some very good points about how they can be a little too pragmatic and conservative at times and too tradition-bound and bureaucratic. That's why civilians are sometimes the people who don't know the issues as well and sometimes are needed to push. However, there has to be this back-and-forth, and I actually like the way the defense transformation debate is going, in the sense that for every NDP study that is too ambitious, there is a correcting mechanism. I actually like the way the services and the OSD debate, the way the Congress and the Pentagon debate, and as long as we don't let any one community get undue influence in this debate, we'll be okay.

DR. THOMPSON: Interesting. Questions from the floor?

AUDIENCE MEMBER: I am Michelle Jennings, U.S. Agency for International Development. I was wondering, although touched on briefly by the first two panelists, could you elaborate on the steps being taken in the transformation process that take into consideration the increased role of the military in humanitarian assistance and disaster response operations and also what considerations are being taken in this inclusive process that you mentioned that integrate the large role of the international humanitarian assistance community and the interagency.

GENERAL DUBIK: I'll take that to start, and then if someone else wants to pick it up. There are several areas I can give you some specifics in. First, during the Millennium Challenge Exercise and experiment that we conducted a couple of months ago, one of the concepts we looked at was establishing a permanent joint interagency control group that was virtually connected. Now, this is not a physical group, but one that was connected virtually. In the experiment, we connected five or six agencies together whose role it was to give advice to the commander in chief, the role player in the same position, and the role player in the commander of joint task force position. The experiment was very successful from several standpoints: First, the group provided good advice to both commanders. Second, the agencies involved found immense value in the establishment and working of this collaborative virtual organization—so much so that they wanted to keep all the equipment we deposited in their offices so that we could establish the environment. That was on the interagency side. To follow on, that part of the experimentation over the next two years will be devoted to refining that concept to such a point where it's no longer the exception, but becomes the rule.

The second aspect on nongovernment organizations, private organizations, that again are present—we hope to establish a similar kind of venue, and we'll at least start in the workshops and seminars side, in the next year to see if we can establish a similar kind of environment for those kinds of organizations, because they have a very important role and in many ways are the dominant role in those kinds of operations where military force is a supporting element of power, not the one being supported. So those are two specifics, and I don't know if anyone else wants to pick it up.

DR. BINNENDIJK: Let me expand just a little bit. As I indicated earlier, I believe this is a very important element of the Defense Department's overall mission. It is not just to win wars, it's to keep the peace and maintain the peace—not everywhere—you have to choose carefully. What we've found in numerous cases in the last 10 years is that our military almost solely has the initial capability to go in and deal with these kinds of humanitarian problems. We have that capability in our active force, and we have it in our reserve force. Very often, in Haiti for example, it is the reserves who come in and play an important role in these humanitarian operations.

Part of the problem in the decade of the '90s was that we had this construct of two major theater wars, which was a very difficult, demanding standard for our military to meet. It did not leave much room conceptually for humanitarian operations. Every time there was an involvement in a Bosnia or a Haiti, it tended to take away from the readiness of the services, and particularly the Army, to do the two major theater war missions. That has now changed a bit, and that is definitely a plus. We also find that servicemen and women who have been involved in these operations come away with a great sense of satisfaction, and the reenlistment rates for people who have served in that environment are way up.

Finally, I would note, as I did earlier, we need to go back and take a look at Presidential Directive No. 56. The core element of that is trying to get the interagencies to work together for precisely these kinds of humanitarian operations, so that other agencies and not just the military are held responsible for pieces of the mission. We need to go back to that in the context of the war on terrorism as well, and refine it, because it's the mechanism we can use to harmonize the interagency process.

DR. THOMPSON: Another question?

AUDIENCE MEMBER: I have two questions to whomever would like to answer them. The first one is the following: I've read several times that the major difference between the situation during the Cold War and the situation now was that, during the Cold War, capabilities were known but intents were not. Right now, the situation would be, according to the officers, exactly the opposite. I mean intents are known—they are very bad—but capabilities wouldn't be. Where I tend to disagree with that analysis, it seems to me that the major unknown is neither about intents nor capabilities. It's about strategies. My first question is: In DoD, is any team working on unconventional ways of using existing technologies, including old technologies?

My second question is about health and security, because I believe in the twenty-first century, this will be one of the major challenges. What I have in mind is not only the natural appearance of about ten new diseases in the last decade, it's also about more than 10 million orphans in Africa who are in the streets and will be the breeding grounds of a number of activities we probably won't like. It's also about the way Russia is losing about 700,000 people every year, and it's also about biological weapons and the military application of the bio revolution. So here again, I'd like to know how important is this question as a whole, not only through bio weapons in the DoD here in Washington. Thank you.

DR. THOMPSON: Why don't we take that second question first. It seems this raises the interesting question of whether our existing national security structure is equipped to deal with certain types of emerging security challenges. Does anybody have any thoughts on that? Dr. Johnson?

DR. JOHNSON: I would say that as we're in this period of transition, what we get is what is available on the shelf. In many ways, what was so comfortable about the Cold War was not that it was bipolar and we had an enemy that we knew and could figure out, it's that the artifacts that we had developed in World War II were perfectly appropriate in a conventional sense in that new environment. Until something forces us to look at those artifacts that are, in many ways, carrier battle groups and air wings and divisions and ask, are those appropriate for the new environment, the approach so far is...

One of my favorite transformational issues is when the Cold War ended and the Navy realized that everybody had moved to the littorals since the Cold War, and we had to go to the littorals because 90 percent of the world's population lives there. I asked them where they were in 1989, if that was so important now. The reason was that the same force had to be moved to a mission that mattered. So, they took this old, large—in the case of moving the ship a very few degrees—and now it's focused on the littorals because they didn't really force a change in the things that mattered to the people that were running those organizations.

It's going to take a very long time to transform ourselves to a point where we're comfortable with new technologies that we've grafted onto processes and organizations, to where we say maybe those organizations and processes are not appropriate in every place along the spectrum of conflict. They may be important in some places, and how do we cover those niches? Because the services have to be designed and equipped and trained and maintained to do the unthinkable, which is a major war. But, at the same time, there are many other things out there. For the first time, we're bumping up against situations where a carrier battle group or division may not be the appropriate response.

DR. THOMPSON: Hans?

DR. BINNENDIJK: The anthrax attack of last year has clearly focused attention in Washington and in the Pentagon on this last question, and I'll just address a piece of it—the bio terrorism part of it. A lot of money and attention is now being focused on this problem. It turns out that most of the detectors for bio sensors that can provide a degree of early warning in the United States belong to the military. It turns out, certainly in the case of anthrax, that most of the vaccines, many of the vaccines that are available, belong to the military. They were designed in the context of force protection. This is clearly now an issue that goes well beyond force protection to national protection. When you think about national protection, the local responders are the firemen and policemen who are on the scene, and they largely don't want federal help unless they really need it. What we have to do now is stretch in both directions. The military has to recognize that it has a role beyond force protection. I believe that's being recognized in order to deal with broader protection against these kinds of threats. We also need to work with first responders in a collaborative way. That is beginning to take place now.

DR. THOMPSON: General Dubik, did you have comment?

GENERAL DUBIK: The reason we're in a position now of facing so many asymmetrical threats is our conventional power, and that goes back, again, to Michael's comment about the paradoxical position that we're in. Certainly, we should adapt some of our current capabilities to be more applicable to current threats, but not so much that the current threats return to their conventional nature. We can transform ourselves all the way into a position where we don't want to be, and the paradoxical give-and-take approach is one that we would all be advised to keep in perspective. We, as a set of military services, have developed a great array of capabilities. They've been developed primarily for the protection of our nation and our allies. They've been developed for reasons to compel our adversaries to do our will, but they are useful in many other arenas. This is all a good thing. We should expand the uses of those in other arenas, pursuant to the new strategic environment, but always with one eye toward the purpose for which we all exist. We are instruments for our nations, and our purpose is to compel people and to protect people. That's the primary purpose. That's our fundamental professional ethos, and while we can do lots of others, we can't erode that ethos. Back to the plenary speaker, don't forget your mission, don't forget your values, but hold on to those.

DR. THOMPSON: Michael, we're pretty much out of time, but before we adjourn, Therese alludes to one of the two technology questions where you said we are seeing rapid growth, which is molecular biology, genetic engineering. Are we in any way prepared to cope with the security challenges that those kinds of revolutions may present?

DR. O'HANLON: In the short-to-medium term, I agree with Hans that we've made a good deal of progress, at least elevating this as a higher priority in homeland security and in military planning. One of the best things about the 1997 QDR, a relatively conservative, cautious document, is that Secretary Bill Cohen did push some of these concepts for battlefield protection as well. Now we're expanding that to homeland security. It's such a big question, I don't know how to properly answer it, but one particular thing concerning Africa is that I agree with the point that we can't allow big parts of the world to be failed states. It's not consistent with our national security interest. It allows safe havens, breeding grounds, sources of income for terrorists, and also allows disease to develop and proliferate. In that regard, let me quickly say two things. One, I'm encouraged by some of what the Bush administration has been doing—the 50 percent increase in foreign aid. Who would have thought you'd get this out of a conservative Republican administration? But I take my hat off to this administration for being flexible and adaptive on that front. I think a lot of that money will go toward helping to rebuild states in Africa as it's increased.

On the other hand, one thing we're not doing enough of is engaging, whether through foreign aid or military operations, with Africa as a continent. Now, DoD is pretty overstretched. You're doing a great job engaging in Europe and Asia with forward presence, peace operations, deterrence, military-to-military exchanges, et cetera. There's not as much going on in Africa. I don't want to add one big new mission to an already overstretched force, but I do think that one program in particular, the Africa Crisis Response Initiative, was very promising in the late Clinton years, and it's now been downgraded. That program allows African militaries to get better at doing some of these things for themselves. We need to make that program much bigger, more oriented toward lethal and difficult operations, which is the other prong in our strategy toward failed states. This is only one small part of the question that you raised, Loren, but too big for me to fully deal with here.

DR. THOMPSON: I understand. Well, unfortunately, we're on a fairly tight schedule today so we're going to have to break. I know there are about two hours worth of questions out there in the audience on this subject. Perhaps you'll have a chance to talk to some of the panelists, but thank you very much for being both diverse and informed in your perspectives.

PANEL 4

BUILDING CAPABILITIES FOR INTERNATIONAL EFFORTS

Co-sponsor: Peter F. Drucker Foundation for Nonprofit Management

Chair: Ambassador Peter W. Galbraith, National War College

International Means: General Montgomery C. Meigs, Commanding General, United States Army, Europe, and 7th Army

Nongovernmental Means: Mr. Howard Roy Williams, President and CEO, Center for Humanitarian Cooperation

Public Security: Ambassador Robert B. Oakley, Distinguished Fellow, Institute for International and Strategic Studies, National Defense University

Panel Charter

The demise of the bipolar world in 1991 altered the traditionally accepted definitions and uses of national power. Suddenly, the potential for large-scale conflict, to include the use of nuclear munitions, diminished, while the probability for involvement in small-scale contingency operations increased exponentially. Prior to 1991, conventional military thought dedicated little effort to developing doctrine and definitions for post-conflict operations. Most military scenarios of this era called for the intervention of overwhelming combat power to stabilize a situation and, once accomplished, departure. Given today's current security environment, this "old school of thought" no longer prevails.

The proliferation of ethnic, tribal, and regional conflicts, beginning in the early 1990s, radically altered the roles and missions traditionally executed by international organizations, nongovernmental organizations, and military forces. In nearly every operation, the United States military finds itself deploying to conflict areas where aid workers are already on the ground. The interaction between these groups will continue to take place, either as coordinated efforts or with all parties working autonomously.

These aid workers, who extend humanitarian and relief aid to troubled regions, consist of field workers from nongovernmental organizations (NGOs)

Left to right: Ambassador Peter W. Galbraith, Mr. Howard Roy Williams, Mrs. Francis Hesselbein, General Eric K. Shinseki, Ambassador Robert B. Oakley, General Montgomery C. Meigs

and international organizations (IOs). In many ways, the military and NGO/IO communities are similar: Both share a commitment to service that goes beyond a routine 9-to-5 work day; both share a sense of mission and purpose to a desired end state; both share the dangers of deploying to the far reaches of the world where, among the dead and dying, they place their personnel in harm's way.

Yet despite these common traits, more often than not each organization functions independently. Each operates under its own set of rules and sensibilities, and each with a suspicion of the other. Due in part to these factors, coordination among these entities is not natural. In particular, NGOs/IOs prize their independence. They pursue their particular mission with their own visions and values. In many ways, their clarity of purpose and homogeneity provide them with an ability to rapidly pursue their objectives. The military structure can be more complicated. The lines of authority from the top to the bottom, while an unbroken thread, encompasses different operational and administrative branches and different services—Army, Navy, Marine Corps, Air Force—each with its own culture, identity, and individual mission. In this environment, friction is always present.

The results of these factors can be damaging. Often the concerned parties work at cross-purposes as they identify and create their own, often unique, solutions to the myriad problems that arise. As a result, unclear coordination in their efforts prods each group to rely on comfortable ways of doing business. This attitude hinders each group from understanding the roles of the other, thus perpetuating misconceptions and suspicions.

Another component of the difficult relationship between the U.S. military and NGOs/IOs is the complexity of the work that both groups perform. The field conditions in which they operate are constantly affected by the current political context, as well as by the nature of the current emergency situation. No two are exactly alike. For these reasons, building capabilities so that each can interface with, and leverage the best practices of, one another becomes a paramount task.

Considering the new operational environment of the post–Cold War era, where military forces and NGO/IO agencies interact in close, sometime overlapping, proximity with one another, both the military and its civilian counterparts must be ready and willing to change their mindsets, to throw away outdated checklists, and to assess the current situation through new and open eyes. Humanitarian relief work is not, nor will it ever be, formulaic. This is not to say that collaborative efforts between the U.S. military and NGOs/IOs have not been, and cannot be in the future, successful. Operation PROVIDE COMFORT, which assisted in returning Kurds from refugee camps in Turkey to their homes in northern Iraq, is widely viewed as a great success. Moreover, civil-military operations in the Balkans and East Timor have gained notoriety and have served as a testing bed for future operations. In this light, military forces and NGOs/IOs must continue to seek ways to improve cooperation and unity of effort mainly through building capabilities not only internally to their own organization but also with their external partners.

Building successful collaborations, unity of effort, and a basis for understanding between the U.S. military and NGOs/IOs requires shared responsibility. How can the functional imperative of the military be balanced with the social imperatives of its civilian partners? The need for cooperation and respect between these two entities is vital. Tough questions must be asked. A direct address of the challenges, misconceptions, roles, perspectives, and results must be explored. The opportunity for partnerships between these groups must become an imperative.

Summary

General Montgomery C. Meigs, Commanding General, U.S. Army, Europe, and 7th Army

• Civil-military relations in international efforts are complicated by varied objectives, cultures, and backgrounds. Creating a common effort in civil-military peacekeeping or peace-enforcement situations depends on three basic elements: the creation of common goals and coordinated ends to be reached through consensus; the building of trust between the key players; and a willingness on the part of the military to lead from behind, which is often contrary to the military's way of doing business.

• The challenges of building capacities for international efforts:

1. Organizations have discordant institutional cultures and differing views of the world.

2. Those serving in humanitarian organizations have seen crisis after crisis in any one effort, whereas military personnel are often the newcomers on the scene.

3. NGOs perceive military goals as different from their own.

4. NGOs are concerned with their donor base and want visibility in the media in order to continue to generate interest in their efforts.

5. Because of varied cultures and experiences, many players in NGOs and private volunteer organizations (PVOs) have a deep distrust of the military.

• In Bosnia, coordinating security was necessary before resettlement could take place. The military was aware that it could not ensure a safe environment if there was random movement into the settlement areas. SFOR brought together all key players to begin coordinating resettlement efforts. Coordination required:

1. Preparing the ground.

2. Negotiating with local officials to ensure they would do at least the minimum required to provide a safe and secure environment.

3. Ensuring that when settlers arrived, the police were on the scene.

4. After the war, long-term security coordination required the military to be in constant contact with humanitarian organizations. The combined effort led to a successful resettlement campaign.

• What are the ways forward, and what have we learned from our experiences?

1. Despite different methods, it is important to emphasize common goals and ends.

2. The establishment of trust between leaders of different organizations must be made through personal contact and interaction, with the military meeting the NGO players on their home ground.

3. Military personnel must show great consistency and patience.

4. The military should and can use staff and facilities in the best interest of coordinating efforts.

5. Cross-training between the military and NGOs allows for better training for soldiers and demonstrates to the NGO community that the military is as committed to progress on common goals in that environment as the NGOs.

Mr. Howard Roy Williams, President and CEO, Center for Humanitarian Cooperation:

• Groups in the NGO community carry with them a considerable degree of arrogance, which in their minds is well earned because they have been willing to go places where no one else wants to go and do good work and achieve incredible accomplishments. However, the danger in their arrogance is that it isolates them from other communities. World situations require more than NGO action. Likewise, it is important for NGOs to learn that whoever helps a victim on a given day is a humanitarian for the day.

• NGOs are in the business of presenting alternatives to negatives in the reality of a given situation.

• NGOs rely upon donors and contributions from the public for their existence; however, those contributions are defined in terms of the immediate reaction to a tragedy, forcing NGOs to focus on the immediate, the real, and the short term.

• NGOs are sometimes accused of not being able to see the big picture. But in reality, the big picture consists of a thousand little pictures; and to the extent that any organization can give you insight into a lot of little pictures, the perception of the big picture is going to be improved.

• The essential question is how to get communities with different cultures, histories, and languages to come together for the common good.

1. We must set up channels of communication between the communities. Although communication channels have worked before, they are episodic, no real patterns have emerged, and there's little predictability. Furthermore, in recent years the military has been more keen on setting up channels of communication than the NGOs.

2. The military must learn that the causes in which NGOs are engaged in are very precious to them, and they are willing to risk their lives to maintain them.

3. Conflict prevention must be a function of a lot of micro-efforts pulling together to accomplish a much larger goal. Awareness of these micro-efforts and seeing them as part of the larger picture would go far in improving coordination efforts.

• The NGO community is multifaceted. Many members of the community feel very strongly that NGOs should have nothing to do with the military because the military is not, and cannot be seen as, neutral. However, there are also members of the NGO community who recognize that if all players are engaged in a humanitarian enterprise, the objectives of that enterprise and the common goal of helping some survive will determine the relevance of the actions.

• What happens in a large humanitarian crisis does impact upon the national security of the United States. NGOs have to feel they are part of the obligation. They are the ones who will be first on the ground, and they will be there after the conflict ends, trying to rebuild. Having been there before and during, there is a tendency to feel isolated from the world community. This isolation cannot be allowed to continue.

Ambassador Robert B. Oakley, Institute for National Security Studies, National Defense University

• Public security in the international context faces many challenges. Just as globalization has taken off with greater technology and better communications, so too have the threats to public security. International crime, terrorism, and narcotics trafficking have all benefited from globalization. As a result, we have a much greater threat to our public security at home just as we do to international public security. Therefore, the challenge can be met only on an international, as well as a national, basis.

• There are two approaches to increasing public security internationally: the soft approach, through humanitarian efforts, etc., and the hard approach, through military, intelligence, and policing efforts. The military must take a hard-line approach to these public security threats, which sets them apart from the NGO community.

• There are three pillars to beating this international security threat:

1. The United States' lead role in increasing international military capabilities in public security in areas where the threat is outside the control of the local government.

2. Civilian law enforcement, which has become increasingly international. Institutions such as Interpol, EuroPol, and the U.N. Drug Control Policy Organization have arrangements with one another, thus establishing multinational operations to combat threats to public security.

3. Intelligence that includes support for military as well as civilian agencies of governments and their operations. The interlocking web of intelligence-sharing is becoming much more important. Better intelligence-gathering and -sharing among agencies are indispensable as we move ahead.

Analysis

Joseph Kruft, Program Director, Peter F. Drucker Foundation for Nonprofit Management

An increase in world conflict has necessitated an increase in humanitarian aid, military operations, and public security. Coordination among the key players—the military, NGOs, and IOs—is an imperative to garnishing greater success in such operations and to fulfilling the overall objective of turning over control to the local authorities, agencies, and people. Such coordination, however, is not a natural relationship. Given the respective organizations' different aims, cultures, languages, and historical suspicion of one another, cooperation and coordination are indeed a challenge.

Nevertheless, all parties agree that building more effective means for capabilities is not only possible, but would be beneficial to all key players, including the local peoples whom they aim to help. Successfully coordinated efforts in Bosnia and other recent operations have demonstrated the advantages to be gained when both civilian and military leaders seek areas of common interest and look for ways to reach the common end.

The panelists—representing the military perspective, the NGO perspective, and the public security perspective—each outlined the sundry challenges facing them in any relief effort, as well as the areas for further opportunity. General Montgomery Meigs, giving the military perspective, cited the military's relatively late arrival into a situation as an obstacle to better coordination. NGOs, who have been on the ground, often from the beginning, and who have seen crisis after crisis, see the arrival of troops as an affront to their mission and efforts. Each group sees the other's goals as different and, at times, incompatible. While the military accuses NGOs of not seeing the big picture, NGOs counter that the big picture, in reality, is made up of hundreds of small pictures, which need to be looked at collectively in order to get a clear view of the situation.

However, General Meigs concluded that, despite their different methods, all parties can find great benefit in persistently emphasizing common goals and ends. Establishing trust between leaders can be accomplished through personal contact and interaction, most effectively if the military is willing to meet the NGOs and IOs on their home turf and if the military is willing to show consistency and patience in its interactions with its civilian partners. A commitment to cross-training military personnel and NGOs would also have far-reaching implications in changing attitudes about the military's seriousness toward operations and common goals.

Mr. Howard Roy Williams, a representative of NGOs, cited NGO's arrogance as a major stumbling block when it comes to cooperation and coordination in efforts. That arrogance often isolates NGOs from other communities. Mr. Williams agreed that NGOs must rely on a donor base for their existence. But the focus remains on the immediate, the real, and the short-term imperatives of a situation. The insight NGOs are able to give an array of little pictures can offer an improved perception of the larger picture.

Mr. Williams, like General Meigs, emphasized the need for proper channels of communication to be established between the leaders and their communities. The military must come to understand that the causes NGOs are engaged in are very precious to them. Likewise, NGOs must recognize that the essential element that is going to determine the relevance of an action or operation is that all players are engaged in the enterprise to help somebody survive.

Added to these challenges is the threat to public security. Ambassador Robert B. Oakley stated that with globalization came a greater security threat at home, as well as on the international level. As a result, the challenge can only be met if it is attacked at both levels. The military must take a focused and hard-line approach to security threats such as international crime, terrorism, and narcotics trafficking. This hard-line approach fundamentally sets the military apart from the NGO and IO communities.

Ambassador Oakley described three pillars to beating international security threats: the U.S. role in security in areas where local authorities cannot control it themselves; the increasing use of multinational operations; and a process for better intelligence-gathering and -sharing among agencies.

The panelists uniformly emphasized the advantages and benefits to be gained through greater understanding, communication, and coordination in civil-military operations. They cited the benefit of cross-training, building personal networks, and establishing communications channels both in the field and at home. The continuing challenges that stand in the way of these efforts will require greater exploration, discussion, and refinement in the years to come.

Transcript

BACKSTAGE ANNOUNCER: Ladies and gentlemen, Dr. Daniel Goure.

DR. DANIEL GOURE: Ladies and gentlemen, it's my distinct pleasure and privilege to introduce Mrs. Frances Hesselbein as the person to introduce the Chair of the next panel. I could go into greater length, but I don't know how I would compete with the introduction given by the Secretary of the Army or her performance and presence on this stage earlier today. So, I will simply introduce her. Mrs. Frances Hesselbein.

MRS. FRANCES HESSELBEIN: Thank you very much. It is my honor to introduce Ambassador Peter W. Galbraith. From 1993 to 1998, Peter W. Galbraith served as the first U.S. Ambassador to the Republic of Croatia, where he actively participated in the negotiation of three agreements that ended the war in the former Yugoslavia. He was the co-mediator and principal architect of the 1995 agreement that ended the war in Croatia by providing for the peaceful reintegration of Eastern Slovenia. From 1979 to 1993, he served as senior adviser to the Senate Foreign Relations Committee, handling the foreign relations authorization legislation in the Near East/South Asia region. His work on Iraqi war crimes against the Kurds was the subject of a 1992 ABC documentary. Ambassador Galbraith is the author of published reports, scholarly articles, and op eds on Iraq, the Kurds, South Asia, security issues, and the

Balkans peace processes. During the Kosovo conflict, Ambassador Galbraith was a frequent commentator for the major U.S. and British networks, logging more than 150 appearances. He is currently on the faculty of the National War College, Ambassador Galbraith.

AMBASSADOR PETER W. GALBRAITH: In 1991, the major participants in the unfolding Yugoslavia tragedy gathered in Lake Bled in Slovenia for a conference. One morning, Slobodan Milosevic, then the president of Serbia; Franco Tudjman, president of Croatia; and Alija Izetbegovic, president of Bosnia, went out fishing together on the lake. They caught a fish and before they could do anything with it, the fish started to talk and explained that it was a magical fish and it would grant each of them one wish. Milosevic, the clever fellow that he was, said, "Well, my wish is that Tudjman and all the Croats will go to hell." Tudjman reacted and said, "My wish is that Milosevic and all the Serbs will go to hell." The Bosnian president looked at the fish and said, "Does this happen all at once?" The fish said, "Yes." The Bosnia president said, "In that case, I'll have a cup of coffee."

Unfortunately, there were no magic fish, either in former Yugoslavia or any place else, and the conflict that broke out in the former Yugoslavia in 1991 was not, of course, new. The world has long been a chaotic place, beset by local conflicts, large-scale human rights violations, and widespread suffering. During the Cold War, these were matters that did not primarily concern the U.S. military. Its task was to prepare for large-scale conflict and, on several occasions, to fight regional wars. Indeed, the first big military test of the post–Cold War world was another conventional, regional war, this time in the Persian Gulf against Iraq. The Bush administration—and I think the military—thought that the war would be like every other. The U.S. would fight and, mission accomplished, withdraw; and, indeed, it proceeded to do just that. One month after the end of the Gulf War, dramatic television pictures of Iraqi Kurds fleeing Saddam Hussein's fury and then dying on snowy hillsides were beamed into homes around the world and around the United States. Outraged commentators, and I have to confess I was one of them, suggested that the administration had lost its moral compass, having called on the Iraqi people to overthrow Saddam Hussein and then abandoning children, women, and men to their fate. Within a few weeks, the U.S. military was back into Iraq, this time negotiating the withdrawal of the Iraqi military and police, facilitating distribution of food and medicine, and setting up transit camps for returning refugees. This became the post–Cold War world's first humanitarian intervention and I would note that, 11 years later, the Kurds today enjoy what is *de facto* an independent state, defended from the air by the U.S. military.

Since the northern Iraq intervention, the U.S. military has been involved in humanitarian interventions in Somalia, Bosnia, Kosovo, Haiti, and East Timor. In each case, the military has facilitated the provision of humanitarian relief, assisted in physical reconstruction, and, in some cases, provided physical security and—the dreaded words—contributed to nation building.

In Afghanistan, winning the war against the Taliban was relatively easy. There is, however, broad recognition that keeping Afghanistan from being a haven for terrorists and extremists will require an extended international presence. As Afghanistan demonstrates, settling disputes among rival warlords, providing humanitarian aid, educating girls, and rebuilding a country are not just good things to do; they can be vital to our national security. All this puts the military in an unusual, unaccustomed, and sometimes uncomfortable role. It has been a dispenser of life-sustaining food and medicine. It has repainted schools and

Ambassador Galbraith

churches. It has hunted down warlords and protected a foreign leader.

In recent cases, other countries have borne much of the burden of nation building, but as we move forward in Iraq and then, as some have suggested, try to clean up the rest of the Middle East, we may find ourselves undertaking these roles largely on our own. These experiences raise many questions. How do the very different cultures of the military, humanitarian organizations, nongovernmental organizations, and the United Nations mesh in complex emergencies? More broadly, what is the role of the military and humanitarian organizations in preventing conflict and in dealing with the consequences of conflict? Are there alternatives to the military taking over key functions such as providing public security?

We may wish that there was a large U.N. civilian peace force that could be deployed, but that really does not exist. More broadly, how do we coordinate the military, the police function, the intelligence function in the promotion of public security, both internationally and as it affects the United States? While it seems to me that real progress has been made in places such as East Timor and Bosnia, one has to note that these are very small places—East Timor with 800,000 people and Bosnia with just 4 million—and they have been very expensive operations. The international community has spent more than $2 million on East Timor and $20 billion on Bosnia.

The question is, how do we handle nation building in bigger failed states? Afghanistan and Iraq—Afghanistan with 22 million, Iraq about the same size,

And what happens if some really large places fail—Pakistan, 140 million, Indonesia, 220 million? To help sort out these questions and to raise and answer others, we have an extremely well-qualified panel.

We have a military man, General Montgomery Meigs, who fought in DESERT STORM, deployed with the 1st Infantry to Bosnia-Herzegovina in October 1996, serving as COMEAGLE in command of NATO's Multinational Division in the north in Operation JOINT ENDEAVOR. He returned to Bosnia-Herzegovina as the SFOR commander in 1998, and took over as the commanding general of the U.S. Army in Europe and the Seventh Army on November 10, 1999. Iraq, Bosnia-Herzegovina, Kosovo—he worked on all of them. From my point of view, very importantly, he was the Army Fellow at the National War College. Please welcome General Meigs.

Mr. Roy Williams is a humanitarian. Currently President and Chief Executive Officer of the Center for Humanitarian Cooperation, he previously worked upstairs in this building as the head of USAID's Office of Foreign Disaster Assistance, responsible for disaster preparedness, relief, and rehabilitation worldwide. Before that, he was with the International Rescue Committee for 12 years in a number of positions, ending up as the Vice President for Overseas Operations. He has worked in Iraqi Kurdistan, Jordan, the Balkans, Kenya, Rwanda, and Southern Sudan. I can't think of anybody better able to talk about the humanitarian issues. Please welcome Mr. Roy Williams.

We have a diplomat. Ambassador Robert Oakley is a Distinguished Fellow at the Institute for National Security Studies at the National Defense University, a position he's held since 1995. Before that, he had a 30-year career in the Foreign Service, having served in a number of high-level positions—Deputy Assistant Secretary of State for East Asia and the Pacific at the time of the Cambodia famine and the Vietnamese boat people crisis; Director of the State Department's Office for Counterterrorism; Ambassador to Pakistan, Congo, then called Zaire, and Somalia. He served as the special envoy for Somalia during the interventions in the Bush and Clinton administrations. He is the co-author of a book on Somalia and the co-editor of a book on peacekeeping. Please welcome Ambassador Robert Oakley.

Gentlemen, thank you for being here and, also, thank you for what you've done. General Meigs.

GENERAL MONTGOMERY C. MEIGS: I was asked to address the issue of creating means, and I had to think a little bit about that and wonder how I was going to define it and cover it in 10 minutes. It came back to me that personal experience might be useful here and a bit of history.

Creating a common effort, based on the complicated and varied objectives, backgrounds, and organizations that one finds in a peacekeeping or a peace-enforcement situation, depends on three basic things: *common goals and coordinated ends*, which, ironically, have to be reached through some degree of consensus between the parties involved in the peacekeeping effort; *trust* between the key players; and a *willingness* on the military's part because, quite often in these situations, the military is the most organized and has the most effective tools for compellance—the military's willingness to lead from behind, which is not our normal way of doing business.

It's interesting to step back a minute, to about 1943, in January, when Dwight D. Eisenhower is reflecting in his diary on his frustration about being considered as indecisive, not bold, and generally behind the momentum in the major decisions made in the campaign in the Mediterranean. This lengthy quotation gives you an interesting insight into the frame of mind that is

General Meigs

required of a military person in these types of operations, i.e., peacekeeping, though this is a conventional setting.

"The truth is that the bold British commanders in the Med were Admiral Cunningham and Tedder, not the English ground commanders. I had peremptorily to order the holding of the forward airfields in the bitter days of January 1943. I had to order the integration of an American corps and its use on the battle lines. I had to order the attack on Pantelleria. And finally the British ground commanders—but not Sir Andrew and Tedder—wanted to put all our ground forces into the toe of Italy. They didn't like Salerno, but after days of work, I got them to accept. On the other hand, no British commander ever held back once an operation was ordered. We had a happy family—and to all the commanders in chief must go the great share of the operational credit." Remember what David Gergen said about teams here. "But it worries me to be thought of as timid when I've had to do things that were so risky as to be almost crazy." And remember David Gergen's comment about self-mastery: "Ho-hum, end of concern, put it away. Never reaches the light of day."

So what's the challenge in a peace-enforcement or peacekeeping situation? First, most of the organizations have discordant institutional cultures. Many of the people that I was dealing with in Bosnia and have helped other commanders deal with in Kosovo and Bosnia have a different view of the world; have different backgrounds. People in humanitarian organizations, for instance, have seen crisis after crisis after crisis. Generally, the military person is a bit of a newcomer to the scene. They perceive that the military goal is different than theirs, or what they see as the overall goal. They have different interests. Nongovernmental organizations generally are very concerned about their donor base. They want visibility in the media in order to continue to generate interest in that donor base, because the donor base is their survival instrument. They can't be seen as being dependent on or subservient to the military actors in a peacekeeping operation. In addition, because of our varied experiences and cultures, and the way we have grown up professionally over the years, and the history that we all share, many of the people in the nongovernmental organizations and the private volunteer organizations don't trust the military.

How do you deal with those problems to create a common effort? I go back to an initiative that General Wes Clark had us launch on, and we sort of negotiated on how to do this and this was our solution. In 1999 we were faced with what we thought was going to be a bow wave of resettlement back into the areas of the Republic of Srpska. We knew that somehow we had to get this coordinated because we couldn't ensure a safe and secure environment if we had random movement into the settlement areas. So we convinced the ambassadors who were involved in this operation—supporting it, reporting on it—and the humanitarian organizations to forward us regional resettlement task forces in each of the major areas of the country and to provide the meals, the location, the coordination facilities for free. Because it was in the interest of the mission, SFOR began bringing all of these actors in and coordinating the effort.

Coordination of that effort required several things: preparing the ground for negotiations with the officials in the receiving localities to ensure that they would do at least the minimum required for a safe and secure environment. Actually, coordination of the move itself—making sure that when the people arrived the police were on the scene, the military was there—in order to ensure that things were done properly, because we couldn't cover everything all at the same time.

After the war—because, as you know, allied force preempted any kind of real resettlement during the activity that was going on in the air campaign—there was, in fact, a resurgence of resettlement, much of it spontaneous, often not even known to be starting by the humanitarian organizations. And because the aid in Bosnia is distributed in the late winter-early spring, as these people fell in on their new locations, their homes, in August and September, we were very concerned about getting them aid prior to the winter that would allow them to stay through the winter so that that resettlement could continue to be successful. To assist in that, SFOR arranged a tour to these locations by all of the concerned ambassadors so they could see firsthand our shared problems and, hopefully, generate a last bit of pocket change and resources to provide the stoves, the cooking fuel, the bedding, and the grain required to keep these people alive and in place during the winter. Coordinating the long-term security required us to be in touch with the humanitarian organizations all the time in case something "went south." That combined effort led to a very successful resettlement campaign in spite of the fact that it couldn't really start until after the war had finished and after the distrust of the situation had calmed down somewhat.

So, what are the ways forward and what have we learned from that experience [that] despite the fact that we have different methods, emphasize common ends? Establish trust with the leaders of these organizations through personal contact. The military actor has to go and meet these people on their home ground—whether it's the Russian Ambassador, the French ambassador, the UNHCR official in your sector—you have to meet them on their home ground so they know you both as a person, [and] as an actor on the stage. The military has to show great consistency and patience. Developing this type of detailed coordination with folks who aren't sure they want to do it requires a lot of effort. It also requires that the military use its strengths in coordinating staff work and facilities to help the effort.

Finally, it's important in our training that we continue to do cross-training with humanitarian organizations. For instance, we are just finishing up the rehearsal for the task force that will go down and replace the current Task Force Falcon in Kosovo. Routinely, we bring in as players members of humanitarian organizations to create the same stresses on that unit that they will encounter down range. That does two things for us. One, it's better training for the unit. Two, it shows the community with whom those soldiers are going to have to deal that we are as serious about progress on common terms in that environment as are they.

MR. HOWARD ROY WILLIAMS: I've been pleasantly surprised to learn that I'm going to have to change the tenor of some of my remarks because of the dynamic that has already emerged in this gathering. That's good. I was going to give you a classic description of the NGO community, what they do, why they do it, and how they do it. But I'll just fill in little bits and pieces of that to the extent that it's relevant.

Basically, I'd rather talk about the NGO community and how it needs to fit into the sort of interactions that are increasingly becoming important when we talk about humanitarian assistance worldwide. I like the phrase *discordant institutional cultures* that General Meigs used. I think that's a fair description. I can narrow it down some. The NGO community carries with it a considerable degree of arrogance. Now, in their minds, that arrogance is well earned, because they, over time, have been willing to go to places where no one else wants to go to do good work, and there is a lot of credit in that, and they've made some remarkable accomplishments. The danger in that arrogance, however, is that it tends to isolate you from other communities. One begins to

Mr. Williams

think that the only people worthy of doing humanitarian work are other humanitarians like themselves. The world is not set up that way. And I think, increasingly, some members of the NGO community and the international community are beginning to accept the realities of the incredible dynamic of Rwanda and Kurdistan where the logistical needs and the needs of the people on the ground were so extreme that no one organization was remotely capable of meeting them.

NGOs are in the business of presenting alternatives to negatives. They do it in many ways and they do it in a variety of situations. They also think in micro terms. Again, General Meigs made an observation, which was very appropriate, that NGOs really rely upon their donors for their existence—their donors and contributions from the public. But those contributions are defined in terms of the immediate reaction to, say, a full page ad in the *New York Times* showing the tragedy that's happening in Kurdistan or Kosovo. And so the NGOs constituency insists that they focus upon the immediate and the real in short terms. Their methodology and approach are very much predicated upon the need to respond to that. Therefore, this does define part of their culture. Now, some see this as a weakness in the NGO community, because they say they're incapable of seeing the big picture. My own sense of it is that the term *big picture* misses the point. Because, in reality, the big picture consists of a thousand little pictures, and to the extent that any organization can give you insight into many of those little pictures, your perception of the big picture is going to be much improved.

So what are we talking about? We are talking about communication and cooperation between the discordant communities. That, to my mind, is the essential of what we are concerned with: how to get communities whose history has been very different, whose sense of obligation has been very different, and whose performance has been very different. Unfortunately, over the last 5 or 6 years, there have been more people killed in the NGO community than were killed in the previous 30. The world has changed. This applies both in terms of the international sector and the local sector. And to that point I might just observe that there are more than 4,000 NGOs operating internationally and hundreds of thousands operating within their own countries. So we're talking about a huge community, but a huge community that has been increasingly subject to the security concerns that affect all of us. Their casualty rates are a function of the fact that they are very much, as General Meigs pointed out, on the front line. That's where their mission demands that they be. So, sometimes when a dialogue emerges between the different communities as to, "Okay, we are going to do this and why aren't you there as well?" there will be misunderstandings as to why the military is not there, why the military is seemingly more concerned with force protection than the objectives of the mission, and so forth.

To sort out the constraints of the language difficulty is going to take time. To my way of thinking, the essential mechanisms for accomplishing this are through setting up channels of communication. Now, these have existed. I can well remember in northern Iraq, for example, there were channels of communication with the military that worked very well, and in Rwanda the same thing, and in Bosnia, not necessarily with the U.S. military, but with UNPROFOR, all kinds of arrangements were worked out. But they all tended to be, unfortunately, episodic and very specifically oriented to the circumstances. There was no pattern to fall back upon for the next time around.

There have been efforts to establish such a pattern. In the case of the U.S. military, the Civil Affairs people have been working very hard to establish the dynamics and rules of engagement, if you will, for dealing with the humanitarian community, and I think they have had a certain amount of success. I think I'm entitled to say that, having worked with the humanitarian community for so long, we are not as keen on doing this as the military has been. So the gulf is still there. The NGOs are still arrogant about the fact that they are humanitarians and no one else can be. I find that a little difficult to accept in terms of reality. If you are a victim in some lace, whoever helps you is the person who helps you, and that person is a humanitarian for a day or for that period. This is something the NGO community has to learn. On the other side, the military has to learn that the assumptions that the NGOs and the international organizations make about humanitarianism are very, very precious to them—so precious that they are willing to risk their lives in order to maintain them. So that has to be understood.

Let me speak about a particular issue, which unfortunately has generated a great deal of discussion. In Afghanistan, now, the wearing of uniforms by the military is presumed to be the thing to do. The absence of uniforms on the part of the military doing humanitarian work has really sent a shock wave through the humanitarian community on the grounds that they are going to be in threat, therefore, the questions of neutrality are in question, therefore, et cetera, et cetera. These are genuine issues. Now, whether or not they are a function of arrogance on the part of the military or a misunderstanding on the part of the humanitarian community is another question. This is the sort of issue that could be negotiated if there were normal, very predictable channels of communication between the communities, which unfortunately, to my knowledge, don't exist.

We talk about conflict response and conflict prevention. I'm not sure that conflict prevention works. I think it does, but I could not demonstrate it. If it does work, it's a function of a lot of small micro-efforts pulling together to accomplish a much larger goal. The trick, it seems to me, is that if there is some awareness of these micro-efforts, to get back to what I was saying before, putting them into the larger objective, then the possibilities or the chance of them working are vastly improved. Overall, the NGO community is a very, very multifaceted organism. There is no question about it. And I'm sure that many members of the NGO community operating right now feel very strongly that there is absolutely no point in having anything to do with the military, because the military cannot be seen as essentially neutral.

On the other hand, many members of the NGO community have moved past that and have recognized that if we are all engaged in a humanitarian enterprise, then the objectives of that enterprise and the fact that we can, in fact, help somebody survive are the essential things that are going to determine the relevance of our actions. There is an effort under ay to organize and regularize channels of communication between the military and the humanitarian community at large, the international organizations, and the NGOs. This is essential if we are going to really function. Humanitarian operations: I my experience, each one is bigger than the last. Each one is more demanding than the last, in simple human terms, in logistical terms, and in financial terms. Donors have been very forthcoming in terms of helping the NGO community, but donors don't see the big picture. They look at their projects, and the community has to respond in terms of their projects. Somewhere, a lot of this has to come together. At some point there has to be an opportunity to discuss the big picture in relation to the small picture, the NGO world in relation to the military world and the international organization world, the world of the press as it focuses on this and the communities.

Getting back to the NGOs, every NGO has a constituency. Whether it's a small town in Iowa or a large city in France, it has a constituency to which it owes a considerable debt of allegiance. This makes it more difficult. That constituency has to be drawn into the communication channel as well. I think it can be done. There have been very, very positive signs and, as I said earlier, some of them have been episodic, but they have had effects while they lasted, and perhaps they laid the seed in the minds of some people that it can be done.

Finally, to underscore what I said earlier, I think the military has been extremely forthcoming in recognizing the need for being prepared to be involved in humanitarian undertakings, and the need that, more often than not, they are going to be far beyond their expectation. I think the point has been made often during this conference that what happens in a huge humanitarian crisis does impact upon the national security of this country. We have been a little slow in recognizing that, but I think it's abundantly clear. The NGOs have to feel that they are part of this obligation. They, no doubt, are the ones who will be first on the ground, and they will be there after the conflict ends, trying to rebuild. Having been there before and during, I fully appreciate the fact that there is a tendency to feel isolated from the world community once you're doing that job. We can't allow that isolation to continue. Thank you.

AMBASSADOR ROBERT B. OAKLEY: Peter, thank you very much for the kind introduction. I think your remarks are right on target, and I wish to make a small point. Roy and General Meigs talked about the interaction and the very positive common ethics dealing with humanitarian affairs, and I'm not going to address that. I'm going to talk about some other things, but we all have to remember Roy's last point. This is part of a much bigger effort where the military and humanitarian communities both have to work themselves out of a job and turn it back over to the people in whose country they are operating; and we can't ever lose sight of that.

I want to talk about public security in an international context, the challenges and the way ahead. It's an increasing problem. Just as globalization has taken off with high-tech, better communications, so have the threats to public security. International organized crime, terrorism, narcotics have all benefited from globalization unfortunately. So we have a much greater threat out ahead, coming in many ways to our public security at home, just as we do to international public security. Therefore, the challenge can only be met on an international as well as a national basis.

It seems to me there are two basic approaches to increasing international capabilities for dealing with public security in the years ahead. First, what I call the soft approach, involving humanitarian, socio-economic, political-diplomatic action—in some cases preventive, and in other cases curative—dealing with conflicts, and acting to improve the basic human conditions and the problems which greatly exacerbate, if not totally cause, the breakdown of public security. I'm not going to talk about the soft approach, but what I call the hard approach, involving military, law enforcement, and intelligence activities to detect, deter, disrupt, or otherwise prevent or protect against public security threats. The three often overlap. General Meigs saw all three of them in Bosnia.

Military action can range from full-scale combat against terrorists, as in Afghanistan, to peace enforcement and peace building in failed states such as Bosnia where public security threats of all kinds flourish. It can also include training or other forms of cooperation with local military in failed states with security threats.

This year, the United States is playing a leading role in increasing international military capabilities dealing with public security. Multilaterally, you look

Ambassador Oakley

at a situation like Afghanistan, where the primary focus is on combat. Nonetheless, you find other elements beginning to come into it as they are now. As Peter said, they do not like to call it nation building. Secretary of Defense Rumsfeld called it "draining the swamp." But they are things that have to be done. The international developmental community, the humanitarian community, and the military are all working closely together in Afghanistan. A lot more has to be done in terms of coordination if we are going to succeed in the long-term effort to stabilize Afghanistan.

Ongoing NATO military operations in Bosnia with SFOR and in Kosovo with KFOR encompass police and other civilian public security activities. They've marked, thanks to General Meigs, increasing attention to organized crime and narcotics as sources of insecurity and threats to public security, both there and abroad, and it also comes back to the U.S. The European Union has created a 60,000-person quick-reaction force for future light interventions of the kind that we see in Bosnia and elsewhere. It includes a special 5,000-person constabulary police component, dealing with this lower end of the problem. Scandinavian countries developed a serious similar capability on the multilateral front. Bilaterally, the United States provides long-term and short-term education and training for thousands of foreign military officers each year in some 150 countries, and it engages most of the countries in bilateral and multilateral military training exercises.

Included in this military education and training are such specialties as antidrug, counterterrorism, and military police functions, as well as the broader improvement of across-the-board capabilities. It substantially enhances the foreign military capacity to deal with public security threats and improves coordination and cooperation with the United States and with each other. The most recent striking example of this has been the U.S. counterterrorist training teams for the Philippines, Yemen, and Georgia. These have been clear, serious terrorist threats beyond the current capacity and perhaps the will of local military forces. Results from the Philippines are already in. The results of Yemen are showing substantial improvement. We don't know yet about Georgia. Yemen is a huge challenge, with hundreds, perhaps thousands, of probable terrorists in mountainous areas outside the control of the local government. Something has to be done to help reestablish governmental control over the long term, and deal with immediate threats. In Pakistan, I wouldn't call it training, but U.S. Special Forces have been working quietly alongside the Pakistani military in the rural areas and have achieved a certain amount of progress there in dealing with the problems of al Qaeda and the Taliban that people thought previously couldn't be gotten at. At the same time, the CIA and FBI are very quietly collaborating with the military, both the U.S. and Pakistani, and the Pakistani police dealing with the al Qaeda terrorist threat. In Afghanistan and Pakistan, they are going to have to deal increasingly with the narcotics problem before we are finished.

Civilian law enforcement is the second pillar to beating this international public security threat. It's becoming increasingly international by means of older institutions such as Interpol, EuroPol, the U.N. Drug Control Policy Organization, as well as new institutions and many ad hoc arrangements. The United States has been the key element of multinational operations to rebuild effective civilian police and other law enforcement capabilities in crime-ridden states such as Bosnia and Kosovo. Most recently, we are starting in Afghanistan, where the Germans have the lead, but the United States is helping. We support the Civilian Police Assistance Unit of the United Nations, which works with scores of countries to rebuild the police forces. Bilaterally, the United States provides various forms of police, judicial, and other law enforcement training to police and judicial institutions in dozens of states, including large-scale programs in critical countries such as Indonesia, Pakistan, and Nigeria. All of these countries had been, could again, be players in international organized crime, narcotics trafficking, and/or international terrorism. The problems are evermore interlocking for mutual reinforcing. Narcotics traffickers, international organized crime, and terrorists reinforce one another. The United States Drug Enforcement Agency has expanded its functions tremendously in the past 15 years as has the FBI, again, to help provide capacity building for other countries as well as to get intelligence of our own.

The third pillar I want to talk about in this sort of international approach to dealing with public security, intelligence. I've arbitrarily created a third pillar because intelligence is so important. Intelligence includes support for military as well as civilian agencies of governments and their operations. Intelligence law enforcement information is usually embedded in military or civilian law enforcement organizations, including ministries of interior and justice, although the U.S. has its own Central Intelligence Agency. The whole function of intelligence—developing it, sharing it—whether it's law enforcement or whether it's intelligence as we have seen in the investigations of al Qaeda, in our own country we have problems in terms of sharing. We have seen the benefits since September 11th of last year of sharing abroad, and the increased volume of interaction has enabled us to detect and put out of business some 3,000 al Qaeda operatives—no mean feat.

This has involved a huge amount of work in Western Europe, also in Central Asia, including a number of Middle East countries: Egypt, Jordan, Saudi Arabia. This is not talked about much. This is the hidden element, all the way out to Southeast Asia, where hit teams have been picked up in Singapore before they could do the damage that they were planning to do to United States installations and personnel. This whole interlocking web of intelligence sharing and law enforcement information sharing is becoming much more important. United Nations Security Council Resolution 1373 gave it a big boost because it provides legal and political cover for countries who understood the need to do these things but had to change their own systems fundamentally in order to do so.

We are working on the same thing here at home—homeland security, how we can work better together, as well as the FBI and CIA, the other intelligence agencies, including their sharing with each other and with the law enforcement agencies. This is absolutely indispensable as we move ahead. In this whole web of activities, whether it's military—including the broad spectrum all the way down to humanitarian operations, which it does very well, but also dealing with organized crime and terrorism in one way or another, either direct combat or civilian affairs operations—or whether it's law enforcement agencies who are doing their thing, sometimes in collaboration with the military as we have seen in places like Bosnia—or humanitarian agencies, it all has to be looked at together because the threats out there are growing; they are not receding. Thank you.

AMBASSADOR GALBRAITH: Bob, thank you very much. First I'd like to invite the panel if there is something further they would like to comment on from the presentations made so far. Roy?

MR. WILLIAMS: One thing, just picking up on Bob's use of the word *intelligence*, I would like to introduce the word *information* because one of the difficulties among the communities has been information flow. Of course, there are always questions of open-source information, classified information, one thing and the other. Part of the many operations has really been compromised by the inability of the communities to arrange for mechanisms by which they can pass information freely and share information freely, information that has an immediate effect upon day-to-day activities. For example, in Kosovo, the meeting that was most attended by all of the NGO community was the one run by the military. Every morning, every NGO that was in Prestina at the time was there, because the military was giving out information on where the mines were, what areas were safe, and what areas weren't safe. Conversely, in that environment the NGOs are more than happy to tell the military things they didn't know because they had been up in the mountains and one thing or another. It wasn't intelligence in the pejorative sense that the NGO community thinks about, it was just a community effort, to use the word in its broadest sense.

AMBASSADOR GALBRAITH: Thank you very much. I was struck by a bit of an irony, though, in one of the points that you made, because you noted that the NGO community sometimes criticizes the military for not being neutral. Yet, we sometimes can see just the opposite. In my experience during the Bosnia war, there was great resentment of the military for not intervening on the part of many of the NGOs that may not have felt the official position of the organization. However, it certainly reflected the views of many on the ground that more ought to have been done to stop an ongoing massacre or genocide. The same thing is maybe even more true in Rwanda, so it can be a very con-fused world.

Before I open it to the audience for questions, I'd like to ask the panelists to come back to the question that I posed in my opening remarks: we figured out at great cost how to do this in the small places, but what do we do about the big places? Do we have the military capability to deal with a major collapse in a place like Pakistan or Indonesia and, indeed, we have one in a large coun-try that Bob knows well—in Congo, the former Zaire? When one talks about public security, how do we deal with, again let's take Pakistan and Indonesia? We know these are countries where terrorism is breeding, and yet there may be parts of these countries—the northwest frontier, some of the outer islands in Indonesia—where government authority is very limited. How do we deal with these bigger issues? Bigger places?

AMBASSADOR OAKLEY: Peter I'll start by saying two things. Places like the Congo, Afghanistan—hopefully not Pakistan, I hope it doesn't get worse—are going to be dangerous, are going to be humanitarian disasters for quite awhile before they can get back on their feet. But, getting them back on their feet requires development of local capacity. It also requires realistic objectives. Frankly, if the objective is to create a multilateral, multiethnic unified demo-cratic state in Bosnia, it takes a lot longer and a lot more resources than sta-bility with reasonable government. The same thing will be true in Afghanistan, to say nothing of what it will be like in Iraq, but we have to build the local capacity. In Pakistan, for example, thanks in part to the help provided by our Special Forces, the Pakistani military is now in the tribal areas where they have never been before, and they bring with them electricity, schools, food, things of this type that the people appreciate because they are not immune to what is happening in the rest of the world. They don't want to live in the Middle Ages forever. Things are beginning to change. The police are beginning to develop in Pakistan. So, it's things of this sort that we are working on in Bosnia as well that we have to think about if we are going to deal with these problems.

MR. WILLIAMS: I'd just like to pick up on that, because we tend to think of these problems in a monolithic sense. I recognize that, obviously at some level of political decision making and policy decision making, that is necessary. I think that, in fact, they exist in a much more fragmented way than we appreciate. During the war in Bosnia, when I was working there, we were able to open factories and start institutions running and keep people in the communities and not have them face the necessity of fleeing simply because there was no fighting in the area at the time. I can think of many examples of that in the Congo as well. The life of the societies in a war is much more fragmented than we tend to realize, and that's where the NGO community is at its best, its strongest, because it operates on the assumption that there are always places to work.

GENERAL MEIGS: I think I'd best confine my comments here to public security because I haven't had the type of experience that Roy and Bob have in a large-scale effort. After all, Bosnia is only the size of Georgia. It's not nearly as big as some of these other problem areas.

Public security is basically a question of returning a responsibility back to the locals, as Bob pointed out, working yourself out of a job. I'll never forget talking to a Republic of Srpska general one day who was very upset. He said, "Look, this is not an underdeveloped country. We had an education system, we had universities, we had a viable economy, we had institutions." Later, speaking to a police official, trying to nudge some things in the legal area, he said, "If you want good judges, it's very simple: pay them, make sure they are independent, and make sure no one can threaten their children." Now, the structures for doing that were existent in the Republic of Serpska and in the Herzegovina area of Bosnia and in the Bosniac area. The trick was creating a safe ground to allow those institutions to come forward and exert their control over the situation.

At one point we were assisting the Bosniacs in chasing down a very unsavory criminal who had assaulted a policeman with his automobile, knocked him down, and beat him almost senseless. Finally, the Bosniac police were fed up with this guy. He had been in court 17 times, and at the last minute, the witnesses would drop out for whatever reason. We finally put enough heat on the Bosniacs that they took him to court, convicted him, and then immediately let him out on appeal. Finally they put him back in jail for 6 months. But that was the first time a mafia don like that had ever been convicted and incarcerated. The trick then is to create the safe ground, provide the training, provide the support, and let them move on to that safe ground and begin to nibble away at these systemic problems that they have. But we can't do it for them.

AMBASSADOR GALBRAITH: Thank you. I'd now like to open the floor to the audience. I would ask that questions be questions and the introductory comments be brief and that you wait for the microphone.

AUDIENCE MEMBER: My name is Larry Juster. I'm with the State Department, Office of Political-Military Affairs. My question is for General Meigs. Sir, what role do you see the military playing in helping to facilitate the coordination of the efforts of the NGOs and GOs in humanitarian operations and postconflict reconstruction? And how do you try to keep that effort transparent, so that the effort remains as neutral and objective as possible? A follow-on is, what has been your experience with the use of civil-military operations centers?

GENERAL MEIGS: Well, first of all it depends on the mission you give the military and that is going to vary from place to place and it will depend to some degree on how aggressive that mission is. The mission in Kosovo and up until recently in Bosnia was to ensure a safe and secure environment, and the military commander was the sole, final interpreter of what that meant pursuant to the latitude allowed him by contributing nations and his own country. So you have to look into what it is that the military is asked to do and how big a player the military is in relation to the civilian organizations that are on the ground. In the case of SFOR, the military is a pretty big player.

Then the question is, how do you create incentive areas that allow the NGOs to come on board and work with you, making it clear that you're one among equals when, in fact, you're really not? That's leading from the back, and I think that's very important. The civil-military operations centers are critical, and the regional resettlement task force was based on those. We had a Civil Affairs organization in each of these headquarters, and while the commander enabled the RTF, the Civil Affairs personnel provided the operational expertise, pushed it forward, and ran it. So, they are vital, they are very, very valuable, and we use the heck out of them, and the reserve components do a terrific job in providing them, because we only have one active battalion in the force structure.

MR. WILLIAMS: One thing I'd like to comment on. You used the word coordination in your question. Using the word *coordination* raises expectations, which are not, quite honestly, going to be realized. The NGO community, as soon as you use that word, run to ground because their boards of directors, their funding sources, and so forth, expect them to be operating independently and responsibly on their own terms. You can get them to work with CMOC, but as soon as you wave the flag of coordination, you're asking for trouble.

AUDIENCE MEMBER: I'm Mike Harwood from the Foreign Service Institute. In March 1994, several of us coming out of Somalia and that operation were given an early draft of Presidential Decision Directive 56, *Managing Complex Contingency Operations*. My question is, based upon your vast experience as practitioners in these kinds of operations, how useful would it be to you as practitioners to get the cogent, well-conceived, comprehensive political-military-humanitarian-type plan from the national strategic level? And also to comment on Hans's point, on the earlier panel, that there is another national security presidential directive that is called [PDD] 56 that's languishing someplace, that would be the son of that particular earlier effort. Again, how useful would that be in your conduct of these kinds of operations down through the operational to the tactical level? Thank you.

MR. WILLIAMS: One of my conclusions, both while working with the NGO community and later with the U.S. government, was that PDD 56 should have been implemented at some point, largely because it struck me that PDD 56 would have given people the opportunity to avoid dodging responsibility for the consequences of their decisions. Creating a larger plan would have been something that gave everyone a means of working together and not being the lead dog and taking full responsibility. As far as I know, it was never implemented, certainly not when I was there or since. But I would have really supported its being implemented.

AMBASSADOR OAKLEY: Based upon my experience and the degree to which it has been implemented, the best is probably Kosovo. It worked out reasonably well. There was a fair amount of advance planning on political issues, military issues, and other issues. To try to look ahead as to where you wanted to be after it was all over, it took a little while to get there. That wasn't true in the beginning. So, for example, if you thought before the war began where you wanted to be when the war was over, and that means back home, you wouldn't have dropped the bridges into the Danube, because that made things much more complicated. I think that we're coming back toward that sort of thinking ahead, at least on the military side.

I was in a big wargame this summer called *Millennium Challenge* and played at the sort of regional combat commander level, and they found they needed such a device. They found it was very important. They brought in a bunch of people from the State Department, including Mr. Harwood and people from the political-military bureau, and they all worked together to craft a broad outline and then implement it as they went along. The implementation had to be done by the military commanders on the ground, together with the civilians on the ground, whether they were from the State Department, from international organizations, or from the humanitarian side. They all had to put their minds together. But we need to have a general outline, coming from the top, of where we want to be after the fighting stops. That is very important.

GENERAL MEIGS: I would certainly agree with that. The interesting thing about Kosovo is it was the second time the lessons learned from Bosnia were applied to the ramp-up to the introduction of KFOR into Kosovo. Here's a story to indicate the dilemma. I showed up as COMEAGLE, which is the northern district commander in Bosnia. I had Annex 1A of the Dayton Peace Treaty. I had an order that got my force into the sector, and then I got a phone call from a very senior military official who is a friend and he said, "Monte, here's my guidance to you, don't get anybody killed and stay out of the press." Now there are advantages to that in that it gives you a wide degree of latitude for what you *can* do. There are certain disadvantages to that. I encountered the same thing when I became COMSFOR because it was my responsibility to determine what *safe and secure environment* meant and what the approximate grounds were for the use of military force, to include lethal force.

It would have been useful to have had a greater consensus between—this is not a factor of this administration; I was serving in the last administration as COMSFOR—a common ground and understanding between the State Department officials that I worked with, the intelligence officials I worked with, and the U.S. guidance to SFOR as it came to me through U.S. channels. That pretty much didn't exist in terms of one common theme, and that complicated things to some extent. So clearly, that is critical. The other thing that is critical is that the mission set has to be based on the consensus of the international coalition. Different members of the coalition have different interests, and they have different rules of engagement. Somehow, there has to be an agreement on what the constructive gray area is for the commander, because that's where all the work is done. That's where all the work gets done with the other organizations, with the other embassies, and in dealing with the hardest core of the people who are on the other side that are trying to frustrate what you're trying to do.

AUDIENCE MEMBER: My name is Philip Hughes from the White House writers' group, and I have a question for Mr. Williams. I'd like you to expand on the key concept of neutrality that is so important to NGO organizations. In the discussion, scenarios have been discussed where NGOs don't trust the military to be neutral. Other scenarios discuss where the military isn't actively interventionist enough for NGOs preferences. We didn't discuss, but I can imagine scenarios where NGOs might actually regard the role of our military as part of the problem—that is, that anybody who is involved in fighting is worsening humanitarian conditions or creating suffering and making no real moral distinctions, or being sort of morally agnostic about the causes for which different combatants are fighting and the role that our forces would be playing. Are there any rules of the road that you can suggest that would help guide the military in what looks like a rather elastic application of the concept of neutrality by NGOs in these scenarios?

MR. WILLIAMS: I keep picking up on words that other people have used. *Elastic* is the one that sticks out in my mind at the moment. There is a big problem with the word *neutrality*. It used to be understood within the NGO community that everything you did, you did from neutral motives. Now, that was fine, because you were describing what the doer did. But I remember working in Bosnia, we would cross over from the Bosniac area to a Croatian area doing exactly the same thing, and people would stone us. We, in our minds, were behaving neutrally, but on the ground, people were thinking that we were taking sides because we had already helped the other people. Right now in the NGO community, there is a very large debate as to the relevance of neutrality, period, as to whether it's possible, period. Now, in the case of the military, if you're wearing a uniform, the presumption is that you are in the pursuit of a political objective for your country's interest. So whatever you do, therefore, cannot be neutral. Now that, to my mind, is kind of tortuous logic, but that is the issue as it's being presented now. In short, it's gotten very elastic, and it's no longer as secure as we used to think it was, even though some organizations insist that that defines how they behave.

GENERAL MEIGS: Let me try another crack at that problem. If I were giving a new SFOR/KFOR commander advice in training, I'd say, to deal with this problem, "Look, you have personally got to engage with the critical humanitarian players in your area of operations personally." I'll give you an example. When I first took over as COMEAGLE, I got to know a great human being named Santiago Perez, who was a UNHCR representative in northern Bosnia. Our problem was that we could never get UNHCR to coordinate their returns with us so that we could be there to secure the darn thing when it happened and help in the preparation, to put the screws to the Serb police so that they would do what they were supposed to do. Because, as Roy pointed out, they have an independent view and they do not want to be subordinate to what we were doing. Santiago asked me to go with him to see a resettlement village, which is something I wanted to do. We went to see about three. At one of them, in these nasty conditions, he showed me a man he had met who had to go around on a four-wheel board that had a scooter motor on it, and his motor was broken down. I said, "Gee, why don't I give you the money so we can go buy this guy a new motor?" He looked at me and suddenly it clicked. And from that moment on, he and I had a very trusting relationship.

Another fantastic person who was operating in Bosnia when I was there was a fellow named Jon Renee Ruiz, who did all the investigations for the Srebrenica massacre. It was not my job to protect him. He worked for ICTY; he was out there on his own. We had had difficult times on occasion with people who would try to suck us into things, and our orders were not to let that happen. But he would go run around in some areas where indigenous Republic of Srpska people would be very upset with him, and the last thing we wanted to do was either have him harassed or have his people injured in any kind of way. So while I could not say, "Jon Renee, I'm gonna have a patrol right with you," because that was contrary to my instructions, he knew that everywhere he went, we were right around the corner. We developed, over a period of time, a very good relationship based on trust. I didn't interfere with his operations; I enabled them. He could trust in the fact that I would do that. I could tell him where I was limited, and we could have an understanding about that. That is a key element on the front end of this thing.

Tie into that what Roy was saying about information. All intelligence becomes information when you go to a counterpart and say, "I don't think it's a good idea that we go here tomorrow." Why not? I'm supposed to do X and Y. "Jon Renee, I just don't think that's a good idea. Why don't you change your plan a little bit? You go over there, I'll go over here. There are some things I have to cake take care of." A light goes on. You haven't violated any security rules, but you have continued to establish this basis of trust and operational integrity.

AUDIENCE MEMBER: My name is Lieutenant Colonel Chris Soljec. I command a U.S. Army Reserve Civil Affairs battalion in Buffalo, New York. My question is in reference to some of the comments made about the permanent feature of the international security landscape—the need for civil-military cooperation in these post-conflict situations, for interagency cooperation. It was alluded to in the discussion about communications nodes, means of information transparency, relationship building as General Meigs pointed out, and it seems that up to this point, at least, we have kind of stumbled along and done this more or less on an ad hoc, post-deployment situation. My question is this: What do you think we could do to build those relationships and train and educate people, particularly the operators, who take policy and implement it on the ground prior to a deployment, so that we can be more effective and the learning curve is a lot less steep? Thank you.

GENERAL MEIGS: Well, we do that to some extent in the mission rehearsal exercises today. We make a very concerted effort to replicate every factor that exists in that area of operations to the people that are going down. And to some extent, we need to incorporate that into our school system, to the extent that we can devote the time and energy to it, because obviously at the Staff College and the War College you're dealing with how to fight a war primarily. Granted, this new strategic environment is going to make new demands on how we allocate that time. Other than that, you could involve humanitarian officials in the ramp-up planning as observers. They probably wouldn't participate as actual doers for the reasons that Roy is pointing out. But, if they understand what you're about and how you're going to do it, that could be very critical, and the Civil Affairs people could be the conduit for that.

AMBASSADOR OAKLEY: A lot of that was done, General Meigs, for Haiti, because General Sheehan, the CINC at the time, and the Assistant Secretary of

Defense for SOLIC (Special Operations and Low Intensity Conflict), who also handles humanitarian operations, found ways to involve the humanitarian community without letting them in on military planning, and actually they had two plans. One was an unopposed landing, which was not too highly classified, and the other one was an opposed landing. But there was so much similarity there, they found a way to do it. The National Defense University has been doing a lot of training with the various combatant commands as well with the representatives of all the different civilian agencies to try to push this forward. There has been less interest during this administration than at the end of the previous administration. They found out from places like Bosnia and Haiti that they needed to do more of it. Hopefully, that will come back again. Whether you call nation building a bad word or not, if you don't leave a place in pretty good shape, then you've defeated your initial objective and your initial reason for going in, but it can be done. I think there is a recognition that it needs to be done, but there are so many demands on the time and resources that people have to recognize that it's more important post-conflict and then push it into the school curriculums all the way through. Otherwise, it produces a nasty situation, and I'm afraid that we may run into that in Afghanistan at the moment.

GENERAL MEIGS: Having done the Afghanistan issue in the 1980s, to find ourselves back in the first decade of the twenty-first century, I'm not sure we want to be back in another 20 years.

MR. WILLIAMS: Two observations in response to that, and they're interconnected. One of the realities against which all of this has to be understood is the large turnover within the communities, both the military community and the NGO community. So the only way, I think, to respond to that is to institutionalize more your objectives.

My concern is that the objectives of the Civil Affairs, the humanitarian side, are not always taken as seriously as they might be in planning operations or even in discussing the criteria backdrop for operations. This is a military issue, of course, but it has been my sense that if we are really going to get someplace where I think we need to be, both those things have to be dealt with in one package.

AMBASSADOR GALBRAITH: I think we have time for one, possibly two, questions.

AUDIENCE MEMBER: My question relates to a comment made by Ambassador Oakley. I want to ask the panel about an area in which I feel that there is a possibility for the armed forces to act in concert with other agencies. The armed forces, in the last two days, have alluded to two aspects. One is attacking the base to remove a base where this type of activity is taking place, like Afghanistan. The other is where they go in after something has happened. When we talk of globalization and crime going global and also the linkage that terrorism usually rides piggyback on the crime syndicates, then we have a very different type of a world that exists out there. Unless we tackle that type of world, I don't think we can ever find a solution to this. So the syndicates, from what I have read, have an annual dollar finance which exceeds $4 to $6 trillion per annum, which is larger than the budgets of three-fourths of the countries listed in the U.N. They have a very, very powerful reach in terms of intelligence, in terms of what they can do—fake passports, all those types of things.

Does the military see roles for itself in tackling this scourge in a proactive manner, or is it going to be allowed to be done by civil agencies? Because in my opinion, if the civil agencies were capable, they would have solved it. So, in the new world that we are in, is there a role for the military to help the civil agencies work on this? That's my question.

AMBASSADOR OAKLEY: I'll just make one brief comment again about Pakistan today. For the first time, we have the Pakistani Army, the Pakistani police, and Pakistani military intelligence working together, and they are working together with the Special Forces, the CIA, and the FBI. Nobody is talking about it, thank God, because the more we talk about it, the more difficult it will be for them to work together. They are making progress, but they have about 25 years to catch up, and it's going to be a very hard, tough, long process, but General Meigs was in the middle of that in Bosnia.

GENERAL MEIGS: One of the problems we had was getting federated intelligence apparatus that worked across all the different agencies. And fortunately, after 9/11, that has been fixed to some extent, and now the trick is to take it into our national doctrine how we do that without a lot of preparation and the immediate entry to planning for one of these operations. You ask a very, very difficult question, but there is no easy answer. First, it depends on national law, and you get differences between nations. In some of these countries, you have this intermediate paramilitary—and by paramilitary I mean an extremely professional, half-military, half-police force—that very easily fits into this niche between the conventional military that is in a peace-enforcement mission and actual civil police. Many times in many situations the civil police don't have the military, the force, to deal with the issues, so they have to call on the military weapon if they can get through the negotiations and the coalition that allow a common effort in this area, which is extremely difficult because of policy and law. One of my frustrations was dealing with the European Union officials and explaining to them that a lot of the money that was causing political perversion in Bosnia was coming out of networks that ran up into their countries, and couldn't they do something under the third pillar of the European Union? They would look at you and say, "Well, we haven't defined that yet." That's a very difficult question, but once you get that sorted out, the next step is in the mandate to the commander, to what degree are you going to give him that kind of enforcement latitude, realizing that every one of the contingents in his force has a different set of rules of engagement limited by national instruction? This is not an easy problem, and it is very difficult when you have operation A and operation B that are somehow connected by this self-healing cellular network of terrorism that we are dealing with. I mean, you put your finger on a real tough problem, but a lot of people much more senior than I am are going to have to work their way through that one.

AMBASSADOR GALBRAITH: Thank you very much. And the hour of 1 o'clock having arrived, I would like to thank our panel for an interesting presentation, based on many years of direct experience that show that these are issues that we will be working with and seeking to refine in the decades ahead. So gentlemen, thank you very much.

CLOSING ADDRESS

TRANSFORMATION OF THE MILITARY INSTRUMENT OF NATIONAL POWER

General Richard B. Myers, Chairman, Joint Chiefs of Staff

Introduction by: General Eric K. Shinseki, Chief of Staff, United States Army

Summary

General Eric K. Shinseki, Chief of Staff, United States Army

- President Bush wrote that all requirements must be transformed. This is a significant challenge and an imperative.
- Fundamental comprehensive change in any institution is more revolutionary than evolutionary.
- President Woodrow Wilson once said, "If you want to make enemies, try and change something."
- Change confronts our biases, it undercuts our most closely held beliefs, it challenges our willingness to take risks. Yet it's essential if we are to grow and remain relevant. Change is the most difficult process that any institution can undertake, and it demands strong, visionary leadership.

General Richard B. Myers, Chairman, Joint Chiefs of Staff

- The security environment that President Eisenhower faced was unprecedented when he took office. He had a conventional conflict going while having to prepare for a potential global, nonconventional, thermal-nuclear conflict. Today we have the opposite situation; we are involved in a global nonconventional war, going against terrorists, while having to prepare for a conventional regional war.

   1. Secretary of Defense Donald Rumsfeld said, "We have to prepare for the unknown, the uncertain, the unseen, and the unexpected."

   2. Eisenhower responded to his security environment by emphasizing the nuclear response and to do this, he had to change the military. Everybody was changing our culture and that had a huge impact on our armed forces.

3. We put so much thought into the nuclear piece that we neglected the conventional piece. It points out that the assumptions that you make can really shape your thinking. And you've got to go back, and you have got to evaluate those assumptions fairly frequently to see if they still stand the test of time.

4. We are still paying the price for being so focused, as successful as it was, on winning the Cold War. It still affects our thinking, our organizations, our structure, and our equipment. For more than 40 years, we were organized, trained, and equipped to defend against the Soviet Union and the Warsaw Pact, and the threat did not change very much. Our thought process did not have the real rigor that is needed in today's environment.

5. Transformation is not just technology. It should not necessarily be about programmatics or budgets. It is not just to seek revolutionary changes through the conduct of warfare. Transformation is not a new concept. It is a continuum of dramatic changes to the ways wars are fought.

• Transformation must occur at the same time that our forces are extremely busy. We need that transformation power now, so we can give our forces and, most importantly, our president the flexibility and options to be agile and responsive to whatever comes our way that would threaten our nation, our citizens, and our liberties.

• The first element of transformation is the intellectual piece. The most important breakthroughs in transformation are going to take place in the minds of our warfighters, planners, service chiefs, and others.

1. We have to learn to adapt to that uncertain environment described by Secretary Donald Rumsfeld. It is the environment that we live in, and probably will most likely live in for some time.

2. Warfighters have to have the intellect to comprehend how the joint force will fight, to comprehend the commander's intent and the joint force commander's intent, and then to recognize how their units' capabilities can fulfill that intent.

3. This will entail taking operational risk—but not recklessness. These are educated and calculated risks.

4. We must encourage and reward subordinates to take risk and support them when they fail. This is not about intellectualism; it is about having a flexible mindset.

• The second element of transformation is the challenge of our operating culture.

1. Proven tactics, techniques, and procedures reinforce service cultures. But in transforming our joint warfighter, we must accept operating in an unpredictable and uncertain environment.

2. Success requires trust and confidence among all our service members, to include the flag and general officers who will lead our joint forces. We

must also extend that trust and confidence outside the military to many other federal departments and agencies.

• Technology also plays a part in transformation.

1. One of the lessons learned from Operation Enduring Freedom in Afghanistan is that technological change must be supported by cultural change.

2. Technological improvements are part of how we can integrate our individual service pieces together better, which is the defining quality of future joint warfighting. In the past, we participated in segregated warfare. In the future, we have to think about how we integrate all of these elements the services bring to the fight into a joint operating architecture.

3. We are working on a joint concept of operations to explain how are we going to fight. Then we can evaluate different systems against that concept. We have to test these systems against an operational architecture.

• We must be able to be responsive to the President's orders when he asks us to do something. We have to enter any situation rapidly and decisively, analyze it, and achieve our objectives. When we can do that, that's what transformation is all about.

Analysis

General Myers' remarks on transformation proved an apt closure to the conference by comparing our current global security environment to that faced by President Eisenhower in the early days of the Cold War, focusing on the essential leadership components of military transformation and highlighting the need for an overarching operational concept for the United States military in today's world. As he noted, transformation is not solely about equipment or platform; it is about changing the way the U.S. military fights.

While the end of the Cold War was an amazing success for the United States, its economic and political systems, and its military strategy, General Myers is correct to emphasize that the nation is still burdened today with strategic vestiges of that conflict. The military remains organized around tactics, doctrine, and equipment that were developed primarily for that conflict. While all of the services have taken steps to appropriately address the challenges of the post–Cold War world and the early twenty-first century, these steps need to be accelerated and must also address the military's underlying culture.

As Mrs. Frances Hesselbein discussed during her address, successful leadership in a time of change requires innovation and fresh thinking. General Myers built on this point with his call for more risk taking and flexibility in the military. Today's security environment requires leaders who can think creatively and learn to adapt to the uncertain environment described by Secretary

Rumsfeld. Senior leaders must encourage, reward, and support subordinates who take creative risks to engender this culture through the services.

This cultural change is essential to true transformation. Underlying that change is building the trust and confidence among the services that is fundamental to truly integrated joint operations. The trust and confidence discussed by General Myers mirrors Mr. Dick Grasso's comments about the importance to success in any organization of building trust and sustaining confidence.

Finally, General Myers addressed many misperceptions by confirming that transformation is truly about changing how the U.S. military fights. The intellectual and culture change will be driven by the newly developed concept for future operations—the blueprint for how the military will fight in the future. Programs, budgets, and technology will be developed to support this concept. How the military will fight must come first and is much more important that what the military will use to fight. This message has wide applicability to the other instruments of national power and provides an appropriate close to the discussion.

Transcript

DR. DANIEL GOURE: Ladies and gentlemen, as the final set of events in this conference, we are going to hear shortly from General Myers, the chairman. I have the distinct pleasure of introducing the individual who is going to introduce him. I was told to be very brief because the general and the chief are on a very tight schedule. I wanted to just come up with a two-word thought here. I heard it this morning. It's not a new idea, but I think it applies here, and that is *change agent*. I can think of no individual in the military who more personifies that in his career and in his leadership in the Army than General Shinseki, so it is distinct pleasure and privilege to introduce the Chief of Staff of the Army.

GENERAL ERIC K. SHINSEKI: Good afternoon, everyone. This has been a terrific two-day gathering, from my point of view, and I'm impressed by your stamina. This afternoon, before introducing our closing speaker for the conference, I would like to just take a minute to express my gratitude and my respect to the co-sponsors of the 2002 Eisenhower National Security Series and this conference. First, to Susan Eisenhower and the Eisenhower family; Frances Hesselbein and Rob Johnston and the Peter Drucker Foundation, and Frances once again, thank you for that wonderful address this morning. Richard Cavenaugh and Gail Fosler and the Conference Board of America, the Office of the Secretary of Defense for Net Assessment, the Honorable Lee Hamilton and Dr. Robert Litwak and the Woodrow Wilson International Center for Scholars, and, finally, Dr. Loren Thompson and Dr. Dan Goure and the Lexington Institute. They have been our workhorses for the past two days, our ringmasters, making sure all of this came together so well. We've been

General Shinseki

privileged to hear from a world-class lineup of speakers and panelists and we've all profited from their insights, their experience, their scholarship, and their candid discussions of the significant challenges facing all of our nations. Please join me in expressing my thanks and the conference's thanks to these distinguished speakers, our co-sponsors, our moderators, and our panelists. Thank you all very much.

In our recently unveiled National Security Strategy, President Bush writes that the major institutions of American national security were designed in a different era to meet different requirements. All of them must be transformed. That is a significant challenge, but it is imperative. Fundamental comprehensive change in any institution is more revolutionary than evolutionary. We are reminded that President Woodrow Wilson once said, "If you want to make enemies, try and change something." Change confronts our biases, it undercuts our most closely held beliefs, it challenges our willingness to take risks. Yet it's essential if we are to grow and remain relevant. Change is the most difficult thing that any institution can undertake, and it demands strong and visionary leadership.

The 2002 Eisenhower National Security Series and National Security Conference is honored this afternoon to welcome that kind of leader, a leader of change, a leader with vision—General Richard B. Myers. On his nomination to the position of Chairman of the Joint Chiefs of Staff, he was described as the embodiment of the transformation with which he will be charged. General Myers is a combat pilot with more than 4,100 hours in six different aircraft; 600 of those hours were in combat in the skies over Vietnam. He served as commander of the 5th Air Force and U.S. Forces Japan, as the assistant to the Chairman of the Joint Chiefs of Staff, as commander of Pacific Air Forces, and at that time as commander-in-chief, North American Aerospace Defense Command and U.S. Space Command. For the 19 months before he assumed his duties as Chairman, he served as the vice chairman of the Joint Chiefs of Staff. General Myers is well versed in the effective use of the military instrument of power—not just in the theory—and he is committed to the important and difficult task of transforming our military for the challenges of today and those yet unforeseen. We are grateful for his strong leadership, for his Midwesterner's penchant for hard work, his common sense and plain talking, and for his more than 37 years of dedicated and courageous service to our nation. Please join me in welcoming the Chairman of the Joint Chiefs of Staff, General Dick Myers.

GENERAL RICHARD B. MYERS: Thank you, Ric [General Shinseki], for the very kind introduction. It's great to be on the same team with you. My thanks to you and your staff for co-sponsoring this event. I thank Ambassador Oakley, Ambassador Galbraith, and many of the co-sponsors who are represented here today by some of their leadership. General Shinseki just went through them, so I'll not go through them again.

Ladies and gentlemen, I'm humbled and intimidated to bat clean-up after such an elite group of who's who in this business we're in. However, I feel I have a connection with almost everybody that spoke to you during this conference. I wish I were half as good a speaker as David Gergen. You're going to wish I was too when I finish here. Dick Grasso allowed me the privilege of ringing the opening bell twice on the New York Stock Exchange. I'm not going to tell you the cumulative decline of the index after I rang the bell, but it was record setting, let me say that, and the people were very nice. The last time I shared a stage with Secretary Mineta, who spoke to you as well, we were saying farewell to Admiral Loy for his great years of public service in the Coast Guard as commandant. We failed in that because the next day he went to work for the Transportation Security Administration.

To make this interesting, I thought I'd talk about a couple of famous people. I'll talk about one in the beginning and one at the end. From my home state of Kansas, the first is obvious, former President Eisenhower, from Abilene. The second person is James Butler, from Hayes City, Kansas. The Eisenhower connection is obvious; after all, the conference is named for him. You've heard the details of the challenges he and his folks faced when he was president and even before. We know that the security environment that President Eisenhower faced was unprecedented when he took office. He had a conventional conflict going while having to prepare for a global nonconventional thermal nuclear-potential conflict. Today we have the opposite situation. We are involved in a global nonconventional war, going against terrorists, while having to prepare for perhaps a conventional regional war.

I know that many of the speakers have talked about the security environment, so I'm not going to dwell on it. Let me just summarize it by a statement made by Secretary of Defense Donald Rumsfeld which captures it all. He said recently that we have to "prepare for the unknown, the uncertain, the unseen, and the unexpected." That about covers it. It's up to General Shinseki and me and some other folks to figure out how are we going to prepare for all those "uns."

General Myers

Eisenhower chose to respond to his security environment by emphasizing the nuclear response. To do this, he had to change the military, and he did. We fielded airplanes like the B–52. The ICBMs became a national priority in those days. In 1957 the Navy Analysis Group published their report on fleet ballistic missiles and their use on submarines. The Army was working with Honest John and so forth. Everybody was changing our culture. Obviously, what took place in that timeframe had a huge impact on our armed forces. In fact, it mesmerized both the United States and the then-Soviet Union by the nuclear arsenals we built up. In our case, we put so much thought into the nuclear piece, it's fair to say that we neglected the conventional piece, and we tried to straighten that out starting in the 1960s.

This points out that the assumptions you make can really shape your thinking, and you have to go back and evaluate those assumptions frequently to see if they still stand the test of time. We are still paying the price for being so focused, as successful as it was, on winning the Cold War. It still affects our thinking. It clearly affects a lot of our organizations and our structure and the equipment we have, and in many respects dominates to this day. Even though we said many years ago we wanted to rid ourselves of that focus, it still dominates our culture and our thinking.

For more than 40 years, we were organized, trained, and equipped to defend against the Soviet Union and the Warsaw Pact. Frankly, the threat didn't change very much. It was a gradual thing, so our thought process, in my view, did not have the real rigor that is needed in today's environment. It seemed like it at the time, but compared to today's environment, I would say it was more like rigor mortis as we came through that process. It was not real rigor. By the time the Berlin Wall fell, we were two generations into our thinking, and it was difficult to change. General Shinseki was talking about that in his introductory remarks.

Let's go back in time; let's put ourselves 50 years ago. This building wouldn't be here, but let's go back. We could still have had a conference years ago called *National Security for the Last Half of the Twentieth Century:*

Anticipating Challenges, Seizing Opportunities, and Building Capabilities. That would have been a good title then, and I bet much of the discussion would probably have been the same. We would have talked about the types of forces we needed, the kind of organizations, doctrine, training, and so forth. So then, like today, we would be talking about transformation.

That is my transition—to tell you what I want to talk to you about briefly—and that is transformation: the key elements of transformation, at least in my view, and the role that transformation should play in our thinking. If you go to just about any search engine and you type in *transformation* and you hit *search*, you'll get about 4.2 million hits. If you decide you just want to search "military transformation," you'll get a much more manageable number of about 430,000 hits. Therefore, transformation is not a subject that you can't find an article or two about. Ideas about transformation abound. My focus is on results. Bear that in mind. I want to make our ability to operate in the battlespace better for our young men and women who are out there in that battlespace. Therefore, I want results. Because it's not going to be transformation that wins our war; it's going to be people.

Let me start out by saying what transformation is *not*. Transformation is *not* just technology. It's *not* about, in the Army's case, putting wheels on vehicles that used to have tracks. That is *not* transformation in and by itself. It's *not* a stealthier airplane. It's *not* a new carrier design. That's not transformation. When it drifts in that direction, the debate then becomes more of a programmatic and a budget debate. Moreover, what we found last year, at least in my view, is that everybody scrambles to look for things they can call transformational. Somebody checks it off on their checklist and it sort of guarantees funding, because now we have called this thing, or this device, or whatever "transformational."

It should *not* be about programmatics; it should *not* be about budgets, necessarily. If it's just an issue of protecting rice bowls, how can we call that transformation? In the same vein, in my view, transformation is *not* just seeking revolutionary changes to the conduct of warfare. We can have, and we have had, dramatic changes to the ways wars have been fought—nuclear weapons, stealth technology, the microchip, and other things. I could go on about things that bring change to us that can be evolutionary, revolutionary, but they can't be the sole focus of our transformation quest. Silver bullet solutions, in my view, are rare.

Finally, I'd say that transformation is not new. It's a continuum we've been on for a long time. Though I would say that after September 11, what is new is the sense of urgency by which we must pursue and transform ourselves. However, transformation is not a new concept for me. It's also important to realize that transformation must occur at the same time that our forces are extremely busy. We can make up all sorts of excuses for ourselves as to why we have to stay as we are today—we have our global war on terrorism, we have folks forward deployed, we are trying to husband forces back here in case we should be asked to do something else. We are a very busy force. In many respects, our operations tempo, our personal tempo is very much wartime-like, as you would expect it to be. But we need that transformation power now so we can give our forces and, most importantly, our president the flexibility and options to be agile and responsive to whatever comes our way that would threaten our nation, our citizens, and our liberties. Therefore, that's what transformation is *not*.

I can't just stop there. I have to go on to tell you what transformation is, so I will do that. The two key elements we need to consider when we think about transformation are the intellectual piece and the cultural piece. This may be different from what some of you have thought about. The first element is the intellectual piece. The most important breakthrough in transforming ourselves is going to take place between the ears of our warfighters, our planners, our service chiefs. All of us have to learn to adapt to that uncertain environment that Secretary Donald Rumsfeld spelled out in all those "uns" that I spoke of earlier. It's the environment we live in and will most likely live in for some time. Therefore, our warfighters have to have the intellect to comprehend how the joint force will fight, to comprehend the commander's intent and the joint force commander's intent, and then recognize how their unit's capabilities can fulfill that intent. Therefore, we have to shed old ways of thinking.

Every day I get presentations on things that reflect those two generations of Cold War thinking that just keep moving along. Some people come in and say, "Here is how we ought to attack this problem," and it's just not responsive to the kind of environment that we face today. Maybe in the question-and-answer session we can go into more detail. I heard General Shinseki say, "This may entail taking some operational risks." That is not about recklessness, but about educated and calculated risk-taking sorts of ventures. We have to weigh all the options, to include the option of what happens if we do nothing in the context of that ultimate objective that is set out there for us. We have to learn to encourage and reward our subordinates to take risks as well. That carries with it the responsibility—once you tell them to be innovative and thoughtful and approach problems differently—that when they fail you don't crucify them. In fact, those are the kind of people you want to keep around.

Intellectualism is all about having a flexible mindset, not one that is etched in the stone that we were so comfortable with up until, well I'd say it's still today for some people. I can see it in the way we approach using various elements of our military power. Again, go back to the briefings in my office that I see from time to time. It is just fascinating to see how people say, "Well, wait a minute, that's our doctrine. That's how we do it." I said, "Does that meet the intent, the objective?" "Well, no, not as well as it should." I say, "Well let's think about another way of doing this then." This is a small example, but it's important. We saw an example of this kind of mental agility in Afghanistan when it was realized that the marines that first went on the ground needed some observers out there. The agreed-upon solution was to put P–3s with great sensor sweeps out there. The P–3 was never designed to be a forward scout element for marines, but that's how they used it. They put a Marine onboard. They put a suite of equipment in the operations center, and the sensors could relay what they saw out there. This was very useful and innovative, and I have to commend the commanders in the battlespace that said, "Yeah, let's try that," and it worked pretty well. Therefore, part of this element I'm talking about is adapting existing capabilities to the new environment.

A second element of transformation I want to talk about is the cultural challenge, and here, I'm thinking of our operating culture. Our service cultures are reinforced by our tested checklist, our proven tactics, our techniques, and our procedures. It's a comfortable environment of known qualities, familiar faces, and verbal shorthand that we all understand. Nevertheless, in transforming our joint war fighters, we have to go beyond that to accept operating in an unpredictable and uncertain environment. While success requires trust and confidence among all our servicemen and women, that includes building better trust and confidence among our flag and general officers, because they're the ones who are going to be leading, in many cases, our joint forces into the crisis, whatever that crisis is. Even harder, we have to extend that trust and confidence outside the military to many other federal departments and agencies, because today, in this new security environment, they are as much of this team and we are as much of their team as never before. We are a team, and that's why we've stood up these interagency task forces out at all the combatant commands, and so forth. We are trying to harness that power.

The first thing we have to do is build trust and confidence among people who say, "I've got this stuff, but I don't know if I can share this with you." Moreover, we've had some great debates in Congress recently regarding intelligence, but that is only one piece of it. There are many other pieces to go with this. It's a challenge that I'm going to take on personally, because one place we can start with is the Capstone Course. I don't know how many folks know about Capstone, but it's been mandated. It's been going on since before Goldwater-Nichols, but was revamped after that. Congress's view was something like, "To enable the services to work better together." That's our guidance, and we have a program today that doesn't go very far toward promoting better-integrated joint warfighting. Therefore, one of the things I have to work on is that Capstone Program, and it probably will trickle down into our joint professional military education that is part of each service's senior service schools, intermediate service schools, and so forth.

We have to invigorate trust and confidence among the components that paid off in the past. An example would be Generals "Fighting" Joe Collins and [American IX Tactical Air Commander General Elwood "Pete"] Quesada in the Second World War. If you remember, Collins' VII Corps was not able to make much progress from Normandy, so he and Quesada got together and came up with an evolutionary idea. They said, "We'll send some guys down there, we'll give them some radios so they'll be able to talk to the aircraft, and see how it works." There were obviously some elements of operational risk in that decision. That wasn't in anybody's playbook, but that's what they did, and they had success with that because they trusted each other, and they got the job done.

We have talked about the intellectual and cultural elements of transformation. They're very important elements that are fundamental if we are going to transform. Let's talk about technology and see what role that plays. Technology plays a part in transformation. One of the things you can go back to right away is the Eisenhower-era B–52. It's as relevant today as it was back then, although in an entirely different context. We upgraded it with the joint direct attack mission, or JDAM. Now we have an aircraft that can go very long ranges, and, in certain environments, can go in and deliver very accurate fire for soldiers on the ground. Technology can help us. I don't think people had conceived about close air support from 20,000 or 30,000 feet a year and a half ago, but that's exactly what we did in Afghanistan. It's a lot different than the kind of close air support that people in my generation grew up with, which is you've got to be pretty much lined up on final and somebody has to see you and say you're clear of hot. In this case, somebody on the ground is looking at the target, passing coordinates, and things happen, and you probably never see anything but the contrails if the weather is good—a much different concept.

One of the points here is that even though we had the technological change, we also had to change the culture a little bit to have that trust. We found out through some friendly fire incidents and so forth, we had some more work to do in this whole area. This is certainly not a panacea, and some of our stuff had not been worked through. Basically, it worked very well. Therefore, technological improvements are part of how we can integrate our individual service pieces together better.

In my view, the term *integrated* or *integrated operations* is the defining quality of our future joint warfighting. It is also my view that in the past we really participated in segregated warfare. DESERT STORM was a hugely successful campaign, but it was largely, not entirely, but largely a segregated and sectored campaign. We had the air war, then we had the ground war, and the ground war had pieces where we had the marines, the coalition, and VII Corps, doing their things. Close air support was a big part of the ground war, but never inside of the troops. It was always beyond the line of sight. In many ways, that was certainly more segregated than we need today. It was not integration in the way I am thinking about it. It was more akin to deconfliction.

In the future, we have to consider how to integrate all of the elements the services bring to the fight. We have to meld these capabilities into a joint operating architecture. We have to integrate, not segregate, our fires and our operational view of the fight. We are looking at the same fight, but it does not happen today. Therefore, if we are going to use our soldiers, airmen, sailors, and marines in a seamless joint campaign conducted by innovative warriors in an unpredictable environment, technology is going to help us do that. Technology is available, and it is not just a hardware or software issue. In my view, it is an issue of culture, trust, and understanding among our warfighters. Think for a moment about the example I used with Quesada and Collins and the P–3s and the marines. In these cases, we sent a person from one unit physically to another unit in the joint team. Those generally are labor-intensive efforts when you are trying to share knowledge and understanding across unit and service boundaries. In this area of shared knowledge, technology offers the greatest promises for transformation. I have talked for a long time about integrating our command, control, communications, intelligence, computers, surveillance, and reconnaissance. We have to do it in a way so that everybody can have a common understanding and knowledge of the battlespace in which they operate. The decisions we're going to have to make today and in the future have to happen a lot faster than they have in the past. Technology is going to help us so that we can do that faster than the enemy.

We are working on a joint concept of operations. The Joint Chiefs have not seen this yet, but we are on a path to put together for the first time how we are going to fight—probably in several different scenarios—and how we are going to fight the best we know. Then we can evaluate different systems as they come forward. How does this fit in the battle space? Does it fit in a way that makes it useful? If it doesn't, then it is rejected early. We can't do that today. People say something is wonderful, but we have to look at it wisely and say, "That's pretty useful," but we don't know because we've not tested it against anything. We have to test things against an operational architecture or concept of operations. We are working to do that to be able to make some of those judgments.

Let me give you one example of where technology really helped. Some of you were probably familiar with this when the Joint Forces Command conducted Millennium Challenge 02. One of the things they considered was web-based tools that enabled us to look at what they call the *joint fires initiative*. It has time-sensitive targets. All the components were in this collaborative environment. They all shared awareness of the battlespace. When a time-sensitive thing came up, they went into the collaboration mode to ask who could service that target. Since it's time-sensitive, we were thinking about servicing the target or creating effects on the target as quickly as possible. There was collaboration on line, and they would decide who would strike the target, who was going to capture the battle damage assessment, and then who was going to execute. This would, in many cases, take less than an hour. If you think about how we do that even today, it's very difficult. It requires a lot more coordination. This doesn't require anybody going physically from one tent to another, or from one command center to another, or across national boundaries. That's what I'm talking about in terms of faster decision cycles. That's part of what a transformed joint warfighting team has to be all about. It's just one of the success stories from that whole experiment.

The bottom line to me is the transformation and, I hope, to you. It's really not a goal. It's a continuum we are on, and it's more a frame of mind than anything you can point to, touch, or feel. Obviously, it's going to have its effects on doctrine, and organizations, and materiel, how we train our leaders, how we train our troops—the whole business. It's obviously going to have all that.

I mentioned two Kansans—one Eisenhower, who would probably have appreciated all these efforts, and another guy named James Butler. You probably wonder what he has to do with a transformed force. Well it was in 1889, 113 ago today, that he was the sheriff in Hay City, Kansas. He got the call, "Hey, we're having a big brouhaha down at the saloon." He goes in, sees about a dozen roughnecks shooting the place up. The local town folks were caught in the cross-fire, and he had to save the day. So he pulled out his revolver, picked out the leader, fired one bullet, shot him dead, and the fighting stopped and things went back to normal for Hay City in 1889.

We have to be just that responsive in the way that we respond to the president's orders when he asks us to do something. We have to enter any situation rapidly and decisively, analyze it, and achieve our objectives. When we can do that, that's what transformation is all about. Well, I don't think you remember James Butler by that name. Wild Bill Hickock was his real name. I don't know how transformational he was, but I thought it was a good way to tie Kansas to this business.

When I measure how we transform, I'm going to measure our ability to integrate our wonderful forces that the services bring to the fight. That's where we are going to get the most power for the punch. Each of the services is involved in its own thinking on how it is going to adapt to this. That's the essence of it for me. It's going to require both the intellectual and cultural piece I talked about. It's going to mean going beyond these existing habit patterns that we have built up for so long that really confine us in many ways. It's going to mean looking for new ways and better ways to do things with and between services, and it's also about trust and confidence. That is the essence. Therefore, we know when we have to count on somebody else, maybe in a different uniform, that whatever we are counting on him or her for, it's going to be there. That's what the trust and confidence is all about.

We have to become more flexible and agile and faster in the way we work as a team. This isn't easy, but this forum will probably go a long way as we write up the proceedings and distribute them and people have a chance to read them. It's going to have a big impact on the world out there—how we think about these things.

I want to thank Dr. Thompson for having set all this up and putting it together. General Shinseki, I thank you for sponsoring it and, more importantly, for your leadership and vision for the United States Army, and the Joint Chiefs of Staffs team for helping make transformation a reality. Thank you very much for that. With that, I'll take your questions and your answers, or questions maybe. Thank you.

AUDIENCE MEMBER: Thank you. My name is Paula Gordon. I have a web site on Homeland Security. There are people who, for whatever reason, are not convinced that there is a difference between pre–9/11 and 9/11. I wonder how you go about explaining or convincing such individuals—whether they are in the coalition, whether they're in the Army, whether they're in the armed forces, or whether they're the public or the media—what the difference is?

GENERAL MYERS: A difference in what sense?

AUDIENCE MEMBER: Why we live in a different world, why we need to have a different kind of focus than we had pre–9/11. What is the balance?

GENERAL MYERS: Okay. I'll give it my shot, and that's a great question. Clearly, we were in the business of transformation before September 11th and, as I said in my remarks, whether that was with a sense of urgency and why that is so important is the question you're asking. Why are we more worried about things today than we were then? If you look at the adversary we're up against, that's one of the big differences. We're up against, in some cases, not other nation's armies, air forces, and navies; we're up against networks that can really bring more harm to us and our friends and allies than armies and navies of the past. As tragic as Pearl Harbor was, fewer people were killed there than at the World Trade Center and the Pentagon on September 11.

If these adversaries, if international terrorists, could get their hands on things like biological or chemical weapons or, God forbid, nuclear weapons or even radiological devices, their willingness to use them is clearly shown. We have good, hard evidence from all the stuff we found in Afghanistan and from the detainees that we questioned that there is no question about their hatred and their quest for these types of weapons. To me, that changes everything, and so the way we are organized and the way we think about organizing ourselves and taking the fight to the enemy has to change along with it.

In the risk equation, the risk has gone way up. I'll give you a concrete example of that without revealing any classified details. We have had clusters of terrorists in places where, because of our inability to do things quickly, we weren't able to go after them. Moreover, the reason we couldn't do things quickly is because we are still organized the way we were in the Cold War, in many cases, or we don't have the right equipment, or we don't have the right relationships in some cases, not only inside our own government but with other governments as well.

Another example is that we have to change the way we set up those wonderful folks that went into Afghanistan and, through classic unconventional warfare methods, actually did the job there. However, they were left trying to win the hearts and minds of the Afghan people without the tools to do it because all of our structure was set up Cold War. If you want to provide military assistance for somebody, "Well, wait a minute, that's somebody else's budget; this has to be approved there or you have to think about this two years ahead of time." Sorry, we didn't think of this two years ago. We have to be more flexible. That's the imperative for me. The stakes are much higher than they've even been. We have wonderful armed forces. The fact that just barely over three weeks after being attacked we took a fight in a landlocked country and we prevailed with very few forces on the ground was a real tribute to us. We can't just rest and say, "Golly, we did a great job." There are many shortfalls that I'm not going to get into here of places we can improve. The people sitting here in uniform and probably half the civilians know what those are. There are things that we have to improve. This is just an entirely different environment, and it will be characterized by those uncertainties that Secretary Rumsfeld discussed. Yes, sir?

AUDIENCE MEMBER: Sir, Major Roger Carstons, Army Special Forces. Sir, as you alluded to and one of our panel speakers alluded to, all four services are developing their own transformation strategies, and as Dr. Binnendijk said, the Joint Staff is trying to weave all those together to try to ensure that they're all working in concert. I wonder if that might not be problematic, if the Army pares down its vehicle weight and yet the Air Force, through the Global Strike doctrine, is still unable to carry the vehicles because they haven't developed strategic lift. Is it better that we come from the bottom up to develop transformation strategies or perhaps should transformation be driven from the top down, from OSD or the Joint Staff, so that we have a chance of achieving a joint integrated approach to transformation?

GENERAL MYERS: That's a good question and getting into the very philosophical. My answer to that would be this: The services have competencies that nobody else has, and they know their forces and their needs. Therefore, some of it has to come up. Some of it, though, in terms of overarching, as I talk about a joint concept of operations, which may not be the right term, but how do we want to fight as a joint force? Some of that has to be agreed upon at a fairly high level, and we are also working on operational architectures that would come out of that concept of operations for command and control, precision engagement—terms that some of us here in Washington understand.

You probably understand. But going down, we need the architectures so we can figure out what fits in. I generally agree with you, and what we tried to do is design.

Take the Reagan Center here, for example. I'm sure the first thing that wasn't thought about when the architects went to work is, "How is the plumbing system going to be designed?" They probably didn't say, "We want a water fountain here and all the electrical outlets here, and, by the way, let's put a building around it." They probably started with the building—asked themselves what is the function—and then later on figured out where the plumbing and wiring went. We operate backwards to that today in the way we do business. We have the wires and the plumbing coming up, and how they fit into the joint fight is sort of an afterthought. We tried to remedy that by demanding that things be interoperable, and in the last couple of years we've done a good job of that. But if you don't know how you're going to put things together in a real fight, then you're at a disadvantage trying to figure out what needs to be interoperable with what, and how, and so forth.

It's a little bit of both, though. The services bring so much, such a wealth of intellectual horsepower to this whole equation. They have to be part of it. Everything that I've talked about has great service involvement, by the way. Eventually the Joint Chiefs of Staff will review some of these things and try to put our best knowledge to use, after they have been through some filters, certainly. I don't know if that helps, but there is not a pure way to do this. I loved it when I reported to the ROTC, and they said, "This is the Military Science building." I said, "Good, I'm an engineer; science I understand." Well, I don't really, but I pretended to for four years. Sir?

AUDIENCE MEMBER: I'm Nicholas Rigg, Department of State, currently at CGSC, Fort Leavenworth. You've talked a lot about U.S. assets. Looking at integration on an international scale, are we looking at assets the European and Asian allies can bring to the table and the specialties that they might have? Are we thinking enough in global terms when we approach transformation, or is that the next step after the current one?

GENERAL MYERS: No, I don't think it can be serial. It has to be parallel, in my view. You can ask some of the other folks. General Meigs knows a lot about this, living in Europe. I don't think it's the first thing we think about, but it needs to be; if not the first, the second, but certainly not in the serial sense. Like I said, we have 90 coalition partners in the war on terrorism. We have 10,000 on the ground in Afghanistan, with 6,000 from other countries in part of the international security assistance force in Kabul. We have another 1,500 on the ground with our folks who are doing the serious soldiering business. Therefore, we have to stay connected. It's a real problem, because everybody in other countries is working their own national interests.

We just came back from a meeting in Warsaw, where we had the North Atlantic Council informal meeting with the defense ministers, and we tried to push this idea of capabilities, and with the majority of the defense budgets going down with our NATO partners, it makes them very hard to transform and stay with us. One of the things that has been put on the table is, "Are there niche capabilities? Does everybody in NATO need a 360-degree military?" We do, but some countries probably don't, but they probably do some things very well. We just had this conversation in our office this morning, and we got some great support from one of the Baltic states in terms of specialized units they can provide in Afghanistan that can then fill a niche that we need. That has to be the model, but we need to think more about this. I don't know what Monte thinks, but we need to be very aggressive, making sure it's a parallel process and not an afterthought. Yes sir?

AUDIENCE MEMBER: Sir, when you talk transformation and you hear warfighters or read doctrine, they often refer to logistics as a burden, and some other folks talk about logistics as an enabler. From your perspective, as you see transformation evolving, are you looking at logistics as a burden or as an enabler for future forces?

GENERAL MYERS: It's clearly the latter. We've written a lot about that in Joint Vision, and we have to revamp the Joint Vision document that we're pushing around now and trying to get people to buy into. Logistics has to be a huge part of it. As we look at potential action in other places in the world, the logistics piece of that is the one that most of the senior folks worry more about than almost anything else. Therefore, almost by definition, that has to be up front. It's essential and a key part, and I didn't necessarily single it out, but it's part of the intellectual and cultural elements that I talked about in thinking about how to do things differently. The Transportation Command at Scott Air Force Base has some great ideas and is pushing some forward-leaning concepts. That's as much a part of how we transform ourselves as anything else. If we don't do that, then we will not be an effective, integrated warfighting force. Yes sir?

AUDIENCE MEMBER: Sir, Lieutenant Colonel Chris Halshee, 402nd Civil Affairs Battalion. With the increased role, as we have seen over the last year, of special operations in both meeting the conventional and unconventional threats and integrating those, what do you think your vision is in terms not only of the structure of special operations but also how we integrate them with the rest of the forces?

GENERAL MYERS: Well, I'm certainly not the expert here, but if we took a poll, I bet we would hear different things. Let me tell you a story. Some of you have heard this story, so pardon me. When I was Commander of U.S. Forces, Japan, we were running this exercise and it was a command post exercise. I'm in the battle cab and people are gathering, and some guy comes in. He has a stack of books this high. I said, "Boy, who are you, and why did you bring all those books?" He said, "Well, I'm your Special Forces representative, and this is our doctrine, and I'm here to make sure we employ our forces in a doctrinally sound, pure manner." He wasn't anybody I was much interested in after that. That may give you a clue where I'm headed.

Two things, one is that template in Afghanistan; you just can't take that template and lay it around the world and say, "Gee, that's our new template. We don't need more Army divisions; we need everybody to be in Special Forces." That is not the answer. It may mean that we uncovered some deficiencies in U.S. Special Operations Command in terms of equipment, and budgets, and stuff that needs to be rectified. It may mean that we need more people here and there and other places. It can certainly mean that. It clearly means that we have to integrate our forces, both black and white SOF and our conventional forces in ways we never thought of before. As I go around talking to people, I'm always confronted with the same mindset. We need some really fresh thinking. Please be one of the fresh thinkers, and don't get deterred when they spear you about 10 times. Just dry off the blood and keep marching forward. Somebody will hear you; I'll hear you. That's as far as I'll go on that. Was there another question over here? Yes sir?

AUDIENCE MEMBER: Sir, I'm Captain Matt Whitehead, I'm a Harvard strategist this year. My question to you is about the effects of globalization on military leadership. We have heard about how the democratization of technology and information has empowered our threat to act at a lower and lower echelon. My question is: How are we in the military going to deal with the fact that smaller and smaller units in our own military are being able to act on the global stage as well? An example would be Afghanistan. You had a handful of E-7s and O-3s who overthrew a country. What is your vision for transforming our personnel management systems to deal with that?

GENERAL MYERS: Everybody talks about my vision. I have my thoughts that I laid out to you, but my vision has to be anything I think. I want General Shinseki to think and we all want to think of this together, so that it will be our vision. I think the Secretary has recognized that the military personnel system, civilian personnel system are relics of an interesting time, but they are not responsive to the kinds of needs we have today, and I have to stop bordering on classified. I can give you great examples of things where we need to have more flexibility so we can train and retain in ways that we cannot do today because we are inhibited by some of our personnel policies, some of which are deeply rooted in statute or in other ways. Therefore, while you're seeing some of that debate in Congress right now on homeland security, I don't know how it's going to come out. That's an extremely important part—all of transformation, if you take the DTLOMS (doctrine, training, leader development, organization, materiel, and soldiers) through the doctrine, organization, and all that business, when you get down to personnel, it all has to be reflected. There is a big personnel piece and a big training piece, and it has to be adaptable and flexible. We have to work with some alacrity in all that we can't do today. Therefore, we are trying to accommodate that. You will probably see several initiatives come out with the next budget. That will move the ball forward. If you have specific ideas, feed them into the system.

AUDIENCE MEMBER: General Conkitis, from Lithuania. Perhaps my question is more in a form of a comment. Regarding specialization, often people tell us that in Lithuania, such a small country, you should specialize. You don't need a 360-degree force. Yet if you look where we are geographically, it concerns me that we may be pushed in the wrong direction. I feel that we can specialize and we do specialize in a specific area, yet at the same time we must have a 360-degree force, just like the United States, for specific reasons of geography.

GENERAL MYERS: That gets to be a very philosophical discussion. We have had these discussions with other members of NATO, especially some of the newer members of NATO, in terms of how much of their gross domestic product they can put into defense. Can they afford a 360-degree military with naval assets and air assets and ground assets that are trained, ready, competent, and can be sustained? It may have to be something you look at in phases. Depending on the outcome of the Prague Summit here in November and Lithuanian status after that point, you may want to consider it in stages. If your country is part of an alliance, you can afford to take some risks in certain areas and then decide what your biggest sovereign risk is and work that piece, but rely on the alliance for other pieces. For smaller countries it's hard to have a competent 360-degree military, especially as you transform and reform your military from what it used to be during the Cold War to what it needs to be in the future. It's probably something you can phase. Good question, and that guy right there probably knows more about that.

I'm getting a cut sign from this guy with the microphone. Thanks very much. Those are some thoughts on transformation. Thanks for the folks that hosted this conference. Thanks again, Rick, for the kind introduction. I thank you all.

DR. GOURE: I have the enviable task of summing up the conference and drawing it to a close in the next 10 minutes. I must be comprehensive, so I will make a couple of points. One was in the last exchange here between General

Myers and the representative of Lithuania. If you think back a decade ago, the idea of having that kind of conversation with representatives from these two countries, on this basis, would have been the height of insanity. It leads to two observations about this conference and the meaning of what we heard today. We have gone from ideas about the consciousness, the relationship between consciousness and culture, violence, predisposition to aggression, and how we can deal with that, all the way across to discussions of specific military capabilities, transformation, their meaning in the larger context. That leaves me with the following observations, and I'll close on these.

The first one is we are getting much better over time at being able to apply military force with speed and precision. I could talk about the problem of having difficulty because it takes an hour for everybody to get together, talk about the target, pick what systems are going to go out and do battle damage—an hour. In the first Gulf War, we were talking three days for an air tasking order. We are now talking about an hour—a 72-to-1 ratio. If that's not transformation, then I'm lost on what the term means, and we are just starting with that. It's very precise and very fast, with increasing knowledge. Contrast the capability of the military with the discussions we have had about the changing environment. We have a lack of precision, a lack of knowledge, a lack of ability to integrate, to synthesize. We have a dilemma. *Paradox* was the term that Michael O'Hanlon used. I like the term. We are in a bit of a paradox. We are getting better, not only in the United States but also in the Western World, at doing the things that the nation asks the military to do—which is fight wars, fight them very effectively, and protect the nation.

There will be much more to do as we go into homeland security and all the rest. However, the world is changing rapidly in unpredictable ways, and our ability to understand it hasn't caught up with our ability to take action. That is, in fact, the strategic problem of the next decade, perhaps even the rest of the century—to understand that world, to be able to then apply strategic principles to it, and, on the basis of that, to understand how to use that military instrument in what way, to what ends, against what adversaries, and with what target in mind. That is going to be a struggle. These things are going in parallels. We can't wait for one, but the other is lagging behind. The world is changing faster than our capacity to understand it or to affect it, if you will.

With that, I want to bring this conference to a close. I would like you to join me in thanking, in particular, the United States Army for its efforts, General Shinseki, General Myers, and the Joint Staff. This, in my view, has been one of the best conferences I've attended in a very long time, and it's been incredibly stimulating. Thank you, General, all the members, the panel, and particularly the support staff, the United States Army, in particular, who were just terrific. Two more things: you have in your packages a questionnaire. When you go out the door, there are boxes to put them in. Please do, because

we are committed to using your ideas to make next year's conference better,
and next year's conference is already scheduled. You can register for it as of
tomorrow. I'm not guaranteeing what is going to be on the program yet, but if
it's anything like this year's program, it's going to be a hell of a show. Thank
you all for attending.

Biographies

Dr. Hans Binnendijk

Dr. Hans Binnendijk is currently the Theodore Roosevelt Chair in National Security Policy and Director of the Center for Technology and National Security Policy. He previously served on the National Security Council as Special Assistant to the President and Senior Director for Defense Policy and Arms Control (1999–2001). From 1994 to 1999, Dr. Binnendijk was Director of the Institute for National Strategic Studies at the National Defense University. Prior to that he was Principal Deputy Director of the State Department's Policy Planning Staff (1993–1994). He also served as Deputy Staff Director of the Senate Foreign Relations Committee (1980–1985). He has received numerous awards for his government services, including two Distinguished Public Service Awards.

In academia, Dr. Binnendijk was Director of the Institute for the Study of Diplomacy at Georgetown University, where he was also the Marshall B. Coyne Research Professor at the Edmund A. Walsh School of Foreign Service (1991–1993). He was Deputy Director and Director of Studies at London's International Institute for Strategic Studies and Editor of *Survival* from 1988–1991. He is author or co-author of about 100 publications and reports, and is a frequent contributor to the International Herald Tribune, the Washington Quarterly, Strategic Forum and Defense Horizons.

Dr. Binnendijk serves on the Board of Overseers of the Fletcher School of Law and Diplomacy, the Studies Committee of the Council on Foreign Relations, the U.S. Committee of the International Institute for Strategic Studies, and the CSIS International Research Council.

Dr. Binnendijk is a graduate of the University of Pennsylvania and received his Ph.D. in international relations from the Fletcher School of Law and Diplomacy, Tufts University.

Dr. Thérèse Delpech

Dr. Thérèse Delpech is currently the Adviser to the High Commissioner for Atomic Energy. From June 1996 until June 1997, she was the Special Adviser to the Prime Minister for Political-Military Affairs. Previously, she served as Research Associate Fellow at the Centre d'Etudes des Relations Internationale (CERI) where her research focused on nuclear matters, nonproliferation, and disarmament. She has recently published L'Héritage Nucléaire (Editions Complexe, 1997) and La Guerre Parfaite (Editions Flammarion, 1998).

Major General James M. Dubik

Major General James M. Dubik hails from Erie, Pennsylvania. He graduated from Gannon University with a bachelor's degree in philosophy in 1971 and earned an ROTC commission in the infantry as a Distinguished Military Graduate. He graduated from the Infantry Officer's Basic Course and Airborne and Ranger Schools at Fort Benning, Georgia, and then was assigned to the 82d Airborne Division, Fort Bragg, North Carolina.

General Dubik served with the 82d Airborne Division from 1972 through 1974 as platoon leader, reconnaissance platoon leader, company executive officer, and brigade staff officer. In 1974, he moved to Fort Lewis, Washington, where he served until 1978 with the 2d Ranger Battalion as company executive officer, civil military affairs officer, company commander, and battalion adjutant.

In 1978, he attended the U.S. Marine Corps' Amphibious Warfare School in Quantico, VA. He then attended Johns Hopkins University for two years where he earned a master's in philosophy. In 1981 he moved to Fort Leavenworth, Kansas, where he attended the U.S. Army Command and General Staff College. In 1982, Major General Dubik became an Associate Professor of Philosophy at the United States Military Academy.

In 1985, he was assigned as the Executive Officer of the 1st Ranger Battalion, Hunter Army Airfield, Savannah, Georgia. In 1987 he moved to Schofield Barracks, Hawaii, where he served as the Inspector General, 25th Infantry Division, then for two years as the Commander of 5th Battalion, 14th Infantry. In 1990, he returned to Fort Leavenworth to attend the Advanced Operations Studies Fellowship, taught at the Army's School of Advanced Military Studies and earned a second master's in military arts and sciences. In 1992, he moved to the Pentagon and became a special assistant to General Gordon Sullivan, Chief of Staff, United States Army, where he also held a fellowship with the Massachusetts Institute of Technology.

In 1994, Major General Dubik commanded the 2d Brigade, 10th Mountain Division, Fort Drum, NY. While commanding the 2d Brigade, he deployed to Operation UPHOLD DEMOCRACY where he served as the commander of U.S. and multinational forces in Northern Haiti. Following command, he was again assigned to the Pentagon as the executive officer to General Dennis Reimer, Chief of Staff, U.S. Army. In 1997, he became the Director of Training, U.S. Army, in the office of the Assistant Chief for Operations.

While the director of training, he completed Harvard University's John F. Kennedy School of Government's Executive Program for National and

International Security. Major General Dubik was then assigned in 1998 as Assistant Division Commander for Support, 1st Cavalry Division. Major General Dubik deployed to Bosnia-Herzegovina with 1st Cavalry Division where he was the Deputy Commanding General, Multinational Division North, and Task Force Eagle. He redeployed from Bosnia-Herzegovina on August 5th, 1999, and was assigned as Deputy Commanding General for Transformation (TRADOC) at Fort Lewis.

In 2000, Major General Dubik assumed command of the 25th Infantry Division (Light), Schofield Barracks, Hawaii. During that time, he completed the National Security Leadership Course at the Maxwell School of Citizenship and Public Affairs, Syracuse University, NY. He is currently the Director of Joint Experimentation at U.S. Joint Forces Command.

Ms. Susan Eisenhower

Ms. Eisenhower has spent 15 years of her career on foreign policy issues, though she came to the field from the business community.

A onetime consultant to IBM, American Express, and Loral Systems, she is best known for her work on U.S.–Russian relations and has lectured on Russia and the West at the Kennedy School of Government's Institute of Policy at Harvard University. Ms. Eisenhower has authored three books, two of which, Breaking Free and Mrs. Ike, have appeared on best-seller lists. She has also edited three collected volumes on regional security issues and penned hundreds of op-eds and articles for publications such as the *Washington Post*, the *Los Angeles Times*, *USA Today*, the Naval Institute's *Proceedings*, the *London Spectator*, Gannett newspapers, and Wolfe Publications. She has provided analysis for CNN, MSNBC, Nightline, This Week, CBS and ABC News, the News Hour, Fox News, and Hardball.

She serves on a number of boards, including the National Trust for Historic Preservation, the National Advisory Council for NASA, the Carnegie Endowment for International Peace, and the Nuclear Threat Initiative.

She has served as trustee of the Rochester Institute of Technology and Gettysburg College. Before becoming President of the Eisenhower Institute, Ms. Eisenhower was President of the Center for Political and Strategic Studies and a Distinguished Visiting Fellow at the Nixon Center.

Dr. Stephen J. Flanagan

Dr. Stephen J. Flanagan is Vice President for Research and Director of the Institute for National Strategic Studies at the National Defense University. He has served as Special Assistant to the President; Senior Director for Central and Eastern Europe at the National Security Council (July 1997–October 1999); National Intelligence Officer for Europe, National Intelligence Council (1995–1997); Associate Director and member of the Policy Planning Staff, U.S.

Department of State (1989–1995); and Professional Staff Member, Select Committee on Intelligence, U.S. Senate (1978–1983).

Dr. Flanagan has also held several academic and research positions, including Senior Fellow, Institute for National Strategic Studies, and faculty member, National War College, National Defense University (1987–1989). He served as Executive Director, Center for Science and International Affairs and as a faculty member, John F. Kennedy School of Government, Harvard University (1983–1987). He served as Fellow on the Council on Foreign Relations International Affairs and as Research Associate, International Institute for Strategic Studies, London (1983–1984).

Dr. Flanagan earned his A.B. in political science from Columbia University in 1973 and his doctorate in international relations from the Fletcher School of Law and Diplomacy at Tufts University in 1979. He is published widely on European, international security, and intelligence issues.

Ms. Gail D. Fosler

Ms. Gail D. Fosler is Senior Vice President and Chief Economist of the Conference Board, the world's leading research and business membership organization.

Ms. Fosler directs the Conference Board's worldwide Economics Research Program, which produces major studies on economic issues and the widely watched *Leading Economic Indicators*, the *Consumer Confidence Index*, the *Help-Wanted Index*, and the *Business Confidence Index*. Her unit now produces leading economic indicators for the United States, United Kingdom, Australia, France, Germany, Japan, Korea, Mexico, and Spain.

The *Wall Street Journal* has twice named Ms. Fosler "America's most accurate economic forecaster." She was also recently awarded the prestigious Annual Blue Chip Economic Forecasting Award for accurately forecasting major economic trends over the last four years.

Ms. Fosler's economic commentary is extensively reported by the global media and has a major impact on financial markets around the world. She is seen regularly on ABC, BBC, CNBC, CNN, and other networks.

Ms. Fosler is a Director of Unisys Corporation, H.B. Fuller Company, Baxter International, and the DBS Holdings (Singapore) and a Trustee of the John Hancock Mutual Fund. She is also a Director of the National Bureau of Economic Research and a past Director of the Institute of Public Administration, the National Association of Business Economists, and the National Economists Club. Fosler is also a member of the Council on Foreign Relations, the Economic Club of New York, and the Economic Advisory Panel to the New York Federal Reserve.

Before joining the Conference Board in 1989, she was Chief Economist and Deputy Staff Director of the Senate Budget Committee. She received her bachelor's degree in economics from the University of Southern California and her master's in finance from New York University.

Dr. Yoichi Funabashi

Dr. Yoichi Funabashi is columnist and chief diplomatic correspondent for the *Asahi Shimbun* and a leading journalist in the field of Japanese foreign policy. He is also a contributing editor to *Foreign Policy*.

He served as correspondent for the *Asahi Shimbun* in Beijing (1980–1981) and Washington (1984–1987), and as American General Bureau Chief (1993–1997). He won the Japan Press Award, known as Japan's Pulitzer Prize, in 1994 for his columns on foreign policy, and his articles in *Foreign Affairs* and *Foreign Policy* won the Ishibashi Tanzan Prize in 1992.

His books include *Alliance Adrift* (Council on Foreign Relations Press, 1998 winner of the Shincho Arts and Sciences Award), *Asia-Pacific Fusion: Japan's Role in APEC* (Institute for International Economics, 1995 winner of the Mainichi Shimbun Asia Pacific Grand Prix Award), *A Design for a New Course of Japan's Foreign Policy* (1993), *Managing the Dollar: From the Plaza to the Louvre* (1988 winner of the Yoshino Sakuzo Prize), *U.S.–Japan Economic Entanglement: The Inside Story* (1987), and *Neibu: Inside China* (1983).

His recent articles and papers in English include "Bridging Asia's Economics-Security Gap" (*Survival*, Winter 1996–1997); "Tokyo's Depression Diplomacy" (*Foreign Affairs*, November/December 1998); "International Perspectives on National Missile Defense: Tokyo's Temperance" (*Washington Quarterly*, Summer 2000); and "Japan's Moment of Truth" (*Survival*, Winter 2000–2001).

He received his bachelor's from the University of Tokyo in 1968 and his doctorate from Keio University in 1992.

Ambassador Peter W. Galbraith

Ambassador Peter W. Galbraith was the first United States ambassador to the Republic of Croatia, having presented his credentials to President Franjo Tudjman on June 28, 1993. Ambassador Galbraith was actively involved in the Bosnia and Croatia peace processes. He participated in the 1993 and 1994 negotiations that led to the March 1994 signing of the Washington Agreement ending the Muslim-Croat War and creating the Federation of Bosnia-Herzegovina.

In 1994 and 1995, he was one of the sponsors of the Z4 Croatia peace process that produced the March 29, 1994, Cease-Fire Agreement and the December 2, 1994, Economic Agreement between the Croatian government and the Krajina Serbs.

From 1979 until 1993, Ambassador Galbraith was a senior adviser to the Senate Foreign Relations Committee, with major responsibilities for the Near

East and South Asia and the Foreign Relations Authorization legislation. Ambassador Galbraith uncovered and documented Saddam Hussein's genocidal campaign against the Iraqi Kurds in the late 1980s, leading to sanctions legislation against Iraq and later contributing to the decision to create a safe-haven for the Kurds. His work on behalf of human rights and democracy in Pakistan earned him that country's high civilian award, the Sitari-i-Quad-Azam.

Mr. David Gergen

Commentator, editor, teacher, public servant, best-selling author, and adviser to presidents for 30 years, Mr. Gergen has been an active participant in American national life. He served as director of communications for President Reagan and held positions in the Nixon and Ford administrations. In 1993, he put his country before politics when he agreed to first serve as counselor to President Clinton on both foreign policy and domestic affairs, then as special international adviser to the President and to Secretary of State Warren Christopher.

Mr. Gergen currently serves as editor-at-large at *U.S. News & World Report* and as a regular analyst on ABC's *Nightline*. He is also a Professor of Public Service at the John F. Kennedy School of Government and Co-Director of its Center for Public Leadership. This fall, he published a book, *Eyewitness to Power: The Essence of Leadership, Nixon to Clinton*.

In the past, he has served in the White House as an adviser to four presidents: Nixon, Ford, Reagan, and Clinton. Most recently, he served for 18 months in the Clinton administration, first as Counselor to the President and then as Special Adviser to the President and the Secretary of State.

During 1984–1993, Mr. Gergen worked mostly as a journalist. For some two-and-a-half years, he was editor of *U.S. News & World Report*. Working with the owner and editor-in-chief, Mortimer Zuckerman, and a revived staff, he helped to guide the magazine to record gains in circulation and advertising. During five years of that period, he also teamed with Mark Shields for political commentary on the *MacNeil/Lehrer News Hour*. The popular political team won numerous accolades for their political coverage.

A native of Durham, N.C., he is an honors graduate of Yale University (A.B., 1963) and the Harvard Law School (LL.B., 1967). He is a member of the D.C. Bar. In addition, he served for three-and-a-half years in the U.S. Navy, where he was aboard ship home-ported in Japan for nearly two years.

In work with his current nonprofit boards, he was elected by the alumni to serve on the Yale Corporation, and he is Chairman of the National Selection Committee for the Ford Foundation's program on Innovations in American government. He frequently lectures in the United States and overseas and holds five honorary degrees.

Dr. Daniel Goure

Dr. Daniel Goure is a Senior Fellow with the Lexington Institute, a non-profit public-policy research organization headquartered in Arlington, Virginia. He is involved in a wide range of issues as part of the Institute's National Security Program.

Dr. Goure has held senior positions in both the private sector and the U.S. government. Most recently, he was a member of the 2001 Department of Defense Transition Team. Dr. Goure spent two years as the director of the Office of Strategic Competitiveness in the Office of the Secretary of Defense. He also served as a senior analyst on national security and defense issues with the Center for Naval Analyses, Science Applications International Corporation, SRS Technologies, R&D Associates, and System Planning Corporation.

Prior to joining the Lexington Institute, Dr. Goure was the Deputy Director, International Security Program at the Center for Strategic and International Studies. At CSIS, Dr. Goure was responsible for analyses of U.S. national security policy, the future of conflict and warfare, the information revolution, counterproliferation, and defense industrial management. He directed analyses of emerging security issues with a special emphasis on U.S. military capabilities in the next century.

Dr. Goure also has done extensive consulting and teaching. From 1990 to 1991, he led a study for the U.S. Institute of Peace on deterrence after the INF Treaty. Dr. Goure has consulted for the Departments of State, Defense, and Energy. He has taught or lectured at the Johns Hopkins University, the Foreign Service Institute, the National War College, the Naval War College, the Air War College, and the Inter-American Defense College.

Dr. Goure is a well-known and respected presence in the national and international media, having been interviewed by all the major networks: CNN, Fox, the BBC, the *New York Times*, the *Washington Post*, the *Wall Street Journal*, the *Christian Science Monitor*, the *Chicago Tribune*, and the *Los Angeles Times*. He has written extensively in more than two dozen journals and periodicals. He is also an NBC national security military analyst.

Dr. Goure holds master's and doctorate's degrees in international relations and Russian studies from Johns Hopkins University and a bachelor's degree in government and history from Pomona College.

Mr. Dick Grasso

Mr. Dick Grasso has been Chairman and Chief Executive Officer of the New York Stock Exchange since June 1, 1995. Since 1988, he had been President and Chief Operating Officer. While continuing in those positions, he became Executive Vice Chairman of the Exchange on January 1, 1991. He is the first member of the NYSE's management to be elected to any of these positions in the NYSE's 210-year history.

After serving in the U.S. Army from 1966 to 1968, Mr. Grasso joined the Exchange in 1968. In 1973 Mr. Grasso became Director of Listings and Marketing, in charge of adding qualified prospects to the NYSE's list of companies. In December 1977, he was promoted to Vice President, Corporate Services, and in November 1981, he was appointed Senior Vice President, Corporate Services. Mr. Grasso became Executive Vice President, Marketing Group, in 1983 and then Executive Vice President, Capital Markets, in May 1986, with responsibility for all financial products and the market data group.

Mr. Grasso serves on the Board of Directors of the Home Depot, Inc., as Chairman of the Economic Club of New York, and Vice Chairman of the National Italian-American Foundation. He serves as trustee of the Centurion Foundation, the New York City Police Foundation, and the Trooper Foundation for the State of New York. He serves as a trustee of New York University, as a member of the New York University Stern School of Business Board of Overseers, the Yale School of Management Advisory Board, the Baruch College School of Business Advisory Council, the National Advisory Board of the Panetta Institute for Public Policy, and the Federal Reserve Bank of New York's International Capital Markets Advisory Committee. He also serves as a member of the board of the Lower Manhattan Development Corporation, the Twin Towers Fund, and the Congressional Medal of Honor Foundation.

Mr. Grasso is a former Chairman of Junior Achievement of New York and a former chairman of the YMCA of Greater New York.

Mr. Grasso has received honorary Doctor of Laws degrees from Fordham University School of Law, Pepperdine University, Graziadio School of Business, and La Salle University, and honorary Doctor of Commercial Science degrees from New York University and from Pace University.

The Honorable Lee H. Hamilton

Congressman Lee H. Hamilton is the Director of the Woodrow Wilson International Center for Scholars. From 1965 to 1999, he served as a member of the U.S. Congress from Indiana's Ninth District. He served as Chairman and was the ranking member of the Committee on International Relations. He served as Chairman, Vice Chairman, and member of the Joint Economic Committee; Chairman and member of the Permanent Select Committee on Intelligence; Chairman of the Joint Committee on the Organization of Congress; Chairman of the October Surprise Task Force; and Chairman of the Select Committee to Investigate Covert Arms Transactions with Iran. He was a member of the House Standards of Official Conduct Committee. His expertise is in international relations and Congress.

Mrs. Frances Hesselbein

Mrs. Frances Hesselbein knows how to help organizations regain their vitality. She transformed a declining nonprofit organization into a thriving vital enterprise that has regained its stature.

Now Chairman of the Board of Governors of the Peter F. Drucker Foundation for Nonprofit Management and Chairman of the Board of Governors of the Josephson Institute for the Advancement of Ethics, her management ideas are studied at institutions like Harvard Business School, which turned her Girl Scouts work into a substantial case study. Mrs. Hesselbein has recently released a new book, *Hesselbein on Leadership* (August 2002).

In January 1998, President Clinton presented Frances Hesselbein with the Presidential Medal of Freedom, the nation's highest civilian honor. President George H.W. Bush appointed Hesselbein to his Advisory Committee on the Points of Light Initiative Foundation in 1989 and to the Board of Directors of the Commission on National and Community Service in August 1991. Hesselbein was the only woman and the only member of the human service sector on this commission. Recognized worldwide, Hesselbein was featured on the covers of both *Business Week* and *Savvy* for her managerial excellence.

Dr. G. John Ikenberry

Professor G. John Ikenberry is the Peter F. Krogh Professor of Global Justice in the Edmund A. Walsh School of Foreign Service, with a joint affiliation in the Department of Government, Georgetown University.

Prior to joining the School of Foreign Service in 2000, Professor Ikenberry taught at the University of Pennsylvania and Princeton University. From 1994 to 1998, he was Co-Director of the Lauder Institute of Pennsylvania. Additionally, he was a Senior Associate at the Carnegie Endowment for International Peace and a Fellow at the Woodrow Wilson Center for International Scholars in Washington, D.C. He is the author of numerous publications, including: *After Victory: Institutions, Strategic Restraint and the Rebuilding of Order after Major Wars, State Power and World Markets: The International Political Economy*, and *Reasons of State: Oil Politics and Capacities of American Government*.

Dr. David Johnson

Dr. David Johnson joined the Washington, D.C., office of RAND Corporation as a senior policy analyst in August 1998. His research interests include: military forces, politics, and technology between the two World Wars;

professional military education (PME); U.S. military doctrine and defense policy; U.S. civil-military relations; the revolution in military affairs (RMA) and military transformation; and military history.

Dr. Johnson is the author of *Fast Tanks and Heavy Bombers: Innovation in the U.S. Army, 1917–1945* and *Modern U.S. Civil-Military Relations: Wielding the Terrible Swift Sword*. He has also authored *Wielding the Terrible Swift Sword: The American Military Paradigm and Civil-Military Relations, From Frontier Constabulary to Modern Army: The United States Army between the World Wars,* and *The Challenge of Change: Armed Forces and New Realities, 1919–1941*.

Dr. Johnson is a 1972 graduate of Trinity University. Additionally, he is a graduate of the U.S. Army Command General Staff College and holds a master's from the Industrial College of the Armed Forces and a master's and doctorate from Duke University.

Dr. Charles Krauthammer

Dr. Charles Krauthammer was born in 1950 in New York City. He grew up in Montreal and was educated at McGill University (bachelor's with First Class Honors in political science and economics, 1970), Oxford University (Commonwealth Scholar in Politics at Balliol College, 1970–71), and Harvard University (M.D., Harvard Medical School, 1975).

From 1975–1978, he practiced medicine as a resident and then chief resident in psychiatry at the Massachusetts General Hospital. His scientific papers include his co-discovery of a form of manic-depressive illness.

In 1978 he moved to Washington to serve as a science adviser in the Carter administration and later speechwriter to Vice President Walter Mondale. In 1981 he joined the staff of the *New Republic* where he was an essayist and editor from 1981–1988. In the mid-1980s, he began writing a weekly syndicated column for the *Washington Post* and a monthly essay for *Time* magazine.

In his first full year as a syndicated columnist, he won the Pulitzer Prize (Distinguished Commentary, 1987). His *New Republic* essays won the highest award in magazine writing, the National Magazine Award for Essays and Criticism (1984).

He has won awards for his writing on everything from the economics of oil (the Champion/Tuck Media Award for Economic Understanding) to religion in civil society (People for the American Way, First Amendment Award). His essays have appeared in dozens of anthologies on subjects ranging from nuclear deterrence to gay marriage. A collection of his essays and columns, *Cutting Edges*, was published in 1985.

He is a regular weekly panelist on *Inside Washington*, Washington's highest rated political TV talk show, and a contributing editor to the *New Republic* and the *Weekly Standard*. He also serves on the editorial boards for several journals, including the *National Interest* and the *Public Interest*.

Ms. Anne O. Krueger

Ms. Anne O. Krueger currently serves as First Deputy Managing Director of the International Monetary Fund in Washington, D.C.

Prior to taking up her position at the Fund on September 1, 2001, Ms. Krueger was the Herald L. and Caroline L. Ritch Professor in Humanities and Sciences in the Department of Economics at Stanford University. She was also the Director of Stanford's Center for Research on Economic Development and Policy Reform and a Senior Fellow of the Hoover Institution. Before joining the Stanford faculty, she taught at the University of Minnesota and Duke University, and from 1982 to 1986 was the World Bank's Vice President for Economics and Research. She received her undergraduate degree (1953) from Oberlin College and her master's (1956) and doctorate (1958) in economics from the University of Wisconsin.

Ms. Krueger is a Distinguished Fellow and past President of the American Economic Association, a member of the National Academy of Sciences, and a Research Associate of the National Bureau of Economic Research. A recipient of a number of economic prizes and awards, she has published extensively on policy reform in developing countries, the role of multilateral institutions in the international economy, and the political economy of trade policy. Recent books edited by Ms. Krueger include *Economic Policy Reform: The Second Stage*, *The WTO as an International Organization*, and, with Takatoshi Ito, *Changes in Exchange Rates in Rapidly Developing Countries: Theory, Practice and Policy Issues*.

The Honorable Jerry Lewis

Representative Jerry Lewis (R-Calif.) is a lifelong resident of San Bernardino County, California, and 30-year owner of a life insurance business. He represents the 40th Congressional District of Southern California, including most of San Bernardino and Inyo Counties.

A member of Congress since 1978, Congressman Lewis is one of the senior members of the House Appropriations Committee. He is Chairman of the Defense Appropriations Subcommittee, the panel with jurisdiction over all national security matters including the entire Pentagon budget—nearly half of all funds appropriated by Congress. In this capacity, he is a forceful advocate of critical defense and aerospace jobs in California. Congressman Lewis also serves on the Foreign Operations Appropriations Subcommittee and the Legislative Branch Appropriations Subcommittee.

Congressman Lewis has personally secured federal funds for critical projects in Southern California, including highway improvements along I-15 and I-40 in the high desert; a revolutionary cancer treatment center and NASA research center at Loma Linda University; access roads and terminal expansion at Ontario International Airport; and construction of the Santa Ana flood control project critical to Orange, Riverside, and San Bernardino Counties.

Congressman Lewis has played an instrumental role in pursuing tough federal clean-air standards, fashioning effective crime and drug legislation, and securing emergency funding for earthquake, flood, fire, and drought relief for California. An innovative housing program he created with San Bernardino County has allowed more than 500 low-income families to buy renovated public housing. He was the driving force in converting the former George and Norton Air Force Bases into successful local employment centers.

Dr. Robert S. Litwak

Dr. Robert S. Litwak is Director of the Division of International Studies at the Woodrow Wilson International Center for Scholars in Washington, and Adjunct Professor of the School of Foreign Service at Georgetown University.

Dr. Litwak is the author or editor of eight books, including *Détente and the Nixon Doctrine, Security in the Persian Gulf, Nuclear Proliferation after the Cold War,* and the recently published *Rogue States and U.S. Foreign Policy.* He served on the National Security Council staff at the White House as Director for Nonproliferation and Export Controls from 1995–1996.

Dr. Litwak has held visiting fellowships at Harvard University, the Russian Academy of Sciences in Moscow, the Graduate Institute of International Studies in Geneva, and the United States Institute of Peace. He is a member of the Council on Foreign Relations. He holds a doctorate in international relations from the London School of Economics.

General Montgomery C. Meigs

General Montgomery C. Meigs is Commanding General, U.S. Army, Europe, and 7th Army in Heidelberg, Germany, a position he assumed in 1998. He also served as Commander of the multinational Stabilization Force in Bosnia-Herzegovina beginning in October 1998.

General Meigs has held a variety of positions during his career including: Commander, 1st Squadron, 1st Armored Cavalry Regiment; strategic planner on the Joint Staff in Washington, D.C.; command of the 2nd Brigade, 1st Armored Division; and Chief of Staff of V Corps and Deputy Chief of Staff for Operations of the U.S. Army, Europe, and 7th Army.

General Meigs commanded the 3rd Infantry Division from July 1995 until its reflagging as the 1st Infantry Division in February of 1996. In October 1996, he deployed with the 1st Infantry Division to Bosnia, serving nine months as COMEAGLE in command of NATO's Multi-National Division (North) in Operations JOINT ENDEAVOR and JOINT GUARD.

He is a graduate of the United States Military Academy and spent one year at the Army's Command and General Staff College. He received a doctorate in history from the University of Wisconsin in 1982.

His awards include the Distinguished Service Medal, the Bronze Star Medal with "V" device, and the Purple Heart.

The Honorable Norman Y. Mineta

Secretary Norman Y. Mineta became the 14th U.S. Secretary of Transportation on January 25, 2001. In that capacity, Secretary Mineta oversees an agency with 100,000 employees and a budget of more than $60 billion.

Prior to joining President George W. Bush's administration as Secretary of Transportation, Mineta served as U.S. Secretary of Commerce under President Clinton, becoming the first Asian-Pacific American to serve in the cabinet. He is the first Secretary of Transportation to have previously served in a cabinet position. Before joining the Commerce Department, he was a vice president at Lockheed Martin Corporation.

From 1975 to 1995 he served as a member of the U.S. House of Representatives, representing the heart of California's Silicon Valley. Secretary Mineta's legislative and policy agenda was wide and varied, including major projects in the areas of economic development, science and technology policy, trade, transportation, the environment, intelligence, the budget, and civil rights. He co-founded the Congressional Asian-Pacific American Caucus and served as its first Chair.

Secretary Mineta served as Chairman of the House Public Works and Transportation Committee between 1992 and 1994. He chaired the Committee's Aviation Subcommittee between 1981 and 1988 and chaired its Surface Transportation Subcommittee from 1989 to 1991. During his career in Congress he championed increases in investment for transportation infrastructure and was a key author of the landmark Intermodal Surface Transportation Efficiency Act of 1991, which shifted decisions on highway and mass transit planning to state and local governments. He also pressed for more funding for the department's Federal Aviation Administration.

Secretary Mineta and his family were among the 120,000 Americans of Japanese ancestry forced from their homes and into internment camps during World War II. After graduating from the University of California at Berkeley, Secretary Mineta joined the Army in 1953 and served as an intelligence officer in Japan and Korea. He joined his father in the Mineta Insurance Agency before entering politics in San Jose, serving as a member of its city council from 1967 to 1971 and mayor from 1971 to 1974, becoming the first Asian-Pacific American mayor of a major U.S. city.

In 1995, George Washington University awarded the Martin Luther King, Jr. Commemorative Medal to Mineta for his contributions to the field of civil rights.

General Richard B. Myers

General Richard B. Myers became the 15th Chairman of the Joint Chiefs of Staff on October 1, 2001. In this capacity, he serves as the principal military adviser to the President, the Secretary of Defense, and the National Security Council. Prior to becoming Chairman, he served as Vice Chairman of the Joint Chiefs of Staff for 19 months.

General Myers was born in Kansas City, Missouri. He is a 1965 graduate of Kansas State University and holds a master's in business administration from Auburn University. He has attended the Air Command and Staff College at Maxwell Air Force Base, Alabama; the U.S. Army War College at Carlisle Barracks, Pennsylvania; and the Program for Senior Executives in National and International Security at the John F. Kennedy School of Government, Harvard University.

General Myers entered the Air Force in 1965 through the Reserve Officer Training Corps Program. His career includes command and leadership positions in a variety of Air Force and joint assignments. General Myers is a command pilot with more than 4,100 flying hours in the T-33, C-37, C-21, F-4, F-15, and F-16, including 600 combat hours in the F-4.

As the Vice Chairman from March 2000 to September 2001, General Myers served as the Chairman of the Joint Requirements Oversight Council, Vice Chairman of the Defense Acquisition Board, and member of the National Security Council Deputies Committee and the Nuclear Weapons Council. In addition, he acted for the Chairman in all aspects of the Planning, Programming, and Budgeting System, including participation in the Defense Resources Board.

From August 1998 to February 2000, General Myers was Commander in Chief, North American Aerospace Defense Command and U.S. Space Command; Commander, Air Force Space Command; and Department of Defense Manager, Space Transportation System Contingency Support at Peterson Air Force Base, Colorado.

As commander, General Myers was responsible for defending America through space and intercontinental ballistic missile operations. Prior to assuming that position, he was Commander, Pacific Air Forces, Hickam Air Force Base, Hawaii, from July 1997 to July 1998. From July 1996 to July 1997, he served as Assistant to the Chairman of the Joint Chiefs of Staff, and from November 1993 to June 1996, General Myers was Commander of U.S. Forces Japan and 5th Air Force at Yokota Air Base, Japan.

Professor Douglass C. North

Professor Douglass C. North, Spencer T. Olin Professor in Arts and Sciences, is also professor of history and a Fellow of the Center in Political

Economy. He was on the faculty of the University of Washington and held visiting chairs at Cambridge and Rice Universities.

In 1993, he was awarded the Nobel Memorial Prize in Economics. He is a Fellow of the American Academy of Arts and Sciences and has served as President of the Economic History Association and the Western Economic Association. His major interest is the evolution of economic and political institutions.

Among his books are: *The Rise of the Western World, Growth and Welfare in the American Past, Structure and Change in Economic History,* and *Institutions, Institutional Change and Economic Performance.*

Dr. Michael E. O'Hanlon

Dr. Michael E. O'Hanlon is a Senior Fellow in the Foreign Policy Studies Program at the Brookings Institution, where he specializes in U.S. defense strategy and budgeting; military technology; Northeast Asian security; Balkan security; and humanitarian intervention.

He is also Adjunct Professor at the Public Policy School of Columbia University and a member of the International Institute for Strategic Studies and the Council on Foreign Relations. O'Hanlon's most recent Brookings publications are *Winning Ugly: NATO's War to Save Kosovo* (with Ivo Daalder) and *Technological Change and the Future of Warfare,* which describes and assesses the hypothesis that a contemporary revolution in military affairs is within reach.

Dr. O'Hanlon's major articles include "Star Wars Strikes Back" (*Foreign Affairs,* November/December 1999); "Unlearning the Lessons of Kosovo" (*Foreign Policy,* with Ivo Daalder, Fall 1999); "China's Hollow Military" (*National Interest,* with Bates Gill, Summer 1999). Other articles include "Stopping a North Korean Invasion" (*International Security,* Spring 1998); "Restructuring U.S. Forces and Bases in Japan," Mike M. Mochizuki, ed.; "Toward a True Alliance" (Brookings, 1997); and "Transforming NATO: The Role of European Forces" (*Survival,* Autumn 1997).

He has a doctorate in public and international affairs from Princeton University; his bachelor's and master's, also from Princeton, are in the physical sciences.

Ambassador Robert B. Oakley

Ambassador Robert B. Oakley has been a Distinguished Fellow at the Institute for National Strategic Studies, National Defense University, since January 1995, where he served as Acting Director from August 1999 until January 2000. During his foreign service career, which spanned three decades, he dealt primarily with Africa and the Middle East and Asia, serving in a wide variety of positions, including Senior Director for Middle East and South Asia on the staff of the National Security Council (1974–1977); Deputy Assistant Secretary of State for East Asia and the Pacific; U.S. Ambassador to Zaire and Somalia; Director of the State Department Office on Terrorism; Assistant to the President for the Middle East and South Asia on the staff of the National Security Council (1982–1988); and U.S. Ambassador to Pakistan (1988–1990).

After retiring in September 1991, he was named Special Envoy for Somalia by the President from December 1992 until March 1993 and again from October 1993 until March 1994.

During his service with the State Department, he received the State Department Distinguished Honor Award. For his service as Special Envoy to Somalia, he received a second State Department Distinguished Honor Award and the Department of Defense Medal for Distinguished Public Service. He is co-author of a book on his experiences in Somalia and co-editor of a book on police intervention in peacekeeping, as well as a number of articles and speeches.

General Eric K. Shinseki

General Eric K. Shinseki assumed duties as the 34th Chief of Staff, United States Army, on June 22, 1999.

General Shinseki graduated with a B.S. degree from the United States Military Academy in 1965. He also holds a master's degree in English literature from Duke University. General Shinseki's military education includes the Armor Officer Advanced Course, the United States Army Command and General Staff College, and the National War College.

Since his commissioning, General Shinseki has served in a variety of command and staff assignments both in the continental United States and overseas, to include two combat tours with the 9th and 25th Infantry Divisions in the Republic of Vietnam as an artillery forward observer and as commander of Troop A, 3d Squadron, 5th Cavalry. He has served in Hawaii at Schofield Barracks with Headquarters, United States Army, Hawaii, and at Fort Shafter with Headquarters, United States Army, Pacific. He has taught at the United States Military Academy's Department of English. During duty with the 3d Armored Cavalry Regiment at Fort Bliss, Texas, he served as the regimental adjutant and as the executive officer of its 1st Squadron.

General Shinseki's 10-plus years of service in Europe included assignments as Commander, 3d Squadron, 7th Cavalry (Schweinfurt); Commander, 2d Brigade (Kitzingen); Assistant Chief of Staff, G3 (Operations, Plans, and Training) (Wuerzburg); and Assistant Division Commander for Maneuver (Schweinfurt), all with the 3d Infantry Division (Mechanized). He served as the Assistant Chief of Staff, G3 (Operations, Plans and Training), VII Corps (Stuttgart).

General Shinseki served as the Deputy Chief of Staff for Support, Allied Land Forces, Southern Europe (Verona, Italy), an element of the Allied Command Europe. From March 1994 to July 1995, General Shinseki commanded the 1st Cavalry Division at Fort Hood, Texas. In July 1996, he was promoted to lieutenant general and became the Deputy Chief of Staff for Operations and Plans, United States Army. In June 1997, General Shinseki was appointed to the rank of general before assuming duties as the Commanding General, United States Army, Europe; Commander, Allied Land Forces, Central Europe; and Commander, NATO Stabilization Force in Bosnia-Herzegovina. General Shinseki assumed duties as the 28th Vice Chief of Staff, United States Army, on November 24, 1998.

General Shinseki has been awarded the Defense Distinguished Service Medal, Distinguished Service Medal, Legion of Merit with Oak Leaf Clusters, Bronze Star Medal with "V" Device with 2 Oak Leaf Clusters, Purple Heart with Oak Leaf Cluster, Meritorious Service Medal with 2 Oak Leaf Clusters, Air Medal, Army Commendation Medal with Oak Leaf Cluster, Army Achievement Medal, Parachutist Badge, Ranger Tab, Office of the Secretary of Defense Identification Badge, Joint Chiefs of Staff Identification Badge, and the Army Staff Identification Badge.

Dr. Loren B. Thompson

Dr. Loren B. Thompson is the Chief Operating Officer of the Lexington Institute, a nonprofit, nonpartisan public policy research organization headquartered in Arlington, Virginia. In that capacity, he directs the Institute's National Security Program and participates in its research on a variety of domestic issues.

Dr. Thompson is a long-time adviser to major defense and aerospace companies, the federal government, and various public policy organizations on national security issues ranging from military logistics and industrial-base trends to nonlethal weapons and infrastructure management. Most of his for-profit consulting activity is conducted through Source Associates, Fairfax, Virginia.

For nearly 20 years, Dr. Thompson has taught graduate-level seminars on strategy and military affairs in Georgetown University's National Security Studies Program, a part of the University's School of Foreign Service. He was Deputy Director of the National Security Studies Program from 1988 to 1995, and holds a doctorate in government from Georgetown University. He has also taught at Harvard University's John F. Kennedy School of Government.

Prior to assuming his present positions, Dr. Thompson was Executive Director of the Alexis de Tocqueville Institution's National Security Program.

During 1994–1996, he represented much of the defense and aerospace industry in Pentagon deliberations on logistics and industrial-base policy in his capacity as director of an ad hoc policy group supported by ten industry associations.

Dr. Thompson is widely cited in the national media, having been interviewed by CBS, NBC, CNN, CNBC, National Public Radio, the *New York Times*, the *Washington Post*, the *Wall Street Journal*, the *Los Angeles Times*, *USA Today*, and the *Economist*.

In a typical year, he authors more than three dozen essays and commentaries on national security topics that appear in public media. During Operation Desert Storm in 1991, he was the on-air military analyst for WUSA, a CBS affiliate in Washington, D.C.

The Honorable Thomas E. White

Secretary Thomas E. White became the 18th Secretary of the Army on May 31, 2001, after nomination to that post by President George W. Bush and confirmation by the United States Senate.

As Secretary of the Army, Secretary White has statutory responsibility for all matters relating to Army manpower, personnel, reserve affairs, installations, environmental issues, weapons systems and equipment acquisition, communications, and financial management. Secretary White is responsible for the department's annual budget of nearly $82 billion. The secretary leads a team of more than one million active duty, National Guard, and Army Reserve soldiers and 220,000 civilian employees. He has stewardship over 15 million acres of land.

Secretary White began his public service career as an Army officer. After graduating from the United States Military Academy at West Point, he was commissioned in the United States Army in 1967, rising to the rank of brigadier general in 1990. His distinguished military career included two tours in Vietnam and service as Commander, 1st Squadron, 11th Armored Cavalry Regiment; Commander, 11th Armored Cavalry Regiment, V Corps; and, Executive Assistant to the Chairman, Joint Chiefs of Staff.

Secretary White attended the Naval Postgraduate School, Monterey, California, and graduated in 1974 with a degree in operations research. In 1984, he attended the United States Army War College, Carlisle, Pennsylvania. Secretary White retired from the Army in July 1990.

From 1990 to 2001, Secretary White was employed by Enron Corporation and held various senior executive positions.

Mr. Howard Roy Williams,

Mr. Howard Roy Williams is presently President and Chief Executive Officer of the Center for Humanitarian Cooperation, an organization focused on achieving coordination in humanitarian work through enhanced cooperation. Mr. Williams was previously Director of the Office of U.S. Foreign

Disaster Assistance (OFDA), Bureau for Humanitarian Response of the U.S. Agency for International Development. As head of OFDA, Mr. Williams oversaw disaster preparedness and relief and rehabilitation programs throughout the world.

Before going to OFDA, Mr. Williams served with the International Rescue Committee (IRC) for 12 years. From May 1996 to January 1998, Mr. Williams was IRC's Vice President for Overseas Policy and Planning. From 1993 to 1996, he was IRC's Vice President for Overseas Programs, and from 1985 to 1993 he was Director of Operations for IRC.

During this time, Mr. Williams led efforts that resulted in the conceptualization, creation, and staffing of IRC's Emergency Preparedness Unit. He helped to establish and staff IRC offices in a variety of places, including northern Iraq, Jordan, the Balkans, Kenya, Malawi, Rwanda, and southern Sudan.

From 1979 to 1985, he served with the International Organization for Migration, formerly known as the International Committee for European Migration.

Mr. Williams has a bachelor's degree from Columbia University. He has also studied at the Columbia University School of Law.

www.ingramcontent.com/pod-product-compliance
Lightning Source LLC
Chambersburg PA
CBHW051954280526
45793CB00005B/718